The Book of the Mirror

The Book of the Mirror
An Interdisciplinary Collection exploring the
Cultural Story of the Mirror

Edited by

Miranda Anderson

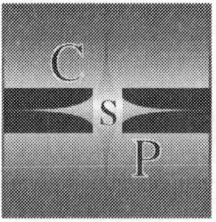

CAMBRIDGE SCHOLARS PUBLISHING

The Book of the Mirror: An Interdisciplinary Collection exploring the Cultural Story of the Mirror,
edited by Miranda Anderson

This book first published 2007 by

Cambridge Scholars Publishing

15 Angerton Gardens, Newcastle, NE5 2JA, UK

British Library Cataloguing in Publication Data
A catalogue record for this book is available from the British Library

Copyright © 2007 by Miranda Anderson and contributors

Cover image © Copyright the Trustees of The British Museum

TABLE OF CONTENTS

PREFACE AND ACKNOWLEDGEMENTS

This book investigates the mirror, as a material object and in visual and verbal imagery, and examines its relationship to ideas of knowledge, perception and human subjectivity in various socio-cultural and technological contexts. Within this book the rich potential of interdisciplinary collections is evident as these essays combine to make the apparently mundane object, the mirror, something we will look at, as well as into, in new ways. The realms of literature, art, history, archaeology, religion and magic are illuminated by the essays, which make apparent surprising parallels and contrasts between different chronological, geographical and disciplinary realms.

Under analysis here are the complex and dynamic relations of particular objects to imagery and to the individuals and societies who both shape and are shaped by them. These essays variously reveal the roles of external and internal factors in constituting human subjects and the permeability of boundaries between us, our technologies, our cultures and our worlds. Whilst several of the essays demonstrate that ways in which human subjectivity can be extended beyond our physical boundaries are represented through the use of the mirror or through other types of mirroring; conversely other essays show that the limits of human subject may also be symbolised by the mirror and mirroring. Resonances of themes echo throughout the book as a whole, although essays have been divided into four parts, in relation to particular focuses: in Part One the mirror is shown as enabling insight into restricted knowledge; in Part Two it signifies perception of God or self-reflection, with both operating on a vertical axis in ontological and epistemological hierarchies; in Part Three the mirror presents worldly perceptions of oneself and others with horizontal analogies and doublings; and in Part Four the mirror is diversely used to create and explore the subject's *re*presentation by art.

The book opens with an introduction by Mark Pendergrast, the author of *Mirror Mirror*, who presents an extensive overview of the history of the mirror, providing a background to the detailed studies in the other essays. In the first essay, Melanie Giles and Jody Joy offer a new reading of Bronze and Iron Age mirrors, which have previously tended to be conceived of as mere objects of vanity, on account of being found in women's graves. They reveal that these objects, with complex identities and histories of their own, were used to signify the supernatural properties of the possessors and thus would have endowed the holder with considerable power. Thus Giles and Joy also make apparent the dangers in critical analysis of hasty generalisations about gender roles. This is followed by Crystal Addey's examination of the use of mirrors for divination in the Graeco-Roman world. Addey explores the differences and similarities between catoptromancy that involved an oracle and catoptromancy in which a God or *daimon* is invoked. She discusses in what ways they were "supernatural" and their different uses of the elemental mediums of light, water, and earth, which are variously employed in combination with the mirror as a means to revelation. Like the earlier two essays in this section, Ross Hulkes's essay upon Seneca's nuanced use of the mirror as a metaphor, reveals its epistemological functionality. In the political realm of Nero's Empire Seneca's writings employ the mirror as a valuably ambiguous symbol that can represent entry into knowledge by the emperor via the philosopher as his moral mirror image.

In the next part, there is a movement in focus away from the practical use of the mirror as an entry into forms of supernatural belief or worldly power and towards the concept of the mirror as a reflector of the liminal state of man within the Christian World. Mark Kauntze charts the inauguration of this movement. He explains how St. Paul's mirror metaphor, that man only sees through a glass darkly, originally referred to the Sayings of the Prophets and functioned as a marker of man's earthly ignorance. Kauntze then goes on to show how this was later positively reinterpreted by Augustine as a metaphor for the mind of man as the microcosm of the Trinity. The essay that follows, which is on Chaucer's use of mirror imagery, also explores the ever increasing emphasis in medieval discourses upon the imaging of God as an active and rational process. This paradoxically heightens the stress on man as fallen, as well as potentially the mirror of God, and depicts women constructed at a double remove from God, in their passions, passivity and vanity. Jacomien Prins's essay explores the continuing evolution of beliefs in man's mirroring of God as evident in Marsilio Ficino's philosophy. In Ficino's Christianisation of Platonic thought it flowered into a belief in a cosmic harmony which was interpretable by man through his smooth and shiny liver's mirroring to his mind of the harmony of the spheres and this world's mirroring of God.

The essays in Part Three concentrate on the relation of mirrors and mirror imagery to perception and doubling. The eminent scientist Richard Gregory introduces this part with his analysis of the technology of mirrors and of how reflection works. This is followed by my essay on early modern mirrors, which compares subject formation by mirrors and by language, as well as exploring the interrelation of social, psychophysiological and technological types of mirroring. Lynn Holden closes this part with her essay on *doppelgängers*, which examines related psychological theories and the cultural and literary phenomenon of the double that allows for a play that can be a source of terror, liberation, and subversion.

The last three essays provide a variety of perspectives on the mirror as a visual metaphor, although all reveal a common concern with the play of presence and absence. Beth Williamson begins with a survey of some of the stereotypical mirror paintings which come to mind: Van Eyck's *The Arnolfini Portrait*, Velaszquez's *Las Meninas*, and Manet's *Bar at the Folies-Bergère*. Williamson offers an invigorating reappraisal of these, and then goes on to examine ways in which the viewer is implicated as a witness by late medieval depictions of the Annunciation, and implicated as a reader by visual techniques in Mary of Burgundy's Book of Hours. Judit Varga's examination of Johannes Gump's curious *Self-Portrait*, argues that it reveals itself as in fact an *Image-Portrait* and so is a disruptive allegory of 17th century Dutch painting in its anxiety about self-presentation as only possible as *re*presentation. Finally, Katherine Shingler's study of Apollinaire's *miroir* reveals it's mimicking of Van Eyck, Velazquez and Manet as also an undermining of the belief in mimetic representation. Thus in this last section the mimesis offered by mirrors and paintings, begins with the ideal of a recreation of presence through the didactic utilisation of these objects, but their employment increases in self-consciousness and finally ends in the high irony of Apollinaire's symbolisation.

This widespread examination of the mirror as an object and in textual and visual imagery reveals that its deployment is related to discourses and beliefs circulating within a particular period, whilst it also interacts with the longer term cultural and psychophysiological capacities and constraints involved in being a human subject. The evolution of the form and functioning of the mirror as a concept is closely interlinked with the evolution of discourses and beliefs concerned with human subjectivity, knowledge and perception, and the authors here collaboratively in this book chart how the meaning of an object and a metaphor is both transformed by and transforms the socio-cultural matrix: the continuities underlying the concept reflect aspects that remain viable in relation to the contexts within which they operate, whilst variations in the manifest forms of concepts reflect the variety of co-evolving structures in play at that moment.

There are many organisations and individuals that are due an acknowledgement for their contribution to this book's making. Most of all, thanks are due to the Bristol Institute for Research in the Humanities and Arts (BIRTHA) for sponsoring the original conference at which many of these essays first took form as conference papers and to Mark Kauntze for organising the funding and the conference. In addition, thanks are due to Perseus Books for permission to use adapted material from Mark Pendergrast's book for the introduction (1-13) and to Maney and the Institute of Materials, Minerals and Mining for permission to publish Richard Gregory's paper (94-104). Thanks are also owed to the British Museum and to Jody Joy and Melanie Giles for arranging the use of the photograph of the Desborough Mirror for the cover image.   Finally, many thanks are due to the Japanese Government (Monbugakusho) and to the Japanese Society for the Promotion of Science (JSPS) for their research scholarships, which respectively provided the editor with the time needed to carry out research and to edit the book. Lastly, the editor would like to thank her family and friends and Janet, Calum and Fiona MacDougall, without all of whom these pages would not now be in your hands.

ILLUSTRATIONS

Figure 1.1.   Bronze mirror types. Line drawings by Jody Joy.

Figure 2.1.   Fresco depicting a scene of catopromancy or lecanomancy.
Room 5, Villa of Mysteries, Pompeii. Photo by Hannah Platts.

Figure 2.2.   Painted representation of a priestess reflected in a mirror.
Room 4, Villa of Mysteries, Pompeii. Photo by Hannah Platts.

Figure 7.1.   Sir Isaac Newton's optical diagram.

Figure 10.1.   *Mary of Burgundy at Prayer*, Hours of Mary of Burgundy.

Figure 10.2.   *Christ Nailed to the Cross*, Hours of Mary of Burgundy

Figure 10.3.   *Virgin Annunciate*, Antonello da Messina.

Figure 10.4.   *St Francis Stigmatised*, Giotto.

Figure 11.1   *Self-Portrait*, Johannes Gump.

Figure 11.2   *Triple Self-Portait*, Norman Rockwell.

Figure 12.1.   "Cœur couronne et miroir", Guillaume Apollinaire.

Figure 12.2.   *The Arnolfini Portrait*, Jan van Eyck.

Figure 12.3.   *Las Meninas*, Diego Velázquez.

Fig.ure 12.4.   *Un Bar aux Folies-Bergère*, Édouard Manet.

INTRODUCTION

MIRROR MIRROR: A HISTORICAL AND PSYCHOLOGICAL OVERVIEW

MARK PENDERGRAST

Strange, that there are dreams, that there are mirrors.
Strange that the ordinary, worn-out ways
of every day encompass the imagined
and endless universe woven by reflections.
—Jorge Luis Borges

It's a morning ritual, something so commonplace that you hardly notice it. Yes, there you are again, perhaps a little bleary-eyed, but it's you, all right, perhaps with a toothbrush in your mouth or a washcloth in your hand. You orient yourself in the world for another day. You're so used to this experience that you rarely think about it. Yet what you have just done is almost unique in the animal kingdom. Your ability to recognize the creature in the mirror as *you* seems to be limited to the higher primates, and perhaps dolphins and elephants. Other animals see only a rival or friend.

Mirrors are meaningless until someone looks into them. Thus a history of the mirror is really the history of looking, and what we perceive in these magical surfaces can tell us a great deal about ourselves—whence we have come, what we imagine, how we think, and what we yearn for. The mirror appears throughout the human drama as a means of self-knowledge or self-delusion. We have used the reflective surface both to reveal and to hide reality, and mirrors have found their way into religion, folklore, literature, art, magic and science.

A Long, Magical History

Humans have been intrigued with mirrors since prehistoric times. The ancient Egyptians, Indians, Chinese, Mayans, Incas, and Aztecs buried their dead with metal or stone reflectors, to hold the soul, ward off evil spirits, or allow the body to check its appearance, before taking the final trip to the afterlife. Because a round mirror can both reflect the sun and become a miniature imitation of it, early metal reflectors came to be associated with sun gods. At the same time, however, secular mirrors were used to apply cosmetics, foreshadowing thousands of years of people peering into the "flattering glass".[1] Yet the magic of mirrors remained. "Scryers" used them to look into the mystic future; mirrors served as a portal to the divine or demonic. Magicians manipulated them to create illusions to impress kings and commoners.[2]

From earliest times, mirrors have also been used for scientific applications. According to legend, Archimedes used mirrors to set fire to Roman ships during the siege of Syracuse, and the controversy over whether or not this feat was possible led eventually to modern solar ovens and generators. Concave mirrors made early lighthouses possible, and the reflecting telescope changed our view of the universe. Today, huge mirrors permit us to peer into ever-more distant regions of space, and light-weight gossamer optics will allow us to delve even farther. Some envision orbiting giant mirrors to manage the earth's climate.[3]

The story of mirrors is also the story of light, that mysterious medium that acts simultaneously like a wave and a particle, imposes a speed limit on the universe, and in a sense *is* the universe, according to Einstein. Yet no one really knows what it is. Sure, it is called electromagnetic radiation, but that only means that it is produced when you run electricity by a magnet. But what *is* light really? Even though it allows us to see, it is itself invisible, traversing space without a trace, unless it bumps into something like dust, which allows us to see that it travels in straight lines. It isn't readily apparent that it has a finite speed—though it does, imposing an apparent speed limit on the universe—or that "it" is an *it* at all. We still really don't understand it, though we know a great deal about how it behaves. The marvel is that humans have tried, with some success, to figure it all out.[4]

As if these mysteries were not enough, visible light is only one octave in the spectrum that ranges from mile-long radio waves to high-energy bursts of gamma rays. After World War II, our ability to explore the universe dramatically expanded as scientists figured out how to make unusual mirrors reflect most of those wavelengths. That story, too, is part of the mirror saga.[5]

From Metal to Glass: Technology Changes Culture

While the first mirror was undoubtedly a still body of water, the first known man-made mirror dates from around 6200 BCE, found at the Çatal Hüyük site in modern-day Turkey. Within another three thousand years, Egyptians and Sumerians created metal mirrors—first copper, then bronze, gold, and silver. Meanwhile, in the Western hemisphere, the Olmecs, Moche, and other cultures made mirrors from anthracite, slat, pyrite, and obsidian.

The ancient Romans pioneered in making glass mirrors by blowing glass bowls and coating their insides with molten lead, then breaking them apart to form poor-quality convex mirrors. During the Middle Ages, this art was nearly forgotten but became popular again, particularly in northern Europe, in time for Jan Van Eyck and others to portray them—and possibly use them as artistic tools—in their paintings of the early 15th century. In that same century, mirror-makers on the island of Murano near Venice perfected the secret art of making larger, flat glass mirrors, backed by a tin-mercury amalgam, creating a demand among royalty and nobility for these expensive, astonishing luxuries. After Louis XIV broke the monopoly in order to make his Hall of Mirrors at Versailles, glass mirrors gradually become more commonplace and cheaper.

People rarely stop to think about the side-effects of technological innovation, but the glass mirror helped to shape the modern secular age. When mirrors were rare, costly, small metal reflectors, they were often symbols of the sacred and divine. But as mirrors became more commonplace, they gradually lost their magic lustre and began to reflect everyday reality and vanity. Mirrors, which had sparked the advance of science ever since the Greeks puzzled over parabolic concave mirrors and why they focused heat and light, were crucial to the final separation of science and magic, which I date from just after the time of John Dee (1527-1609), one of the last great believers in scrying as well as optics and astronomy.[6] As the seventeenth century broke, the science of optics and mirrors had advanced to the edge of modernity. In the new century, there would be no more "natural magic." Many people would continue to believe in the supernatural, but it would be divorced from the natural.

Since its inception in the Middle Ages as a secret Italian guild, followed by the 17th century French industrial espionage that broke the monopoly, the glass mirror industry has grown to huge proportions, with the modern float glass factory running a constant river of molten and then solid glass over an ocean of liquid zinc. The common glass mirror also had an unforeseen, revolutionary impact on Renaissance literature and art. With the advent of cheap industrialized glass and modern methods of applying reflective material to it, mirrors have now become common objects even in the poorest homes. They have been used creatively by architects and home decorators, and in the 20th century, glittering mirrors helped transform America into a pleasure-seeking, vain, celebrity-driven society. Psychologists, advertising men, police, and voyeurs peer at us through one-way mirrors.

Mirrors ushered in the earliest human civilizations, and now they point us into the future—while simultaneously allowing astronomers to peer ever further back into time. The history of mirrors covers a vast territory, from the creation of the universe (perhaps along with alternate mirror universes) to the first hominids to the Hubble Space Telescope and beyond. The cast of quirky characters looking into and manipulating mirrors is equally diverse.

A Personal Adventure

When I first conceived of researching mirrors, I knew it would be interesting, but I didn't realize in how many directions it would take me. I examined ancient Egyptian mirrors in the Louvre, walked through the Hall of Mirrors at Versailles, looked at myself in an Aztec divining mirror at the British Museum, stumbled through a century-old mirror maze in Lucerne, buried myself under books and manuscripts in various archives and libraries, visited a French nudist colony (few mirrors, as I suspected), lay on my back to see the world's largest kaleidoscope in an upstate New York silo, looked at myself as I really am (not flipped right-to-left) in a "True Mirror" in Manhattan, clambered to the top of a new 300-foot diameter radio telescope in rural Green Bank, West Virginia, gazed down into the vast pool of the 200" mirror on Mt. Palomar, ventured under the University of Arizona football stadium to see Roger Angel's Mirror Lab, and lived at a Vedanta Monastery while tailing John Dobson, the extraordinary missionary of amateur telescope mirror makers.

As I type this sentence, I am looking into my own eyes in the hinged "PC mirror" attached to the side of my computer monitor. This device is sold by a New York company primarily as a sales tool for telemarketers—if you smile winsomely people are more likely to buy your product. I put the mirror on my computer, however, not to sell something, but to remind me of my own humanity. Right now, I see a man in his mid-fifties, greying around the temples, who needs a haircut and who, though he hates to admit it, looks a bit like Woody Allen. I am confessing all this, because this essay is not only a history of mirrors but also, like all essays, a reflection of a particular person who lurks somewhere behind the words.

One overarching theme of the history of our intimacy with reflective surfaces is that as human beings we use mirrors to reflect our own contradictory nature. On the one hand, we want to see things as they really are, to delve into the mysteries of life. On the other hand, we want the mysteries to remain mysteries. We yearn for definitive knowledge, yet we also revel in imagination, illusion, and magic. The German poet Rainer Maria Rilke may have been right when he wrote, "Mirrors: still no one knowing has told / what your essential nature is."[7] In J.K. Rowling's Harry Potter fantasy novels, the Mirror of Erised shows us "the deepest, most desperate desire of our hearts."[8] In a way, all mirrors are like that. Ultimately, what we see in them depends on what we bring to them.

Mirror Mazes

As I groped my way through the mirror maze in Lucerne's Glacier Garden, I kept bumping into a mirror where it appeared that I was walking down a long corridor framed with Moorish columns. At the far end of the corridor, I saw a young man approaching. He kept disappearing as both of us turned corners or pursued blind alleys. Finally, I bumped into another mirror, turned right, then left, and there he was again, now quite close. He reached out and, as he touched my face tentatively, he asked, "*Sind sie echt?*" In German, he was asking me if I was real. I laughed and said "*Ja*," and he laughed too. But for a confusing moment of disequilibrium, he wasn't joking. That's what mirrors can do to us human beings. They can jolt us out of reality or fantasy with equal ease.

My younger brother once worked in a factory where he was the only white laborer. One day he caught a glimpse of himself in a mirror down a hallway and thought, "What is that white boy doing here?" Then he realized he was looking at himself. Most of us have had experiences like that, moments of shock when we see a stranger before recognizing ourselves. When it once happened to Sigmund Freud on a train, it caused him "profound displeasure." In researching the history of mirrrors, I had more than my share of such moments, though I generally found them intriguing.

The Prague mirror maze atop Petrin Hill, known as the Bludiště, was built in 1891. "I see my back at the end of one aisle," I wrote in my journal there, "my side in another, and I can look sideways at myself writing in this notebook. It is strange to turn everywhere and see yourself. There is a big fly in here with me, whacking against the glass, buzzing madly." At the end of the maze is a superb gallery of funhouse mirrors installed in 1911, which turned out to be the real attraction. Children shrieked and giggled, while adults flirted and laughed. One mirror makes you look like a dwarf with cute little knees but a very long body. Another stretches your head into grotesque shapes. As in the Lucerne mirror maze, the laughter here rippled over barely concealed anxiety. *Do I really look like that? Could this be a part of who I am in my dreams?* Later, at the London Natural History Museum, I saw a woman in a low-cut blouse look at herself in a distorting mirror, where she saw her breasts absurdly stretched downwards. She gasped and backed away, exclaiming, "I've seen the future!"

Who Do You See in the Mirror?

And so we come back to the question the earliest hominid faced in the still water after the rainstorm. This is the question of identity, of essence, of soul that concerned the ancient Egyptians, Chinese, and Aztecs. It is even at the root of the questions asked by astronomers who have turned their big mirrors out towards space. Who are we, and what is our place in the universe? This brings us into the realm of psychology, where we must pick carefully amongst unproven theories and scientifically valid concepts.

In 1964 Chicago psychologists Arthur Traub and J. Orbach created the "adjustable body-distorting mirror," a plexiglass reflective surface about four feet high that could be adjusted to bend as a convex or concave mirror in various ways. Subjects stood seven feet from the mirror and saw themselves at first as "tall, with pin head, large elongated body and legs tapering to tiny feet," then as "short with enormous horned head and tapering legs". When subjects were asked to adjust the mirror so that they looked normal, they had an unexpectedly difficult time. "Many subjects declare . . . that they have forgotten precisely what they look like," wrote Traub and Orbach.[9]

A 1968 experiment shows how most people can hallucinate when staring at themselves in a mirror. Psychiatrist Luis Schwarz and psychologist Stanton Fjeld placed subjects two feet from a 16-inch square mirror, illuminated only by a tiny bulb three feet behind them, and then tape-recorded their impressions over the next half hour in what amounted to perfect scrying conditions. "It is a transparent face, jelly . . . like a cloud changing its form completely . . . the nose is large and the ears smaller and smaller . . . now I am bald," a man identified as "neurotic" reported. But a "normal" male said, "My eyes are whole caves with dancing skeletons," while another observed, "I see several faces . . . They change one from another . . . Their hair cut is changing . . . are holy men . . . a Japanese . . . a Negro." Yet another normal male saw himself gradually fading: "The image is darker and darker . . . disappears . . . the mirror . . . and I see a deep black."[10]

Some mirrors are intended to manipulate. A recent article in *Chain Store Age* offers the case study of Sally, who tries on a pair of capri pants in a store's dressing room. "Alas, the sole mirror and bad lighting make Sally look pale and fat," and she leaves without buying anything. The moral? Store managers should "spend money on mirrors (and lots of them)," along with good lighting.[11] Although no department stores will admit it, rumor has it that they sometimes use slightly convex mirrors that make people look slimmer.   Bruce Newman and Susan Larson of Assist Technologies in Lake Carmel, New York, sell the four-inch square, hinged PC Mirror that is attached to the side of my computer. Intended for use in workplace cubicles, the mirror can be useful in various ways, such as warning of a boss's approach or permitting a quick appearance check before a meeting. But its primary purpose is to help telephone sales people to "smile while you dial," on the assumption that the smile can be "heard" in a more pleasant tone of voice. Company-sponsored surveys claim an average eight percent increase in sales after PC Mirror installations.[12]

Apes, Elephants and Dolphins Face the Mirror

One morning in 1964, when 22-year-old grad student Gordon Gallup looked at his own reflection while shaving, he considered that it would be interesting to see whether other species of animals could recognize themselves in mirrors. Five years later, as an assistant professor of psychology at Tulane, he got the chance.[13]

Gallup put four preadolescent chimps—two female, two male—into separate cages and placed a full-length mirror outside each cage for ten days. At first, they reacted as they would to a stranger—bobbing, vocalizing, threatening, or adopting submissive postures. On the third day, however, he noticed a dramatic change. In the mirror, the chimps began to examine the inside of their mouths, to groom the hair on their foreheads, to pick their noses, to examine their genitals—taking advantage of the mirror to see otherwise inaccessible areas. They made faces, blew bubbles, and manipulated food wads with their lips. It was obvious to Gallup that they knew they were looking at *themselves* in the mirror, but he needed to be able to prove this subjective impression to skeptical colleagues.

Gallup devised a test. He anesthetized the four chimps and marked an eyebrow ridge and top half of the opposite ear with an odorless red dye. He did the same thing with a male and female chimp with no previous mirror experience. When the chimps awoke, they were monitored to make sure they weren't touching their red marks. Then mirrors were introduced. The four experienced chimps immediately took notice, touching the red marks repeatedly, and then looking at that finger. One of them even smelled the finger. The two other chimps showed no mark-directed responses.   In subsequent experiments, Gallup did the same test on macaques and rhesus monkeys, habituating them to mirrors for two weeks before trying his mark test. They failed. In a two-page paper published in *Science* on January 2, 1970, Gallup summarized his experiments, concluding, "Recognition of one's own reflection would seem to require a rather advanced form of intellect." He added that this ability might imply a "concept of self" that set humans and the great apes apart from other species. That fly I met in the Prague mirror maze might wear itself out, buzzing and banging against its image, but it will never figure out who that other hardheaded fly is.

Gallup and others have subjected all kinds of animals to the mark test with mirrors. Orangutans passed with no problem. To everyone's surprise, however, no gorillas touched the red marks. Only Koko, the famous gorilla who has learned sign language, clearly identified herself in a mirror, according to her owner. Bonobos, the endangered, peaceful apes of the Congo, knew themselves in mirrors. But all monkeys flunked. Gallup left a mirror with a pair of rhesus monkeys for 18 years, and they still didn't get it.

Elephants apparently failed the mark test in the late 1980s, but ten years later, in Nevada, animal behaviorist Patricia Simonet tested two performing Asian elephants—Bertha, a veteran in her forties, and 8-year-old Angel, although Angel got little chance to see herself, since the dominant Bertha hogged the mirror. Within 20 minutes of the mirror's introduction, Bertha stopped flapping her ears and trumpeting at the other elephant in the mirror and apparently began examining herself. During the mark test, white children's face paint was applied to a brow and temple, behind one front leg, and on one hip, all visible to Bertha only in the mirror. With her trunk, she touched the marks 15 times during the two hours of testing.

Dolphins also know themselves in mirrors, according to a 1999 study by Lori Marino, an Emory University psychology professor, and Diana Reiss, director of marine mammal research at New York Aquarium.[14] They marked Pressley and Tab, two teenaged bottlenose dolphins, with non-tactile black magic marker and used a variety of control circumstances. In order to qualify for self-recognition, the dolphins had to 1) spend more time at the mirror when marked, 2) display no "social" behavior as if towards another dolphin, and 3) swim immediately to the mirror and expose the mark. Pressley and Tab passed the test, obviously contorting their bodies in front of the mirror in order to observe marks under their chins or sides. When they marked Pressley's tongue, he opened and closed his mouth in front of the mirror as he never had before. Gordon Gallup, Marino's former mentor, is still skeptical, since dolphins have no hands or trunks with which to touch their marks. "It is entirely possible," he told me, "that the dolphins have learned that they have control over the behavior of the 'other' dolphin in the mirror, and therefore when they see the image with a mark they change their orientation to the mirror so that they can see it better."[15]

No one denies, however, that dolphins are smart. Like humans, they have large brains, but they have meager frontal lobes, which are crucial to humans. Marino believes this may be a case of evolutionary convergence, in which different species arrive at the same survival strategy by independent paths, like the flying ability of bats and birds. The convergence is probably not toward the specific trait of mirror self-recognition, she says, but to a "certain level of complexity in how they process information."[16]

Becoming Aware of Yourself

In a 1972 issue of *Developmental Psychobiology,* Beulah Amsterdam published the first mirror-recognition study for human babies, "Mirror Self-

Image Reactions Before Age Two."[17] She described how she had tested 88 children between the ages of 3 months and 24 months by putting a spot of rouge on one side of the nose and seeing if they touched it while looking in the mirror. Early on, babies seemed to recognize their mothers in the mirror, but not themselves. By six months, infants were smiling and playing with themselves in the mirror, but they treated the reflection as another child. At one year, they began to search behind the mirror for their mysterious playmate. Finally, Amsterdam concluded "from 20 to 24 months, 65 percent of the subjects demonstrated recognition of their mirror images." Subsequent research has substantiated her findings, indicating that most children's brains first register that they are observing themselves sometime during the latter part of their second year, when they become coy, embarrassed, clownish, or self-admiring in front of the mirror.

What exactly does mirror self-recognition imply? Gordon Gallup believes self-recognition means self-awareness. "You become the object of your own attention. You are aware of being aware. And that, in turn, allows you to make inferences about comparable states of awareness in others."[18] Gallup doesn't deny that other animals such as dogs or even fleas may have alternate forms of self-concept, but the brain's capacity to allow us to know we are looking at ourselves appears to place us—along with higher apes and perhaps elephants and dolphins—in a unique category, and this simple ability to recognize ourselves in a mirror seems to be essential to the human enterprise.

Can it be a coincidence that toddlers develop language and begin to say *I, me*, and *mine* about the same time they learn mirror self-recognition? Or that the frontal lobes develop dramatically in the second year of life? Or that they reach Piaget's level of understanding "object permanence" (remembering and seeking out hidden objects) and begin to engage in pretend play? Or that they begin to act like strong, self-willed individuals in the "terrible twos"? Or that they begin soon afterwards to develop empathy for others and moral standards? Or that their autobiographical memories supersede the period of "infantile amnesia" around the age of three?

In the late 1800s, Charles Horton Cooley, a Michigan sociologist, theorized that the human sense of self is created in infants through social interactions. Cooley—who was himself a shy semi-invalid—called this the "looking-glass self" because he believed that our self-concept is a reflection of what we perceive others think of us.[19] His disciple, George Mead, concluded, "it is impossible to conceive of a self arising outside of social experience."[20] Gallup, suspecting that Cooley and Mead were onto something, gave the mark test to chimpanzees that had been raised in complete isolation, after habituating them to mirrors. As he predicted, they failed to identify themselves. Similarly, the famed Wild Boy of Aveyron, captured in the French woods in 1799, reached behind a mirror to find the boy he thought was hiding there. The Wild Boy never learned mirror recognition, nor did he learn to speak.[21] Perhaps such abilities must be developed during the crucial developmental period when the brain is growing and establishing new branches, connections, and synapses.

Of course, mirrors are not necessary for self-awareness. Blind people know perfectly well who they are, for instance. Thus Sidney Bradford, blind before his first birthday, was an intelligent, self-assured 52-year-old when his sight was restored by a cornea transplant in 1958. He became fascinated by mirrors, often preferring to see the world in their reflection rather than directly. But Bradford couldn't get used to his own face in the mirror and shaved by touch in the dark as he always had. [22] The ability to recognize oneself in a mirror correlates with (but does not cause) essential human traits such as logic, creativity, curiosity, the appreciation of beauty, and empathy, leading directly to tool use, scientific experiments, story-telling, poetry, art, theater, law-making, philosophy, religion, and a sense of humor. In other words, as humans evolved, the ability to *think*— to ponder themselves in mirrors, among other things—helped them to survive.

"Without self-awareness," Emory University primatologist Frans de Waal observes in his 1996 book, *Good Natured*, "we might as well be folkloric creatures without souls, such as vampires, who cast no reflections. Most important, we would be incapable of cognitive empathy, as this requires a distinction between self and other and the realization that others have selves like us."[23] As one would expect, other species that display mirror self-recognition also show the capacity to empathize, which is the very essence of the Golden Rule, to treat others as you would be treated. Dolphins, for instance, are famed for helping injured people. On the other hand, the ability to put oneself in someone else's shoes also permits deception and cruelty. What would sadists know about exquisite torture unless they could imagine what it felt like? As Jane Goodall discovered with her beloved chimps, they could murder as well as comfort one another, whatever their motivation.

Sex also seems to be connected with mirror self-recognition, from the ancient Egyptians to the modern brothel ceiling. Bonobos and dolphins are highly sexed animals always ready for intercourse. Pan and Delphi, the two half-brother dolphins, always enjoyed sexual play with one another, but when mirrors were available, their libido went wild, so that in one half-hour session, they attempted to penetrate one another 43 times. In all cases, they assumed positions so that they could watch themselves in the mirror, breaking off if their bodies drifted out of sight, then resuming sex play in front of the mirror.[24]

Self-awareness may lead to more satisfying sex, but it also makes humans, and perhaps some other animals, aware of their mortality. Humans want to believe in a humanistic deity—a mirror image of sorts—who will guarantee us immortality in heaven. Fear of death may account for the religious impulse, but

I think there's more to it. Our search for meaning and our innate reverence for this world in which we live are also probably related to self-awareness and mirrors.

The Mirrorless Biami Garden of Eden

Throughout the developed world, mirrors are commonplace. "The profundity of what takes place in a mirror is in perpetual danger of being lost through familiarity", notes science writer Adrian Desmond.[25] My history of mirrors was in part an attempt to untarnish our mirrors, allowing us to look into them with fresh wonder and to help us understand their extraordinary place in human history. Sometimes, however, I admit that I have thought we might be better off without mirrors, especially when I read that hundreds of thousands of people a year pay for botox injections to smooth their facial wrinkles with a paralytic poison, or when I consider other such attempts to manipulate image and deny mortality.[26] But without mirrors, we would still be human. It is not the blank slate of the mirror that I deplore – it is what we sometimes reflect in it.

Let me leave you with the parable of anthropologist Edmund Carpenter's encounter with the Biami, an isolated New Guinea tribe.[27] "It was important to us to film the reactions of people totally innocent of mirrors," Carpenter wrote in 1975. "Such people exist in New Guinea, though they number only a handful and are disappearing like the morning mist." A few Biami men had mirror shards, but they were too small to show a face and were used only as light-reflectors. They lived near swift rivers but no standing bodies of water in which they could see themselves. "Certainly their initial reaction to large mirrors suggested this was a wholly new experience for them," Carpenter observed. "They were paralyzed: after their first startled response—covering their mouths and ducking their heads—they stood transfixed, staring at their images, only their stomach muscles betraying great tension." Carpenter interpreted their reaction as the "terror of self-awareness," and he portrayed their looking into mirrors as something like Adam and Eve eating the apple in the Garden of Eden, then suddenly becoming self-conscious and covering themselves.

"Western man," Carpenter asserted, "values, above all else, the isolated, delimited, aware self," whereas for traditional New Guinea tribes, "there was no isolating individualism, no private consciousness." As appealing as this romantic assessment may be, I don't buy it. Anthropologist William Mitchell, who did extensive field work with New Guinea tribes, says, "I never met any "primitive" male or female who didn't know who he or she was, and acted upon it."[28] Though the Biami did not have mirrors, they had the human capacity to recognize themselves in them, and the human need to consider and manipulate their image. After all, the men already applied elaborate face-paint to one another in preparation for war. "In a matter of days," Carpenter was forced to report, "they groomed themselves openly before mirrors." When they first beheld the miracle of their own reflection, the Biami may have felt genuine terror, as Carpenter surmised, but perhaps they also felt awe, wonder, and dawning comprehension.

In the developed world, we would do well—as we look into the myriad mirrors that surround us daily and as we use innovative scientific mirrors to look ever farther into the reaches of space and time, to send messages ever more quickly over beams of light, to direct deadly laser weapons—to learn from the Biami. Mirrors *should* inspire terror, wonder and comprehension.

Notes and References

The material in this chapter is adapted from Mark Pendergrast, *Mirror Mirror: A History of the Human Love Affair with Reflection* (New York: Basic Books, 2003).

[1] See Richard Gregory, *Mirrors in Mind* (London: Penguin, 1997); Christine Lilyquist, *Ancient Egyptian Mirrors* (Munich: Deutscher Kunstverlag, 1979); Bruno Schweig, *Mirrors: A Guide to the Manufacture of Mirrors and Reflecting Surfaces* (London: Pelham Books, 1973); Benjamin Goldberg, *The Mirror and Man* (Charlottesville, VA: Univ. Press of Virginia, 1985); Sabine Melchior-Bonnet, *The Mirror: A History*, trans. Katharine H. Jewett (NY: Routledge, 2001).

[2] Lynn Thorndike, *A History of Magic and Experimental Science*, 8 vols. (NY: Macmillan, 1923-1958); Theodore Besterman, *Crystal Gazing: A Study in the History, Distribution, Theory and Practice of Scrying.* (Kila, MT: Kessinger, reprint, [1924]). Benjamin Woolley, *The Queen's Conjurer: The Science and Magic of Dr. John Dee, Adviser to Queen Elizabeth I.* (NY: Henry Holt, 2001).

[3] Goldberg, *Mirror and Man.*

[4] Jacob Abbott, *Light.* (NY: Harper & Brothers, 1871); Richard P. Feynman, *QED: The Strange Theory of Light and Matter.* (NY: Penguin, 1985); Thomas D. Rossing and Christopher J. Chiaverina, *Light Science: Physics and the Visual Arts* (NY: Spring, 1999); David Park, *The Fire Within the Eye* (Princeton, NJ: Princeton U. Pr., 1997).

[5] Nigel Henbest and Michael Marten, *The New Astronomy.* (Cambridge: Cambridge U. Pr., 1983); Wallace Tucker, and Riccardo Giacconi, *The X-Ray Universe* (Cambridge, MA: Harvard U. Pr., 1985).

[6] Wooley, *The Queen's Conjurer.*

[7] Rainer Maria Rilke, *Ahead of All Parting: The Selected Poetry of Rainer Maria Rilke*, translator Stephen Mitchell (New York: The Modern Library, 1995), 467.

[8] J.K. Rowling, *Harry Potter and the Sorcerer's Stone.* (NY: Scholastic, 1997).

[9] Arthur C. Traub and J. Orbach, "Psychophysical Studies of Body-Image," *Archives of General Psychiatry*, v. 11, 1964, 53-66; J. Orbach and Arthur C. Traub, "Psychophysical Studies of Body-Image," *Archives of General Psychiatry*, vol. 14, Jan. 1966, 41-47.

[10] Lui Schwarz and Staton P. Fjeld, "Illusions Induced by the Self-Reflected Image," *Journal of Nervous and Mental Disease*, vol. 146, no. 4, April 1968, 277-284.

[11] Suzanne Barry Osborn, "Little Things Make a Big Difference," *Chain Store Age*, June 1, 2000, 36.

[12] http://www.pcmirror.com/, Bruce Newman (president of PC Mirrors) in phone interview with author, Jan. 30, 2001.

[13] Gordon Gallup (psychology professor at SUNY Albany), interview with author in his office, August 2000 and phone interviews; Gordon G. Gallup, Jr., "Can Animals Empathize? Yes," *Scientific American*, vol. 9, Nov. 1998, p. 66-71; Gordon G. Gallup, Gordon G., Jr., "Chimpanzees: Self-Recognition," *Science*, vol. 167, Jan. 2, 1970, 86-87.

[14] Diana Reiss and Lori Marino, "Mirror Self-Recognition in the Bottlenose Dolphin: a Case of Cognitive Convergence," *PNAS*, v. 98, n. 10, May 8, 2001, 5937-5942; Lori Marino (psychology professor at Emory University) interview with author, Oct. 9, 2002.

[15] Gallup phone interview with author, Nov. 2, 2002.

[16] Should we treat animals that recognize themselves in mirrors in an especially humane manner? So Steven Wise argues, but he also makes the case for many other animals who don't pass the mark test, including honeybees. Steven M. Wise, *Drawing the Line: Science and the Case for Animal Rights* (Cambridge, MA: Perseus Books, 2002).

[17] Beulah Amsterdam, "Mirror Self-Image Reactions Before Age Two," *Developmental Psychobiology*, v. 5, no. 4, 1972, 297-305.

[18] Gordon G. Gallup, Jr., "Self-Awareness and the Evolution of Social Intelligence," *Behavioural Processes*, v. 42, 1998, 239-247.

[19] In 1949, Jacques Lacan incorrectly theorized that infants go through a "mirror stage" between 6 and 18 months of age in which they discover their mirror image and believe it is themselves, thus dooming them to a life of alienation from their true selves. As Lacan put it: "This jubilant assumption of his specular image by the child...[exhibits] the symbolic matrix in which the *I* is precipitated in a primordial form, before it is objectified in the dialectic of identification with the other." Jacques Lacan, *Écrits: A Selection* (London: Tavistock Publications, 1977).

[20] George H. Mead, *Mind, Self and Society from the Standpoint of a Social Behaviorist* (Chicago: U. Chicago Pr., 1934).

[21] Harlan Lane, *The Wild Boy of Aveyron*. (Cambridge, MA: Harvard U. Pr., 1976).

[22]The story ends tragically. With his sight restored, Bradford became self-conscious, lost his self-confidence, and died within two years. Richard Langton Gregory and Jean G. Wallace, "Recovery from Early Blindness: A Case Study," *Experimental Psychology Monograph No. 2*, 1963.

[23] Frans De Waal, Good Natured: The Origins of Right and Wrong in Humans and Other Animals (Cambridge, MA: Harvard U. Pr., 1996).

[24] Reiss and Marino, "Mirror Self-Recognition in the Bottlenose Dolphin."

[25] Adrian J. Desmond, *The Ape's Reflexion* (NY: Dial Press, 1979).

[26] David Noonan and Jerry Adler, "The Botox Boom," *Newsweek*, May 13, 2002, 50-58.

[27] Edmund Carpenter, "The Tribal Terror of Self-Awareness," in *Principles of Visual Anthropology*, ed. Paul Hockings (Hague: Mouton Publishers, 1975).

[28] William E. Mitchell (emeritus anthropology professor), email correspondence, July 21, 2002.

PART I:

MIRRORS OF ANTIQUITY

CHAPTER ONE

MIRRORS IN THE BRITISH IRON AGE: PERFORMANCE, REVELATION AND POWER

MELANIE GILES AND JODY JOY

In 1984, archaeologists excavating the Iron Age cemetery at Wetwang Slack, East Yorkshire, came across three remarkable graves, dating between the fourth and first centuries BC.[1] Like other burials nearby, they consisted of a single inhumation in a grave pit, surrounded by a square-cut ditch, from which chalk and silt had been used to cover the burial in a low mound. However, these barrows were larger than normal and set apart, lying to the west of the main cemetery. Grave goods within this cemetery included pots (usually containing a sheep humerus, representing a joint of mutton), or small items of jewellery such as a brooch, bracelet or necklace. However, all three of the new burials contained the dismantled remains of two-wheeled vehicles (chariots or carts), complete with their horse gear. Significantly, whilst the two men were buried with elaborately decorated bronze scabbards and swords, the woman was interred with a decorated bronze canister or box, and an iron mirror.

Mirrors are one of the prestige objects manufactured by smiths and artisans, during the middle-late Iron Age (c. 400 BC – 43 AD) and are found in both Britain and Ireland, as well as elsewhere on the Continent. They are made of iron or bronze polished plates and finished with bronze fittings, including looped handles and rims. Both complete examples and damaged fragments have been found in a variety of contexts: pools and lakes, as well as graves. However, their frequent association with female burials has often led to them being dismissed as a mere accoutrement, or "attractive vanity" of high status women, who are all too often marginalised in representations of Iron Age society.[2]

In this paper, we seek to challenge this passive and superficial view of both object and individual, by characterising these objects and exploring the context of their deposition. Since these Iron Age communities were pre-literate, we will use anthropological analogy to explore their potential use and meaning, and to prompt us to think differently about the relations between people and things in the prehistoric past.

Mirrors in the British Iron Age

The earliest mirrors from Britain and Ireland were made of iron, and date between the 4th and 1st centuries BC. Five examples are known from East Yorkshire: two from Arras,[3] two from Wetwang Slack[4] and one from Garton Slack.[5] There are also three mirrors thought to date to the 1st century AD including an iron mirror handle from the Carlingwark Loch hoard, Kirkcudbrightshire[6] and a fragment of iron mirror from a layer behind the hillfort ramparts at Maiden Castle.[7] An iron mirror found in an inhumation on Lambay Island, Co. Dublin is also likely to be of 1st century AD date.[8] Most of these examples consist of a roughly circular iron plate, once polished, varying between 165mm to 198mm diameter. In examples such as the Lady's Barrow from Arras, cast and decorated bronze fittings are used to join the iron handle to the plate. These handles are straight, measuring up to 154mm long, and are either round or square in section. This distinctive profile led Fox to classify them as part of a "bar-handled" type of mirror, most commonly found in the north of Britain.[9]

In contrast, bronze mirrors are made of a polished bronze plate, which is sometimes rimmed, and a cast bronze handle. Whilst the reflective surface of the front plate may have been improved by a variety of finishes, such as tin sweat, cementation, wiping, dipping or even plating, systematic metallurgical analysis has yet to be undertaken.[10] However, many of the bronze mirrors have intricate La Tène style decoration engraved into the back of the main plate, and these highly decorated mirrors are amongst the most recognisable objects of the later British Iron Age. The majority come from burials in the south of England dating between the 1st century BC and the 1st century AD. Two distinct regionally and temporally significant groups, from the southeast and southwest of England, can be identified from depositional context, form, size and decoration (Figure 1.1).[11]

Based on burial evidence, bronze and iron mirrors have been interpreted as the personal property of high status Iron Age women.[12] For example, the mirror burial found at Portesham in Dorset contained, in addition to a decorated bronze mirror, the crouched remains of a mature woman, pottery and joints of meat, three brooches, a knife, a bronze pan and a toilet set.[13] Burials with mirrors are also sometimes seen as the female equivalent to a small number of male burials containing weapons such as swords, shields and spears.[14] Evidence from recent finds suggests that these generalisations may be overly simplistic. Whilst it is true that the vast majority of mirrors have been identified as coming from female burials, a recent find from the Scilly Isles consisted of an unsexed inhumation burial containing, among other things, a bronze mirror and a sword.[15]

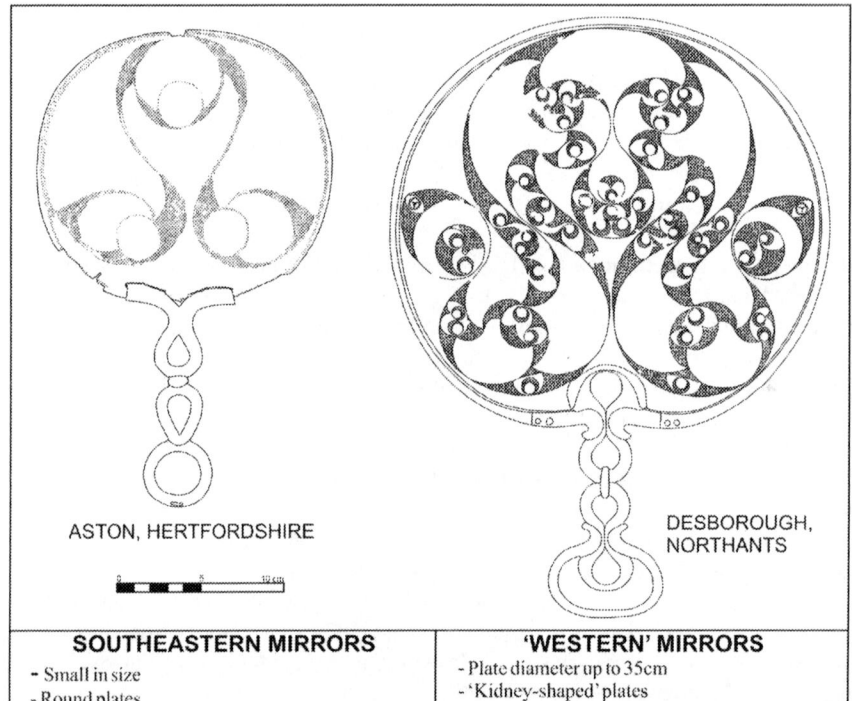

ASTON, HERTFORDSHIRE

DESBOROUGH,
NORTHANTS

SOUTHEASTERN MIRRORS	'WESTERN' MIRRORS
- Small in size - Round plates - Found in cremation burials dated 80-20BC, alongside pottery and brooches. - Decoration constructed using minimal number of motifs. Areas filled with inconsistent hatching.	- Plate diameter up to 35cm - 'Kidney-shaped' plates - Where evidence exists, deposited in ground AD 40-60. Often in graves - Complex decoration using many, repeated motifs. Design constructed using compasses. Basket-hatching.

Figure 1.1. Bronze mirror types. Line drawings by Jody Joy.

Archaeologists have therefore begun to question the ways in which we interpret such grave goods: they cannot be seen as direct reflections of either the status or gender of the deceased. The dead do not bury themselves: the living do,[16] and the motives of mourners may have been very complex. They may have used the funeral to demonstrate their own status, gaining prestige and authority by gifting a celebrated artefact or inherited antique to the deceased. The power and reputation of the object may also have been drawn upon to deal with important or unexpected "bad" deaths, which tore a rift in the social fabric. Such gifts may also have been used to close debts with the deceased (lest they return to look for reparation) or to appeal for intercession on behalf of the living, once the deceased had entered the world of the ancestors. For many prehistoric communities, the dead appear to have been regarded as active in people's lives, and grave goods may have been used to equip them for these new tasks or roles.

The manner in which a mirror is deposited will therefore depend upon a large number of factors, including the status and identity of their owner. Recent work in anthropology has shown how social relationships tend to cluster around certain objects.[17] Some artefacts can be seen to take on the characteristics, or personality, of people.[18] Objects can act as a medium through which people are able to tell their life story.[19] Objects can also be conceived as possessing a life history or biography.[20] They are made or "born". They have a "life", during which they accumulate meanings and associations as they are exchanged between people, and "act" in certain contexts.[21] These meanings can 'change' and are "renegotiated" throughout the object's life-history.[22] Objects age like people; they become damaged and worn as they are used and they eventually "die" when they are broken, or deposited. Mirrors had the potential to become biographical objects; they are complicated and durable and are likely to have led complex lives. It is possible to infer something about the potential life-paths of mirrors from their physical form, through evidence for use, wear and repair, production and deposition. In this next section we will use the idea of an object life to examine some of the potential meanings and social relationships which clustered around bronze mirrors during their lifetime.

Mirror Making

The process of making a complicated artefact like a mirror would have involved the coming together of a number of people and the coordination of many different resources at each stage of manufacture. First, the raw materials for iron and bronze would have had to be obtained. Whilst iron is difficult to source metallurgically, we know that the bronze handles and plates were often made of copper alloys from different sources, using different ores. [23] Metallurgical analysis also suggests that many bronze mirrors may have been recycled from other artefacts: this is not unusual in an Iron Age context and bronze is easily recycled.[24] It is not presently possible to identify the recycling of iron, unless other substances are caught up in the matrix from the parent artefact, but it is likely that iron was also recycled.[25] Mirrors, then, were created in a world in which many things were regenerated when they reached the end of their usefulness.

Once procured, the metals were worked by specialist smiths. The iron mirror from Wetwang was solely the work of a blacksmith, who would have forged plate and handle together. However, the iron plate from Maiden Castle was bound with a bronze rim, secured by a small bronze clasp,[26] and both of the mirror plates from Garton Slack and the "Lady's Barrow" at Arras are conjoined to their iron handles with bronze fittings.[27] These composite objects would have therefore demanded the skills of both iron and bronze smithing, from one or more smiths. First, the plate and handle would have been forged out of blooms which had been partially worked into currency bars or ingots: reheating, drawing out and hammering the metal into the desired shape. Where bronze fittings were used, these would have been moulded in wax, around which a clay mould was pressed. The mould was fired by heating, during which the wax model melted and drained out, to be replaced by molten bronze. Once cool, these rough casts were filed and polished to remove dribbles and seams, and – in the case of one of the Arras mirrors – finished with fine, punched dot decoration.

Bronze mirrors are almost unique in the context of Iron Age craftwork, as they combine both cast and sheet-metal components and it is possible that a number of different individuals were involved in making such a mirror. The plates and handles required different skills to make, as did marking out, and inscribing the intricate decoration on the plate. Plates were made from an ingot of cast bronze which was hammered flat and cut to shape, the handle was cast using the *lost wax* technique described above, and the plate was decorated by inscribing or chasing lines into the surface of the mirror.[28] Each mirror is an individual artefact[29] and the processes of making individual mirrors would have varied. However, the overall effect of a mirror when the components are brought together suggests a design plan. Elements of the design of the handles and plate decoration are often the same and when the plate, handle and rim are attached the decoration on the plate is not significantly obscured.

There is evidence from some of the mirrors that implies a sequence of events in their making. The handle was probably made before, or at the same time, as the plate was decorated because often elements of the decoration on the handle are incorporated into the designs inscribed onto the plate. The plate and handle would have been joined by wedging the plate into a pre-cast slot in the handle. This joint was sometimes secured with rivets or pins and the addition of a copper-alloy rim, or binding around the edge of the plate. We know the plates were decorated and polished before they were attached to the handle because the decoration on a number of the mirror plates lies underneath the handle or the rim. When a mirror found at Birdlip in Gloucestershire was restored by the British Museum, they discovered an area underneath the handle which had been used to practice some of the techniques used to inscribe the decoration onto the visible areas of the plate.[30] The practice area conformed so well to the shape of the top of the handle that the person decorating the plate must have known the shape of the handle and how it was going to be attached.

Mirror makers must have been, or had contact with, the metalworkers who made and decorated the component parts. Mirrors could have been made for and by, an individual, a group of people, or a social group. In the later Iron Age there was an emerging group of people identifying themselves as socially different. These people expressed their identities in new ways in which they presented themselves to others, through dress, appearance and adornment, and the conspicuous consumption of food and drink.[31] The production of mirrors in the late 1st century BC to the early 1st century AD echoes this apparent heightened concern for personal appearance, and may have been used to inspect the decoration of the body, hair and clothing, or to monitor appearance, gesture and posture. The sociologist Foucault saw such self-surveillance as a way in which particular ideals about the body were effectively inculcated and reproduced.[32] For Mauss, objects and tools like the mirror developed what he described as specific "techniques of body care", which were intimately tied up in people's sense of identity and how it was performed to others.[33] The possession and use of the mirror may therefore have been an important way in which status was reproduced. In addition, by orchestrating the making of a mirror a person could demonstrate the social relationships and resources they could co-ordinate. Thus, throughout its lifetime, the mirror helped reproduce certain ideals about personhood and appearance, as well as becoming a symbol of identity, and the relationships and resources people had access to.

Mirror Form

The forms of the different components of a mirror are similar to, and could be seen to refer to, a number of other items of Iron Age material culture. For example, like the iron mirrors with bronze fittings, middle to late Iron Age horse gear from East Yorkshire also used a combination of iron bars and bronze rings or links, and iron swords were frequently sheathed in decorated bronze scabbards.[34] These similarities evoked relations between families of objects, and suites of craft skill. Meanwhile, the sheet metal of the bronze mirror plates could refer to sheet metal objects like bronze shields and cauldrons. Similar decoration to the mirror plates is found on other objects such as some sword scabbards and harness fittings. The shape of the rim binding is like a torc, it is also similar to bronze binding around wooden shields and other unidentified wooden objects. Finally, the handles of many of the mirrors are similar in form to horse bits when they are laid out flat. People encountering mirrors could have made these associations and linkages between the mirror and other objects. The mirrors combine into one artefact these referents of other items of material culture and could stand for an idealised sense of continuity with the past, present and future. As inherited heirlooms or gifts, they also embodied a lineage of associations and events in which they had played a part. Mirrors may not therefore necessarily reflect the status of the individual in a grave; they may be representative of the whole community and its history.

Deposition

There are many parallels between the treatment of people and mirrors in funerary contexts. Iron Age burials often contain brooches, found near to the neck or shoulder, or even in front of the face or at the knees, indicating that the bodies were interred with some kind of clothing or shroud, secured and decorated by brooches.[35] Brooches are also found in association with mirrors, sometimes still attached to the bottom, or terminal loop, of the mirror handle. For example, in 2000, two metal detectorists found a highly decorated mirror near Shillington in Bedfordshire, with a silver brooch attached to the loop of the handle and the fragmented remains of an urn and some other pottery vessels. These remains probably came from a disturbed cremation burial dating to 80-20 BC.[36] A brass brooch was also found attached to the loop of the Portesham mirror handle.[37]

The brooches could have been used to close, or secure organic bags or cloth. A number of the mirrors, like those from Chilham Castle or Holcome, have been found in an area of organic staining, suggesting that they were indeed contained in a bag, or wrapped in cloth. Patches of mineralised cloth on the Wetwang Slack mirror[38] can be compared with impressions of wood on the mirror from Garton Slack,[39] suggesting these two iron examples were contained respectively in a bag and wooden box. Such coverings would have acted to protect the mirror plate from corrosion and damage in life,[40] as well as from jealous eyes.[41] As part of the funerary rite, it could also be seen as analogous to the preparation of the body, and its wrapping in a shroud secured with a brooch, or placed in a coffin. By gradually concealing both corpse and/or mirror from public view, both were withdrawn from the world of the living in a similar manner.

Decoration

Bronze mirrors are often decorated using a small number of compass-drawn motifs of repeated and distinctive forms which are arranged into complex, intricate and free-flowing designs. This has been termed the "mirror-style".[42] The La Tène artwork on mirrors has been described by the art historian Martin Jope as deliberately ambiguous, combining abstract forms with a restless allusion to natural phenomena, such as bird beaks and the faces of owls or cats.[43] Mirror decoration animates the object by disorientating the viewer, acting to deceive the eye.[44] Beyond possible references to nature, mirror decoration also possesses its own internal logic which refers to the reflective properties of the plate. The overall design is often arranged so that it has vertical symmetry; each half of the decoration is a mirror image of the other. The designs also show equal concern for the areas on the mirror surface which are not decorated.[45] The individual motifs, filled with basket-weave hatching, are arranged in such a way in order to frame and create blank areas of distinctive and repeated forms. The inscribed areas can be seen to evoke the reflective properties of the mirror by framing and creating distorted images of themselves. The decoration on mirrors therefore not only acts to deceive the eye, but also to reinforce the reflective qualities of the mirror plate.

The anthropologist Alfred Gell envisaged two ways in which art can be utilised.[46] First, it is used in ritual where it is displayed to express political power and legitimise associations with the supernatural. Secondly, art objects are produced for exchange. We can see mirrors, concealed by their coverings or bags, being revealed with great ceremony, releasing their power and conferring it on participants in the performance. These physically impressive and powerful objects would also have made very prestigious gifts. Thus, through their physical resemblance to other items of Iron Age material culture, the different component parts of a mirror act as referents to these objects and throughout their lives mirrors would have accumulated a history through the people and events they were associated with. It is this life-story that would have been one of the factors which determined whether a mirror was going to be recycled, placed in a grave or disposed of in some other way. The skills of the person(s) that made a mirror, the visual impact of the object, and the social and physical history they accumulated throughout their lifetimes would have given some mirrors powerful "auras".[47]

There are therefore all sorts of reasons why a particular individual may have been buried with a mirror. One reason could be that the mirror was the possession of that individual in life but as we have already noted, mirrors may not directly reflect the status of the individual in a grave. Mirrors may be gifts to or from important individuals. Mirror burials may also be representative of and perform a function for, the whole of the community. A mirror could also have been placed in a grave to help the occupant perform a certain task in another place. A useful analogy is provided by Etruscan mirrors, which were placed in tombs to aid in the release of the soul in its journey to the after world.[48] The history and power a particular mirror had accumulated during its life may therefore have determined whether it was selected to perform such a role.

Interpreting mirrors

Although the final depositional context of mirrors is clearly important, during their life they may have had a range of roles and meanings. Wear patterns suggest many were suspended from the handle when not in use, perhaps from a belt on the body or pegs on the walls of roundhouses. Although they would have been impressive at a distance, catching and reflecting light, they

were meant to work most powerfully upon the viewer close-up. We have
already touched on the use of the mirror to inspect appearance and reproduce
certain bodily ideals, but they may also have been used to reveal aspects of the
self which were not normally visible, or reflect on transformations which
emerged after rites of passage, such as initiation. Some of them would have
been too heavy to hold single-handedly, and were designed to be held either by
an attendant,[49] or in some settings, by figures of authority, for others to gaze
into.

The burnished metal of these planar discs would never have provided a clear
surface in which the face could be seen as an accurate reflection. As such, they
are unlikely to be merely tools of personal vanity. Instead, they would have
reflected a shadowy world, a play of light and darkness, exaggerated by the La
Tène art which drew the viewer into a maze of decoration. This pleasing
entanglement of design could be playful, witty and mischievous, as elements of
vegetation and animals' features were glimpsed before becoming lost in
abstraction.[50] The sheer dexterity embodied in the crafting of this object, and its
complex engraving and embellishment, can be seen as part of a "technology of
enchantment",[51] exuding a "halo-effect" of power which captivated or ensnared
the viewer.[52] However, Jope noted that the overall effect of this compass-drawn
mirror art was of arrested movement, pent-up flow: the coiled spring of forces
under tension. The skilled use of asymmetry also led to more disorientating
effects in some mirrors: slewed, swaying rhythms, crazed and leering faces
which would have overwhelmed and confused the viewer.[53] In his work on
Oceanic art, Thomas has considered such complex, decorated objects as being
capable of committing a kind of psychological warfare on the recipient, with
powerful visceral as well as visual effects. [54] Supernatural power or
cosmological energy is often attributed to objects with luminous or brilliant
qualities,[55] like the mirrors. Perhaps this explains why they were so carefully
wrapped or contained; concealing these objects from uninitiated or vulnerable
eyes, because of their potential danger, whilst enhancing the drama and effect of
their revelation. In later prehistory, such encounters may well have been
enhanced by psychotropic drugs or alcohol, episodes of fasting or even
heightened emotional states like grief.

It is therefore possible that both the polished fronts and decorated back-
plates were used to gain insights into aspects of the Iron Age world. Mirrors not
only transpose left and right, but permit viewers to see both ahead of and behind
themselves at the same time.[56] It is possible that this physical quality is the
source of the metaphor which links mirrors with the power to see both back into
the past and forward into the future. For example, Tibetan Oracle priests use
mirrors to assist their prediction of future events,[57] this use of mirrors for
augury is known as catoptromancy. In contrast, the Bakongo people of the

Congo River investigate past misfortunes using mirrors which can reveal the use of witchcraft and other invisible sources of harm.[58] In other societies, their power is drawn upon to heal or curse people, spy upon others, bind oaths and cast spells.[59] Interestingly, South American Ayahuasca shamens believe that through the manipulation of the mirror-world of reflections, the physical world will be altered accordingly; inverting the norm of the mirror as the visual echo of the physical world.[60] Mirrors can therefore act as powerful metaphors for understanding the world, whilst as objects, they can be both sites of human agency *and* be perceived to possess agency themselves.

In particular, mirrors seem to have a special role in relation to the dead or the spirit world. The Fang people of Gabon take hallucinogens before using mirrors to access visions or contact the ancestors: under the influence of such drugs, perhaps it is not surprising people glimpse the 'family face' reflected in their own features.[61] Meanwhile, the Bakongo people also used their mirrors to transmit power across dimensions and invoke ancestral intercession.[62] It is therefore possible that the inclusion of mirrors in Iron Age graves was similarly used to aid communication and contact with the deceased. Mirrors are frequently seen as objects which are able to work at the boundaries of states of being: thresholds between worlds which are both liminal and dangerous. As with several other groups, the Bakongo explicitly draw an analogy between mirrors and the reflective surface of lakes, pools or streams: both are viewed as a film separating the world of the dead from the world of the living.[63]

This is significant, since several of the bronze mirrors and one iron example were deposited in watery contexts such as lakes or bogs. Along with springs, such natural sources of water may well have had sacred importance to many Iron Age communities.[64] Interestingly, the art historian Jope believed that some of the Celtic art on mirror-backs was designed to symbolise or mimic flows of water, pools and islands.[65] These twin themes – the power of mirrors in dealing with the dead, and their analogy with water as boundaries between worlds – come together in the latest mirror burial to be found in East Yorkshire.

Death, mirrors and water

In the spring of 2001, a new chariot burial was discovered on the opposite side of the valley from the earlier inhumations.[66] The burial proved to be that of a mature woman, who was interred with horse-gear decorated with red enamel and coral, and another iron mirror, laid against her drawn-up legs. Interestingly, the barrow was situated close to the village pond, which (like others in the region) was probably a small, clay-lined mere in later prehistory. These features would have held standing bodies of water, whose surfaces may have been very similar to the murky, shadowy face of the iron mirror.

The proximity of this burial to a water source fits a larger pattern identified by Bevan who noted that many of the square barrow cemeteries dating to this period were deliberately placed near, or even in, the watercourses known locally as "Gypsey Races".[67] The word 'gypsey' is derived from the Scandinavian word to "gape", describing the way in which the porous chalk land yawns open to release powerful springs, through which the "races" begin to flow in later winter or early spring.[68] These streams are strongly seasonal and sometimes disappear dramatically into the ground through sinkholes. Bevan suggests that these bodies of water were perceived as the medium which flowed between the overworld of the living and the underworld of the dead.[69] Their association with burials may have been used to both speed the departure of the deceased and enable their transformation and return as members of the ancestry.[70] Regenerative properties may have been attributed to these streams because of their rich mineral content, which brought fertility to the land and new life to its inhabitants. However, the waters were also dangerous; their unpredictability and violence meant that in the Medieval period, property and livestock were frequently damaged in the ensuing floods.[71] As with all significant forces, the power of the water was double-edged: destructive and violent as well as fertile and lifegiving. If the surfaces of mirrors *were* seen as analogous to these bodies of water, this dangerous and ambiguous quality would also have been conferred upon the object.

Returning to Wetwang Slack, the association between the reflective surface of water and the mirror was reiterated in its wrapping in a bag or covering made of otter fur:[72] an animal which symbolised the ability to move between the realms of land and water, this world and the next. The bag also appears to have been decorated or tied with a tassel of tiny blue-glass beads. In the cemetery across the valley, larger blue glass bead necklaces were only found with mature women, so the beads may be used to evoke both the female gender and advanced age of both the Wetwang woman and her mirror.[73] The osteoarchaeological analysis revealed that she was probably in her senior years, having survived childbirth, making her a rare and valued repository of knowledge and lore.[74] At 5 foot 7 inches in height, she would have been a striking figure, and this was compounded by a dislocated shoulder which was never re-set, but fused out of place – an impressive feat of recovery and strength. The preliminary analysis suggested that this woman may also have been distinguished from birth by a facial haemangioma: a misgrowth of the blood-vessels which would have left one half of her face blood-red, lumpy and swollen in texture.[75] Red enamel and coral decorates much of the bronzework during this period, from swords and scabbards, to shields, boxes and brooches.[76] Rather than interpreting this as a disfigurement, her community may have regarded it as a sign of other-worldly favour, as if she had been "enamelled" by the gods and empowered by this potent or sacred colour. This may explain why – as an important, powerful elder – she was entrusted with the mirror, as someone who was attuned to, and able to intervene with, these other worlds.

Conclusion

To conclude, Iron Age mirrors, whether made of iron or bronze, were beautiful, powerful, and potentially terrifying or dangerous objects. They were used in the preparation and presentation of the body and in prestigious displays, but may also have been associated with the powers of augury and insight into the past, or access to ancestral or spiritual worlds. Their decoration and wrapping appear to have been integral to their powerful effect upon people in a variety of social settings and performances, as they were revealed or concealed from view. As complex objects, they were also evocative through their similarities with other objects and embodied a series of important relationships which had come together in their making. Evidence of wear and repair also brought to mind the chain of hands through which they had passed before they were deposited. Mirrors may have had identities, names or lineages of their own: some were accorded "burial" rites which appear analogous to those of humans, whilst others were paired with specific individuals in death. This paper has therefore challenged the view that these objects were associated with idle vanity and passive femininity: mirror bearers were active and instrumental agents whose identity and power in life and death, were forged, in part, through their relationship with these objects.

Notes and References

[1] J.C. Dent, "Three cart burials from Wetwang, Yorkshire", *Antiquity* lix (1985): 85-92.

[2] C. Fox, *Pattern and Purpose: A Survey of Early Celtic Art in Britain* (Cardiff: The National Museum of Wales, 1958), 84.

[3] I. Stead, *The Arras Culture*. (York: York Philosophical Society, 1979), 81-82.

[4] Dent, "Three cart burials": 85-92. J.D. Hill, "A new cart/chariot burial from Wetwang, East Yorkshire", *Past (The Newsletter of the Prehistoric Society)* 38 (2001): 2-3.

[5] T.C.M. Brewster, *The Excavation of Garton and Wetwang Slacks* (Malton, East Riding Archaeological Research Committee, 1980), 228.

[6] Fox, "Celtic Mirror Handles in Britain, with special reference to the Colchester Handle" *Archaeologia Cambrensis* 100 (1948): 22-44, 26.

[7] R.E.M. Wheeler, *Maiden Castle, Dorset. Reports of the Research Committee of the Society of Antiquaries of London No XII* (Oxford: Oxford University Press, 1943), 272.

[8] R.A.S. MacAlister, "On Some Antiquities discovered upon Lambay Island", *Proceedings of the Royal Irish Academy* XXXVIII (1928-9): 240-6, 244. Fox, "Celtic Mirror Handles": 22-44, 25.

[9] Fox, *Pattern and Purpose*, 98.

[10] Thomas Eley, Cambridgeshire County Council, *pers.comm.*

[11] A.P. Fitzpatrick, "A 1st-century AD 'Durotrigian' inhumation burial with a decorated Iron Age mirror from Portesham, Dorset", *Proceedings of the Dorset Natural History and Archaeological Society* 118 (1997): 51-70, 60. A. Fox & S. Pollard, "A decorated bronze mirror from an Iron age settlement at Holcolmbe, near Uplyme, Devon", *Antiquaries Journal* LIII (1973): 21-41, 32-3.

[12] G.C. Dunning, "An engraved bronze mirror from Nijmegen, Holland; with a note on the origin and distribution of the type", *Archaeological Journal* 85 (1928): 69-79. Fox, *Pattern and Purpose*, 98. E.M. Jope, *Early Celtic art in the British Isles* (Oxford: Oxford University Press, 2000). R.A. Smith, "On a Late-Celtic mirror found at Desborough, Northants, and other mirrors", *Archaeologia* 61(B), (1909): 329-46.

[13] Fitzpatrick, "A 1st-century AD 'Durotigian' inhumation burial": 51-70.

[14] B. Cunliffe, *Iron Age Britain* (London: B. T. Batsford Ltd/English Heritage, 1995).

[15] C. Johns, "Iron Age sword and mirror cist burial from Bryher, Isles of Scilly", *Cornish Archaeology* (2006): 1-80, 41-2.

[16] E. Leach, "Discussion", *Space, Hierarchy and Society: inter-disciplinary studies in social area analysis, BAR Supplementary Series 59,* ed. B.C. Burnham & J. Kingsbury, 119-124. (Oxford, British Archaeological Reports, 1979).

[17] A. Gell, *Art and agency: an anthropological theory* (Oxford: Clarendon Press, 1998). C. Gosden, "Making sense: archaeology and aesthetics", *World Archaeology* 33(2), (2001): 163-7.

[18] D. Battaglia, *On the bones of the serpent: person, memory and mortality in Sabarl Island society* (Chicago: Chicago University Press, 1990). N.D. Munn, *The fame of Gawa: a symbolic study of value transformation in a Massim (Papua New Guinea) society* (Cambridge: Cambridge University Press, 1986). M. Strathern, *The gender of the gift* (Berkeley: University of California Press, 1998).

[19] J. Hoskins, *Biographical objects: how things tell the stories of people's lives* (London & New York: Routledge, 1998).

[20] I. Kopytoff, "The cultural biography of things: commoditization as process", *The social life of things: commodities in cultural perspective,* ed. A. Appadurai. (Cambridge: Cambridge University Press, 1986), 64-91.

[21] Y. Marshall & C. Gosden (eds.), *World Achaeology: the cultural biography of objects,* Vol. 31(2), (1999).

[22] Ibid., 169.

[23] J. Bayley, "Analysis of the engraved mirror and associated brooch", 61-2: Table 1, in A.P. Fitzpatrick (ed.) "A 1st-century AD 'Durotrigian' inhumation burial": 51-70. M. Farley, "A Mirror Burial at Dorton, Buckinghamshire", *Proceedings of the Prehistoric Society* 49 (1983): 269-302, Table 1. J.P. Northover, "Analysis of Celtic mirror I from Rivenhall", *Rivenhall: investigations of a villa, church and village, 1950-197, Volume 2—specialist studies and index to volumes 1 and 2,* ed. W.J. Rodwell & K.A. Rodwell,

33-5. (London: CBA Research Report 80, Chelmsford Museums Service and the Council for British Archaeology, 1993).

[24] See Bayley, 62.

[25] Roger Doonan, University of Sheffield, *pers.comm.*

[26] Wheeler, fig. 89: 2

[27] Brewster, 245. Stead, *The Arras Culture*, 81-2.

[28] P. Lowery & R. Savage, "Celtic design with compasses as seen on the Holcombe Mirror.", *Celtic art in ancient Europe five protohistoric centuries: proceedings of the Colloquy held in 1972 at the Oxford Maison Francaise*, ed. P.M. Duval & C.F.C. Hawkes, 219-31 (London: Seminar Press, 1976). P. Lowery, R. Savage & R.L. Wilkins, "Scriber, graver, scorper, tracer: notes on experiments in bronzeworking technique" *Proceedings of the Prehistoric Society* 37 (1971): 167-82.). P. Lowery, R. Savage & R.L. Wilkins, "A technical study of the designs on the British mirror series." *Archaeologia* 105 (1976): 99-126.

[29] Jope, 147

[30] Fox, *Pattern and Purpose*, 91, Plate 58a. Jope, Plate 245e.

[31] J.D. Hill, "The end of one kind of body and the beginning of another kind of body? Toilet instruments and 'Romanization' in southern England during the first century AD", *Re-constructing Iron Age Societies*, ed. A. Gwilt & C. Haselgrove, 96-107. (Oxford: Oxbow Monograph, 1997). J.D. Hill, "Romanisation, gender and class: recent approaches to identity in Britain and their possible consequences", *Britons and Romans: advancing an archaeological agenda*, ed. S. James & M. Millett, 12-8. (York: Council for British Archaeology Research Reports 125, 2001). S. Jundi, S. & J.D. Hill, "Brooches and identities in First Century AD Britain: more than meets the eye?", *TRAC 97. Proceedings of the seventh annual Theoretical Roman Archaeology Conference, Nottingham 1997*, ed. C. Forcey, J. Hawthorne & R. Witchen, 125-37 (Oxford: Oxbow Books, 1997).

[32] M. Foucault, *The history of sexuality. Volume 3: The care of the self* (London: Penguin, 1990).

[33] M. Mauss, "The notion of body techniques", *Sociology and Psychology: Essays of Marcel Mauss,* trans. B. Brewster. (London: Routledge, 1979), 97-123.

[34] Stead, 47-55.

[35] M. Giles, *Open-weave, close-knit: archaeologies of identity in the later prehistoric landscape of East Yorkshire*, Unpublished PhD thesis, University of Sheffield, 2000.

[36] J.D. Hill, "Shillington, Bedfordshire: Iron Age silver brooch, bronze mirror and pottery fragments (P&EE 79)", *Treasure Annual Report 2000*, 15-6. (London: Department of Culture, Media and Sport, 2000).

[37] Fitzpatrick, 21.

[38] J.S. Dent, *Wetwang Slack: an Iron Age cemetery on the Yorkshire Wolds,* Unpublished MPhil thesis, University of Sheffield, 1984.

[39] Brewster, 245.

[40] Fox & Pollard, 19.

[41] C.f. J. Brück, "Material metaphors: the relational construction of identity in Early Bronze Age burials in Ireland and Britain", *Journal of Social Archaeology* Vol. 4 (3), (2004): 307-333.

[42] J.M. De Navarro, "The Celts in Britain and their art.", *The Heritage of early Britain*, ed. M.D. Knowles, 56-82. (London: G. Bell & Sons Ltd, 1952), 79.

[43] Jope, 137-48.

[44] C.f. C. Gosden, "Making sense: archaeology and aesthetics", *World Archaeology* 33(2), (2001): 163-7, 164.

[45] Fox, *Pattern and Purpose*, 48-53.

[46] A. Gell, "The technology of enchantment and the enchantment of technology", *The art of anthropology: essays and diagrams*, ed. E. Hirsch, 159-86. (London & New Brunswick, NJ: The Athlone Press, 1999), 175.

[47] C.f. W. Benjamin, *Illuminations.(The work of art in the age of mechanical reproduction* (London: Fontana, 1973: 1992 edition), 211-44.

[48] Jope, 123.

[49] Fox, "Celtic Mirror Handles in Britain": 24.

[50] Jope, 147.

[51] Gell, "The technology of enchantment and the enchantment of technology." In *Anthropology, Art and Aesthetics* ed. J. Coote & A.Shelton, 40-63. (Oxford: Clarendon Press, 1992) 43.

[52] Gell, *Art and agency*.

[53] Jope, 139

[54] N. Thomas, *Oceanic Art* (London: Thames and Hudson, 1995), 87-88.

[55] H. Morphy, "From Dull to Brilliant: the Aesthetics of Spiritual Power Among the Yolngu", *Man (New Series)* 24 (1989), 21-40.

[56] S. James & V. Rigby, *Britain and the Celtic Iron Age.* (London: British Museum Press, 1997), 39.

[57] D. Tseten, "Tibetan art of divination", *Tibetan Bulletin* (March-April 1995), http://www.tibet.com/Buddhism/divination.html.

[58] P. Samford, "Searching for West Afrian Cultural Meanings in the Archaeological Record", *African-American Archaeology* (Newsletter of the African-American Archaeology Network) No. 12 (Winter 1994), http://www.diaspora.uiuc.edu/A-AAnewsletter/Winter1994.html.

[59] R. Burton, *Personal Narrative of a Pilgrimage to Al-Madinah and Meccah*, http://etext.library.adelaide.edu.au/b/burton/richard/b97p/b97p.html . (Memorial edition of 1893 original, rendered into electronic text, 2003). D. Henness, "The magic mirror: a Fijian folk-tale", *Folklore* 14 (1913): 233-4.

[60] M.C.Y. Lumby, "The Realm of Visions: Towards an Evaluation of the role of near-death experience in Ayahuasca Psychotherapies", University of Cambridge, Department of Social Anthropology Fieldwork Report 1 (1997), http://www.maps.org/research/lumbyreports1.html

[61] W.J. Fernandez, *Bwiti: An Ethnography of the Religious Imagination in Africa* (Princeton, New Jersey: Princeton University Press, 1982).

[62] K.P. Smith, "Through a Clouded Mirror: Africa at the Pan-American Exposition", Buffalo Museum of Science, (2002), http://www.sciencebuff.org/africa_at_the_pan_am_introduction.php.

[63] Smith, "Through a Clouded Mirror".

[64] M. Aldhouse-Green, *The Gods of the Celts.* (Thrupp, Stroud: Sutton Publishing, 2004).

[65] Jope, 138 & 140.

[66] Hill, "A new cart/chariot burial": 2-3.

[67] W. Bevan, "The dead can dance: Iron Age square burials and landscape in East Yorkshire.", *The loved body's corruption: archaeological contributions to the study of human mortality*, ed. J. Downes & J. Pollard (Glasgow: Cruithne Press, 1999), 69-93.

[68] A. H. Smith, *The Place-Names of the East Riding of Yorkshire and York.* (Cambridge: Cambridge University Press, 1937).

[69] Bevan, "The dead can dance".

[70] Giles, 169.

[71] Giles, 111.

[72] Hill, *pers.comm.*

[73] Giles, 141.

[74] A. Havercroft, A. *The Wetwang Chariot Burial. Interim Report.* Beverley: The Guildhouse Consultancy, 2001.

[75] The British Museum. The Wetwang Chariot Burial: what did she look like? COMPASS Tours Online. http://www.thebritishmuseum.ac.uk/compass/index.html.

[76] Jope, 214-5.

CHAPTER TWO

MIRRORS AND DIVINATION: CATOPROMANCY, ORACLES AND EARTH GODESSES IN ANTIQUITY

CRYSTAL ADDEY

Divination was a widespread phenomenon in ancient Graeco-Roman religion: the Oracle at Delphi, the most famous oracular sanctuary in ancient Greece, operated for at least a thousand years, with kings, civic officials and private individuals consulting the oracle for advice.[1] Many other types of divination were also widely practised in the Graeco-Roman world: for example, haruspicy, the examination of the entrails of sacrificial animals, is a divinatory practice attested from at least the eighth century BC to the late antique period (fourth to sixth centuries AD). Other types of divination practised included augury, astrology and dream incubation. The practice of divination using mirrors was called Catoptromancy, a name derived from the Greek word *katoptron*, which means "mirror", or "reflection"; since one looks into a mirror as one would look into a reflective pool. Catoptromancy involved divination by images seen reflected on a shining surface, usually a mirror, but sometimes water or another analogous reflective medium. Although this was not a particularly well-known or prevalent form of divination in antiquity, there are some notable and striking instances of its use recorded in various literary sources. Pausanias, a travel writer, Artemidorus, a writer on dream interpretation, and Iamblichus, a Neoplatonist philosopher, all refer to Catoptromancy; their accounts allow a glimpse into the ancient practices and rituals involved in this type of divination.

It seems clear that two types of Catoptromancy were practised in Graeco-Roman antiquity. The first type, generally practised at oracular temples and sanctuaries, used mirrors by lowering them into water. The prophet or prophetess would then utter an oracle based on his or her vision in the mirror. The second type of Catoptromancy invokes a god or *daimon* (semi-divine being) to appear as a luminous vision by using reflective surfaces to conduct light; the god or *daimon* would then give the practitioner oracular information. The French scholar Andre Delatte argues that the first type made no appeal to supernatural power but relied on the natural ability of any glittering surface to encourage divination by exciting the imagination, whereas the second kind of catoptromancy had a very clear religious character, and employed invocations to both gods and *daimones*.[2] I would like to offer a few suggestions regarding the interpretation of these two types of Catoptromancy.

Catopromancy at Oracle Sites and in Mystery Cults

Pausanias' *Description of Greece*, a second century AD travel guide, gives us the clearest extant account of the first type of Catoptromancy.[3] In his discussion of the sanctuary of Demeter at Patras he discusses an oracular ritual utilising the practice of Catoptromancy:

τοῦ δὲ ἄλσους ἱερὸν ἔχεται Δήμητρος· αὕτη μὲν καὶ ἡ παῖς ἑστᾶσι, τὸ δὲ ἄγαλμα τῆς Γῆς ἐστι καθήμενον. πρὸ δὲ τοῦ ἱεροῦ τῆς Δήμητρός ἐστι πηγή· ταύτης τὰ μὲν πρὸς τοῦ ναοῦ λίθων ἀνέστηκεν αἱμασιά, κατὰ δὲ τὸ ἐκτὸς κάθοδος ἐς αὐτὴν πεποίηται. μαντεῖον δὲ ἐνταῦθά ἐστιν ἀψευδές, οὐ μὲν ἐπὶ παντί γε πράγματι, ἀλλὰ ἐπὶ τῶν καμνόντων. κάτοπτρον καλῳδίῳ τῶν λεπτῶν δήσαντες καθιᾶσι, σταθμώμενοι μὴ πρόσω καθικέσθαι τῆς πηγῆς, ἀλλ᾽ ὅσον ἐπιψαῦσαι τοῦ ὕδατος τῷ κύκλῳ τοῦ κατόπτρου. τὸ δὲ ἐντεῦθεν εὐξάμενοι τῇ θεῷ καὶ θυμιάσαντες ἐς τὸ κάτοπτρον βλέπουσι· τὸ δέ σφισι τὸν νοσοῦντα ἤτοι ζῶντα ἢ καὶ τεθνεῶτα ἐπιδείκνυσι. τούτῳ μὲν τῷ ὕδατι ἐς τοσοῦτο μέτεστιν ἀληθείας

[Next to the grove is a sanctuary of Demeter; she and her daughter are standing, but the image of Earth is seated. Before the sanctuary of Demeter is a spring. On the side of this towards the temple stands a wall of stones, while on the outer side has been made a descent to the spring. Here there is an infallible oracle, not indeed for everything, but only in the case of sick folk. They tie a mirror to a fine cord and let it down, judging the distance so that it does not sink deep into the spring, but just far enough to touch the water with its rim. Then they pray to the goddess and burn incense, after which they look into the mirror, which shows them the patient either alive or dead. This water partakes to this extent of truth][4]

Pausanias' description does not say whether the mirror was lowered into the spring vertically or horizontally. It is interesting to note that this oracle was not consulted on any matter concerning the inquirer, as with most oracular practices in the ancient world, but rather just for cases of illness. There seems to be a parallel here with the purposes of the divinatory practices at sanctuaries of Asclepius, where sick people went to receive cures and advice about their health through dream incubation, by sleeping in the temple in order to receive an oracular dream. Unfortunately, Pausanias does not fully describe how the oracle was produced, neither mentioning whether a prophet or prophetess uttered the oracle nor explaining how the actual ritual worked. Generally, oracular practices in antiquity involved the consultation of a prophet or prophetess who was thought to utter the words of a deity, in some cases while in a trance-like state. Therefore, presumably, a prophet or prophetess composed their oracle from the observation of the vision in the mirror and was believed to utter the words of a divinity, most likely Demeter, since this ritual is located in her temple. However, Pausanias does not give any details and therefore does not tell us whether the prophet was in a trance-like state or not.

Yet there are various details in his account that are extremely interesting. For example, the catoptromantic ritual is associated with the spring by the temple and linked specifically with the water of the spring. As we have seen, the Greek word *katoptron* can mean "reflection" as well as "mirror," indicating the connection between mirrors and water because of their common reflective qualities. Many Oracles in ancient Greece and Asia Minor had a spring near the temple, which served a variety of divinatory purposes other than the reflective revelation described in Pausanias' account. For example, the Pythia, the prophetess at Delphi, drank from the Kastalian spring located near the temple before uttering oracles.[5] There was also a spring at the Oracle at Claros from which the prophet drank before uttering his prophecies; the spring water was thought to have oracular power which inspired the prophet.[6] Again, there was a spring at the Oracle of Didyma, which the priestess bathed in before delivering oracles.[7] Pausanias asserts that at Hysiae, there was a half-finished temple of Apollo and a sacred well and in former days oracles were obtained from the well by drinking from it.[8] In the very elaborate ritual preparations of the Oracle of Trophonius in Boeotia the consultant had to bathe in the river Hercyna and then had to drink from two springs; the priests called the water from these springs, the water of Forgetfulness (*Lethe*) and the water of Memory (*Mnemosyne*) respectively.[9] Therefore, from these examples it appears that the ritual Pausanias describes is linked with hydromancy, divination practised by looking into water, and lecanomancy, divination practised by observing water or oil in a bowl or basin. This is confirmed by the emphasis in the text upon the water as the instrument which partakes in the truth. Thus, water was a common feature at oracular sites and was often involved in oracular rituals, including Catoptromancy.

Another notable feature of Pausanias' account is that the Catoptromantic ritual occurs at a temple of Demeter. Demeter was an ancient Greek goddess associated with the earth, fertility and crops.[10] Pausanias tells us that there were statues of Demeter, her daughter Persephone and the goddess Earth, or Ge, at this temple.[11] The earth was often linked with water in ancient Greek thought: both were thought to possess prophetic power.[12] For example, the earth goddess

Ge was said to possess the Delphic Oracle long before the god Apollo did; the legendary origins of this Oracle are linked with this ancient earth goddess.[13] Indeed, Ge is often considered to have been the prophetess *par excellence*.[14] The practice of Catoptromancy was not only linked with the prophetic power of water, through its shared reflective properties and other uses in oracular rituals, but more surprisingly, it was also linked with the prophetic power of the earth.[15] Artemidorus' *Oneirocritica*, an ancient handbook of dream interpretation from the second century AD, states that the mirror is associated with the earth and, incidentally, it is associated with foretelling death for the sick, in a discussion of the meaning of mirrors in dreams:

νοσοῦντας δὲ ἀναιρεῖ· γήινον γάρ ἐστι τὸ κάτοπτρον, ἐξ οἵας ἂν ᾖ πεποιημένον ὕλης.

[But it [the mirror] portends death for the sick. For the mirror belongs to the earth, whatever the material it may have been made from.][16]

Oracular practices using mirrors were associated with earth goddesses and their chthonic power. One reason that the mirror might be associated with the earth is that both were viewed as feminine and thus connected with feminine aspects of divine power. Indeed, Artemidorus also suggests that the mirror is a symbol of a woman:

εἰ μὲν τύχοι ἐρῶν γυναικός, οὐ τὴν ἐρωμένην ὄψεται ἀλλ' ἵππον ἢ κάτοπτρον ἢ ναῦν ἢ θάλασσαν ἢ θηρίον θῆλυ ἢ ἐσθῆτα γυναικείαν ἢ ἄλλο τι τῶν σημαινόντων γυναῖκα.

[if he is in love with a woman, he will not see his beloved in a dream, but rather a horse, a mirror, a ship, the sea, an animal that is female, a piece of feminine apparel or anything else that signifies a woman.][17]

Thus, the use of Catroptromancy at oracle sites was linked with water and the earth, both of which were thought to possess prophetic power. In addition, mirrors were associated with earth goddesses because they were perceived as feminine.

The other reference to mirrors in Pausanias' work is very revealing in these respects. Although it does not comprise an explicit account of Catoptromancy, it is very interesting in the light of these associations between Catoptromantic rituals, the earth, earth goddesses and water. Pausanias describes a sanctuary at Lykosoura in Arcadia which is dedicated to a mysterious goddess to whom he refers simply as Despoina, "the Mistress" ["τὸ ἱερὸν τῆς Δεσποίνης"].[18] He enigmatically describes Despoina as follows:

ταύτην μάλιστα θεῶν σέβουσιν οἱ Ἀρκάδες τὴν Δέσποιναν, θυγατέρα
δὲ αὐτὴν Ποσειδῶνός φασιν εἶναι καὶ Δήμητρος. ἐπίκλησις ἐς τοὺς
πολλούς ἐστιν αὐτῇ Δέσποινα, καθάπερ καὶ τὴν ἐκ Διὸς Κόρην
ἐπονομάζουσιν, ἰδίᾳ δὲ ἐστιν ὄνομα Περσεφόνη . . . τῆς δὲ
Δεσποίνης τὸ ὄνομα ἔδεισα ἐς τοὺς ἀτελέστους γράφειν.

[This Mistress the Arcadians worship more than any other god, declaring that she
is the daughter of Poseidon and Demeter. Mistress is her surname among the
many, just as they surname Demeter's daughter by Zeus the Maid. But whereas
the real name of the Maid is Persephone . . . the real name of the Mistress I am
afraid to write to the uninitiated.][19]

Pausanias reports that this temple was associated with the goddess Demeter,
along with Despoina, as altars to both goddesses stand in front of the temple.
The statues of the goddesses were constructed from one piece of stone, which
was dug up from the earth within the sanctuary "in obedience to a dream"
["ἀλλὰ κατὰ ὄψιν ὀνείρατος λέγουσιν"].[20] The fact that the statues were
constructed from the same piece of stone clearly reflects the link between the
goddesses, whilst the oracular dream instructing the Arcadians to dig the stone
from the earth indicates a connection between these goddesses, the earth and
oracles. Pausanias then alludes to a mirror displayed on the right wall of the
temple:

ἐν δεξιᾷ δὲ ἐξιόντι ἐκ τοῦ ναοῦ κάτοπτρον ἡρμοσμένον ἐστὶν ἐν τῷ
τοίχῳ· τοῦτο ἤν τις προσβλέπῃ τὸ κάτοπτρον, ἑαυτὸν μὲν ἤτοι
παντάπασιν ἀμυδρῶς ἢ οὐδὲ ὄψεται τὴν ἀρχήν, τὰ δὲ ἀγάλματα τῶν
θεῶν καὶ αὐτὰ καὶ τὸν θρόνον ἔστιν ἐναργῶς θεάσασθαι. παρὰ δὲ
τὸν ναὸν τῆς Δεσποίνης ὀλίγον ἐπαναβάντι ἐν δεξιᾷ Μέγαρόν ἐστι
καλούμενον, καὶ τελετήν τε δρῶσιν ἐνταῦθα καὶ τῇ Δεσποίνῃ
θύουσιν ἱερεῖα οἱ Ἀρκάδες πολλά τε καὶ ἄφθονα.

[On the right as you go out of the temple there is a mirror fitted into the wall. If
anyone looks into this mirror, he will see himself very dimly indeed or not at all,
but the actual images of the gods and the throne can be seen quite clearly. When
you have gone up a little, beside the temple of the Mistress on the right is what is
called the Hall, where the Arcadians celebrate mysteries, and sacrifice to the
Mistress many victims in generous fashion.][21]

This fascinating passage states that those exiting the temple who look into the
mirror can see themselves only dimly or not at all, but the statues of the
goddesses can be seen very clearly. This suggests the mirror has some special
significance since it is not reflecting what one would expect, that is, the person
standing in front of it most clearly and the statues of the gods in the background

less clearly because they are more distant. Rather this mirror reflects the statues of the gods most clearly, showing the divine that lies behind the human. The fact that immediately following this comment Pausanias describes the Arcadian mystery ceremonies devoted to Despoina seems significant: it raises the possibility that the mirror displayed on the temple wall had some connection with these mystery ceremonies.

Mirrors were certainly linked with the mystery ceremonies held in honour of Dionysus. A fresco in Room 5 of the Villa of the Mysteries at Pompeii, which depicts scenes from Dionysiac Mysteries, shows a young satyr looking intensely into a cup, which is held by a Silenus, a mythical creature who was a follower of Dionysus.[22] Behind the satyr looking into the cup, another young satyr holds up a mask, a cultic object sacred to Dionysus, and a girl to the satyr's right looks frightened (Figure 2.1). It is generally believed that this is a scene of Catoptromancy. Some scholars argue that the satyr is a medium who tells the Silenus what he sees on the shining surface; the Silenus then interprets the vision as an oracle for the girl, who looks terrified because of the content of the oracle.[23] It has been suggested that this scene may also be linked with another Silenus, standing to the left of the frightened girl, who plays a lyre and sings a divinely-inspired song, possibly relaying the oracle.[24] A similar scene on a Praenestine bronze mirror depicts a Silenus looking into a vessel and reporting his vision and a female figure playing a lyre and singing the oracle.[25] The adjacent room, Room 4, also contains frescoes depicting Bacchic scenes that are thought to be linked with the frescoes of Room 5. According to the interpretation of Brenda Longfellow, in the southernmost corner of the east wall in Room 4, a painted representation of a rectangular mirror rests on a painted cornice in the right-hand corner of an architectural vista, above a mural depicting a priestess (Figure 2.2). This representation of a mirror is tilted so that the reflection of a red-skinned figure is partially visible.[26] The similarities with Pausanias' account of the mirror in the temple at Lykosoura are striking: both mirrors are placed to the right-hand side of the wall (which may be significant given that omens appearing on the right were considered to be auspicious in antiquity) and both reflect effigies of deities. Given this evidence and its location in a temple, it is likely that the mirror described by Pausanias would also have been considered a sacred object and it may have also been used in the mystery ceremonies devoted to Despoina.

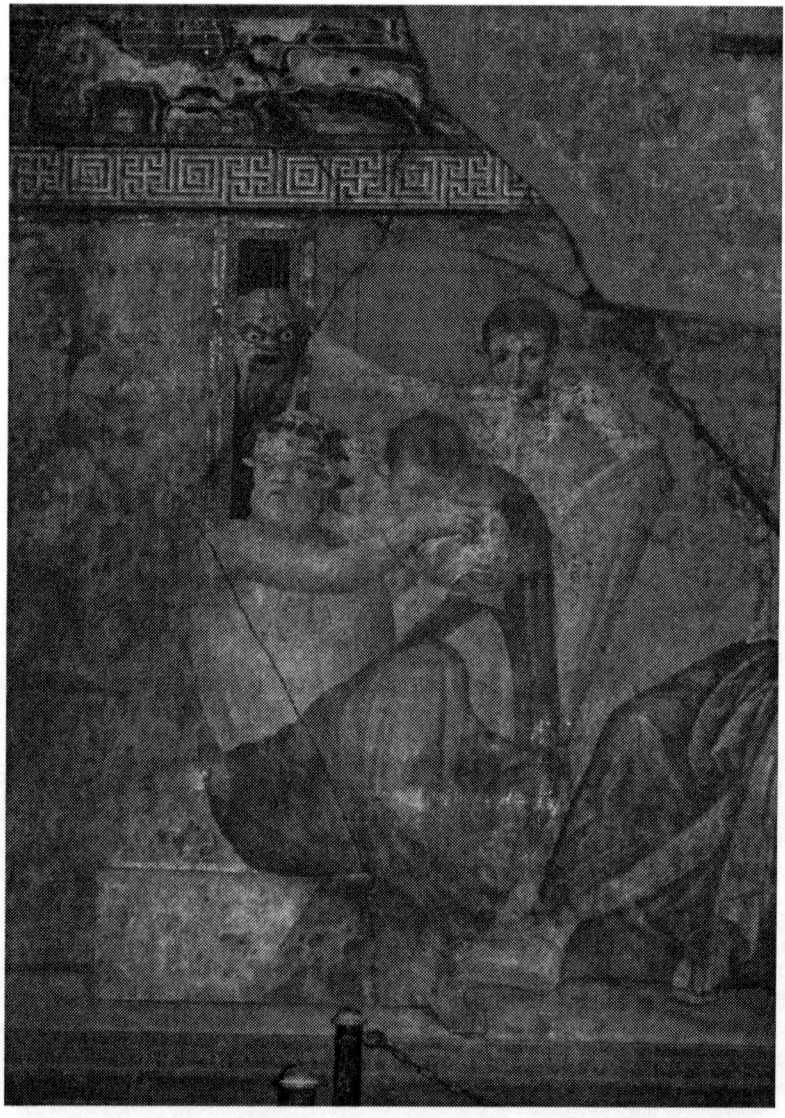

Figure 2.1. Fresco depicting a scene of catopromancy or lecanomancy in Room 5 of the Villa of Mysteries at Pompeii. Photograph: Hannah Platts. Reproduced by permission from Ministero per i Beni e le Attivà Culturali Soprintendenza Archeologica di Pompei.

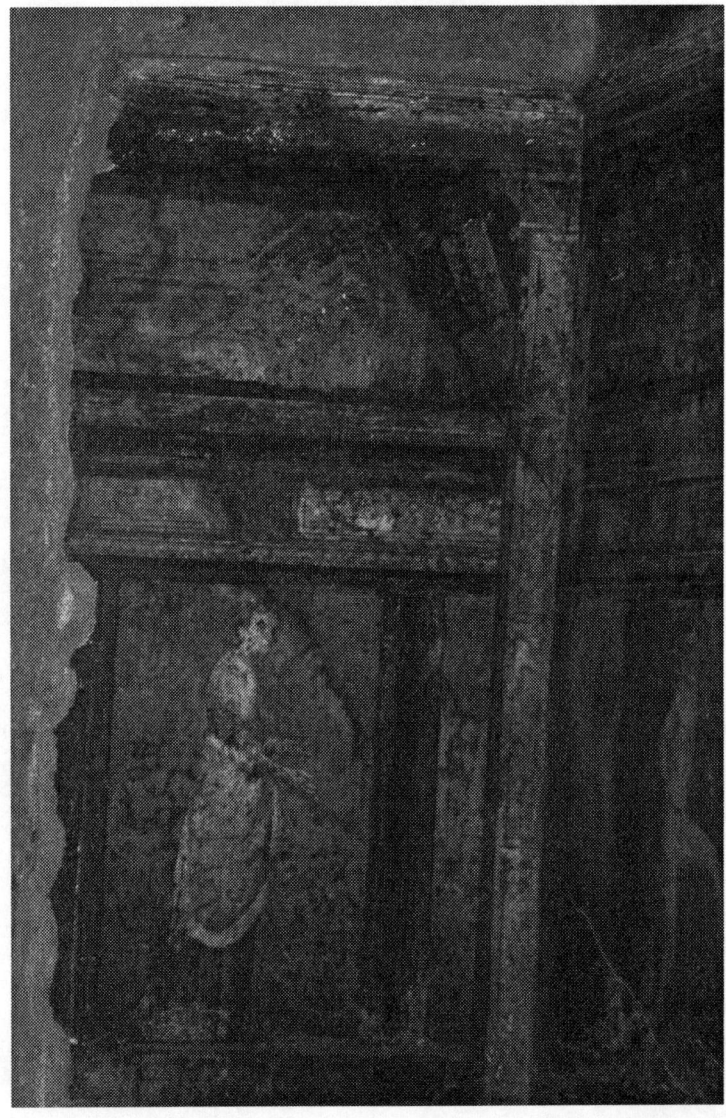

Figure 2.2. Painted representation of a mirror in Room 4 of the Villa of Mysteries at Pompeii. Photograph: Hannah Platts. Reproduced by permission from Ministero per i Beni e le Attivà Culturali Soprintendenza Archeologica di Pompei.

Thus, a complex web of associations is apparent in the use of mirrors in ancient Graeco-Roman religion and divination. This first type of Catoptromancy practised at oracular temples was clearly connected with earth goddesses, particularly Demeter, and with ancient Greek religious conceptions of the prophetic power of water and the earth. These links suggest that Catoptromancy was perceived as having a feminine and chthonic nature, at least as it was practised at oracle sites. Catoptromancy, and mirrors in general, also lead us to aspects of Graeco-Roman cults which are obscure to us: the feminine and chthonic power of Greek goddesses was linked with mystery cults which remained, and still remain, shrouded in secrecy and obscurity because of their initiatory nature. All initiates had to take an oath of silence, and so a thick veil of secrecy obscures the nature of these ancient Graeco-Roman mystery cults. Yet Pausanias' description of the mystery cult at Lykosoura, as well as the depiction of the mirror and the reflecting cup in the frescoes at the Villa of Mysteries at Pompeii, raise the possibility that mirrors played a significant role in the mystery cults of antiquity. However, the use of the mirrors is also shrouded in the secrecy of initiation, resulting in the tentative nature of the conclusions drawn here.

Catopromancy in private, ritual practices: "evoking the light"

The second type of Catoptromancy involved the invocation of a god or a *daimon* to appear as a luminous vision on a reflective surface, by using water to conduct light. The invoked being was believed to provide oracular information. This type of Catoptromancy is discussed especially by the Neoplatonist philosopher Iamblichus in the third century AD in his work, *On the Mysteries.*[27] This type of Catoptromancy Iamblichus calls, "evoking the light" ["φωτὸς ἀγωγή or φωταγωγία"].[28] Although Iamblichus does not specifically refer to a mirror in his description, it is clear that the practices he alludes to can be classified as Catoptromancy, since they entail divination by images seen on a reflective surface.

According to Iamblichus, the use of water or any other transparent, reflective surface for "evoking the light" is just a means to an end; any accessory or instrument that one can shine and conduct light through seems to be appropriate:

Ἐνίοτε δ᾽ αὖ καὶ δι᾽ ὕδατος ἄγουσι τὸ φῶς, ἐπειδὴ διαφανὲς ὂν τοῦτο εὐφυῶς διάκειται πρὸς ὑποδοχὴν τοῦ φωτός. Ἄλλοτε δ᾽ εἰς τοῖχον αὐτὸ ποιοῦσιν ἐπιλάμπειν, ταῖς ἱεραῖς τῶν χαρακτήρων καταγραφαῖς προευτρεπίζοντες ἕδραν ἀρίστως εἰς τὸν τοῖχον τῷ φωτί, καὶ ἅμα ἀποστηρίζοντες αὐτὸ ἐνταῦθα ἔν τινι στερεῷ χωρίῳ, ὥστε μὴ ἐπὶ πολὺ διαχεῖσθαι.

[Sometimes, moreover, they also conduct the light through water, since this, being transparent, is naturally well suited for the light's reception. At other times they cause it to shine on a wall, having expertly prepared in advance a place on the wall for the light with sacred inscriptions of magical symbols, and at the same time fixing the light on a solid place so that it will not be too diffused.][29]

Iamblichus emphasises this point repeatedly: any instrument which conducts light is appropriate.[30] In this form of Catoptromancy, water and mirrors are merely potential instruments for conducting the light and can be used interchangeably. Iamblichus' explanation of the operation of this type of divination depicts these instruments as having metaphysical and psychological effects: the light illuminates the soul vehicle of the practitioner and acts as a conduit for the divine light which surrounds the soul; then the divine appearances within the soul vehicle, set in motion by the gods' will, take possession of the imaginative power within us.[31] In other words, the imagination is illuminated from the outside by the gods, and this ultimately causes the appearance of divine visions on the reflective surface, where they can then be interpreted. Iamblichus emphasises that the imagination acts as a passive receptacle in its role of transmitting divine visions.[32]

The later Neoplatonist philosopher, Damascius, also refers to an "evoking the light" ritual where a wall is used as the reflective surface upon which the light is shone.[33] These types of rituals are also attested to in the *Greek Magical Papyri*, a collection of papyri from Graeco-Roman Egypt containing a variety of magical formulae, hymns and rituals.[34] However these rituals do not seem to utilise a reflective surface, such as a mirror or water, but instead simply use a lamp.[35]

Conclusion

The nature and scarcity of the evidence makes it difficult to draw firm conclusions about these two types of Catoptromancy; however, I would like to suggest some modifications to Delatte's distinction between these two types. Delatte argued that the second type of Catoptromancy, "evoking the light," had a far more "supernatural" and religious character than the first type. The use of terms such as "supernatural", and the distinction between religion and magic, have been widely contested and debated in recent academic research.[36] I propose that Delatte's distinction between them is anachronistic, since both types of Catoptromancy could be classified as being "religious," the first type as much as the second, due to the fact that it was used at oracular sites consecrated to specific deities. As we have seen, the prophet or prophetess at Patras was thought to utter the words of a divinity, most likely Demeter. A more accurate categorisation would seem to be a distinction drawn between them in terms of the first type being a public ritual, which any individual could utilise in a recognised public institution, and the second type being a private ritual, undertaken by individuals possibly in secrecy. These individuals often laid claim to special skills, but the extant evidence is too scarce to allow a clear picture of their status and precise identity.

Another distinction between these types would seem to be the natural phenomena that are utilised in conjunction with them. In the first type of Catoptromancy, this is clearly water; whilst in the second type, it is more predominantly light, and water only functions to replace the mirror rather than being used in conjunction with it. The first type of Catoptromancy is very clearly connected with the prophetic qualities of water and the earth, and is linked with the worship and cult of earth goddesses, particularly Demeter. At the oracle sites, the prophet or prophetess looks into the mirror-in-water, which imperfectly reflects divine truth. The second type is connected with light; a phenomenon which, for Iamblichus at least, acted as a conduit and means of reflecting divine beings. Iamblichus tells us that one uses the reflective surface, representative of the mirror, to focus or direct the light, but looks at the light rather than the mirror.

Similarities are also apparent between the two types, since the mirror seems to be interchangeable with any shining, reflective object in both types of ritual. In addition, both types use the mirror or a similar reflective surface to inspire the human soul of the prophet or practitioner. Although in the first case it enables the practitioner to utter oracles, whereas in the second case it enables the perception of divine visions, in both cases the practitioner was thought to be the recipient of divine truth. As we have seen, it was a complex yet fascinating network of associations that surrounded the use of mirrors in both types of divinatory practices in the ancient world. This shared network of associations suggests the falsity of too bold an overstatement of the distinctions between the two types. For both types of Catoptromancy, the water related public type at oracle sites and the light evoking private type, share the same ultimate aim: to use elemental phenomena to gain a vision of truth and knowledge from the gods.

Notes and References

I wish to express my warmest thanks and gratitude to my supervisor, Gillian Clark, and to the editor of this work, Miranda Anderson, for their valuable assistance and suggestions. I also wish to thank Mark Kauntze who organised the Interdisciplinary Conference on Mirrors at the University of Bristol, at which this paper was originally presented, and the other speakers and participants at the Conference. I also wish to thank Hannah Platts for supplying the photographic material from the Villa of the Mysteries, and both Shelley Hales and Hannah Platts for their valuable advice and assistance with the Villa of the Mysteries material.

[1] Joseph Fontenrose, *The Delphic Oracle* (Berkeley: University of California Press, 1978), 5 – 6; H.W. Parke, *A History of the Delphic Oracle* (Oxford: Blackwell, 1939), 4.

[2] André Delatte, *La Catoptromancie Grecque et ses Dérivés* (Paris: Bibliothèque de la Faculté de Philosophie et Lettres de L'Université de Liége, 1932), 8–9.

[3] K.W. Arafat, *Pausanias' Greece: Ancient artists and Roman rulers* (Cambridge: Cambridge University Press, 1996), 8, suggests that Pausanias' work was written between the 130s and approximately 175-80 AD. Cf. John Elsner, "Pausanias: A Greek Pilgrim in the Roman World" *Past and Present* 135 (1992): 3–29.

[4] Pausanias *Description of Greece* VII.21.11-12, trans. W.H.S. Jones (Vol III Loeb Classical Library, 1966).

[5] Pausanias *Description of Greece* X.24.7, trans. W.H.S. Jones (Vol IV, Loeb Classical Library, 1965).

[6] Iamblichus *On the Mysteries* III.11 (124.8 –126.3), trans. Emma C. Clarke, John M. Dillon & Jackson P. Hershbell (Atlanta: Society of Biblical Literature, 2003); Pliny *Natural History* II.106.232, trans. H. Rachkham (Vol I, Loeb Classical Library, 1938); Tacitus *Annals* II.54, trans. J. Jackson (Vol III, Loeb Classical Library, 1931).

[7] Iamblichus *On the Mysteries* III.11 (127.6 – 7).

[8] Pausanias *Description of Greece* IX.2.1, Vol IV.

[9] Pausanias *Description of Greece* IX.39.7-8, Vol IV.

[10] For oracles urging Greeks to worship Demeter, cf. H.W. Parke, 330.

[11] Pausanias *Description of Greece* VII.21.11, Vol III.

[12] W.R. Halliday, *Greek Divination* (London: Macmillan, 1913), 121 – 123; Cf. A. Bouché-Leclercq, *Histoire de la Divination dans L'Antiquité* (Paris: Ernest Leroux, 1880), Vol II, 252: "Gaea devait donc être, aux yeux des Hellènes des premiers âges, la divinitié prophétique par excellence, et nous verrons les théories des âges postérieurs lui rendre peu à peu le privilège exclusif d'alimenter l'inspiration des oracles." Cf. also Mircea Eliade, *Patterns in Comparative Religion* (London: Sheed and Ward, 1958), 199 – 202, 239 – 262, for an extensive discussion of this subject which includes parallel mythological and religious ideas from other cultures.

[13] Aeschylus *Eumenides* 1 – 8, trans. H.W. Smyth (Vol II, Loeb Clasical Library, 1932); Euripides *Iphigenia Among the Taurians* 1259–1269, trans. D. Kovacs (Loeb Classical Library, 1999); Plutarch *Moralia* 421C, trans Frank Cole Babbit (Vol V, Loeb Classical

Library, 1936); Apollodorus *The Library* I.4.1, trans. James G. Frazer (Vol I, Loeb Classical Library, 1921); Cf. Fontenrose, 3.

[14] Cf. Jules Herbillon, *Les Cultes de Patras* (Baltimore: John Hopkins, 1929), 30 –31.

[15] Cf. for example Pausanias *Description of Greece* IX.10.6, Vol IV.

[16] Artemidorus *Oneirocritica* (The Interpretation of Dreams), 2.7, ed. Roger A. Pack, *Artemidori Daldiani Onirocriticon Libri V*, 108 (Leipzig: Teubner, 1963); trans. R. White (Park Ridge: Noyes Classical Press, 1975).

[17] Artemidorus *Oneirocritica* (The Interpretation of Dreams) Book 4, Introduction, ed. *Roger A. Pack, Artemidori Daldiani Onirocriticon Libri V*, 240 (Leipzig: Teubner, 1963); trans. R.J. White (Park Ridge: Noyes Classical Press, 1975).

[18] Pausanias *Description of Greece* VIII.37.1, Vol. IV.

[19] Pausanias *Description of Greece* VIII.37.9.-10, Vol. IV.

[20] Pausanias *Description of Greece* VIII.37.2-3; 37.4, Vol. IV.

[21] Pausanias *Description of Greece* VIII.37.7-8, Vol. IV.

[22] Elizabeth de Grummond, "Bacchic Imagery and Cult Practice in Roman Italy," in *The Villa of the Mysteries in Pompeii: Ancient Ritual, Modern Muse*, ed. Elaine K. Gazda, 81–82 (Michigan: Ann Arbor, 2000), argues persuasively that the fresco cycle may depict a Bacchic ritual and have a firm basis in reality since a number of cultic titles found on a second century AD inscription might plausibly be used to describe figures in the Pompeian paintings. She follows many other scholars who also hold this view.

[23] Cf. Richard A.S. Seaford, "The Mysteries of Dionysus at Pompeii" in *Pegasus: Classical Essays from the University of Exeter*, ed. H.W. Stubbs, 59, 62-64 (Exeter: University of Exeter, 1981); Nancy T. de Grummond, "Mirrors, marriage, and mysteries," in *Journal of Roman Archaeology Supplementary Series No. 47*, ed. C. Stein and J.H. Humphrey, 73-75 (Portsmouth: Rhode Island, 2002); Delatte, 189-190. Cf. also the interpretation of James W. Jackson, "Villa of the Mysteries, Pompeii,": "The Silenus looks disapprovingly at the startled initiate as he holds up an empty silver bowl. A young satyr gazes into the bowl, as if mesmerized. Another young satyr holds a theatrical mask (resembling the Silenus) aloft and looks off to his left. Some speculate that the mask rather than the satyr's face is reflected in the silver bowl. So, looking into the vessel is an act of divination: the young satyr sees himself in the future, a dead satyr. The young satyr and the young initiate are coming to terms with their own deaths. In this case the death of childhood and innocence."
http://www.art-and-archaeology.com/timelines/rome/empire/vm/villaofthemysteries.html

[24] Nancy T. de Grummond, 74.

[25] Cf. Nancy T. de Grummond, 62–85, especially 68 (Figure 12), who examines many Etruscan and Praenestine bronze mirrors which seem to depict prophetic scenes involving many of the following motifs: the figure of a satyr or a Silenus, the use of the lyre, the gesture of reception of the prophecy, the use of lekanomancy and catoptromancy, the presence of an assistant / medium and a mediator / interpreter. She provides a detailed comparison of these motifs with those depicted on the frescoes in Room 5 of the Villa of the Mysteries at Pompeii.

[26] Brenda Longfellow, "Liber and Venus in the Villa of the Mysteries," in *The Villa of the Mysteries in Pompeii: Ancient Ritual, Modern Muse*, ed. Elaine K. Gazda, 121-122 (Michigan: Ann Arbor, 2000).

[27] Iamblichus *On the Mysteries* III.14.

[28] Iamblichus *On the Mysteries* III.14 (132.7-9).

[29] Iamblichus *On the Mysteries* III.14 (134.2-7).

[30] Iamblichus *On the Mysteries* III.14 (134.8-10).

[31] Iamblichus *On the Mysteries* III.14 (132.9-14).

[32] Iamblichus *On the Mysteries* III.14 (133.1-7). Cf. Emma C. Clarke, *Iamblichus' De Mysteriis: A manifesto of the miraculous* (Aldershot: Ashgate, 2001), 85.

[33] Damascius *The Philosophical History* Fragment 75F, trans. Polymnia Athanassiadi (Athens: Apamea Cultural Press, 1999).

[34] Hans Dieter Betz, introduction to *The Greek Magical Papyri in Translation*, ed. Hans Dieter Betz, xli (Chicago: Universtiy of Chicago Press, 1986), who states that the extant texts date mainly from the second century BC to the fifth century AD.

[35] *Papyri Graecae Magicae* IV.930 – 1114, trans. W.C. Grese and E.N. O'Neil; VII.540 – 578, trans. Jackson P. Hershbell in *The Greek Magical Papyri in Translation*, ed. Hans Dieter Betz, 56, 133-134 (Chicago: University of Chicago Press, 1986).

[36] Since J. Goody, "Religion and Ritual: The Definitional Problems" *British Journal of Sociology* 12 (1961): 142-157, many scholars tend to view the dichotomy profane-sacred (or: supernatural) as a Western ethnocentric construct. Cf. also H.S. Versnel, "Some Reflections on the Relationship Magic-Religion" *Numen* 38 (1991): 178, 193. Social anthropologists, ethnologists and Classicists have long debated the meaning and possible definition of "magic" and its relationship with, and possible distinction from, "religion." The literature on this matter is vast, and this is intended as a brief summary rather than an exhaustive account. The debate began with Sir James Frazer, *The Golden Bough* (London, 1911-15), 222: "By religion, then, I understand a propitiation or conciliation of powers superior to man which are believed to direct and control the course of nature and human life...It is true that magic often deals with spirits, which are personal agents of the kind assumed by religion; but whenever it does so in its proper form, it treats them exactly in the same fashion as it treats inanimate agents, that is, it constrains or coerces instead of conciliating or propitiating them as religion would do." Frazer opposed magic and religion on the basis that magic compels and coerces divine beings, whereas religion propitiates them. The second classical approach to magic was to explain it in terms of social categories: cf. Émile Durkheim, *Les formes élémentaires de las vie religieuse* (Paris: Quadrige, 1912), 62, for whom religion is the communal cult and beliefs of a group, the expression of collective identity. Magic, on the other hand, is an individual, private practice, which may be secret and a potential threat to group identity. Marcel Mauss, *A General Theory of Magic* (London: Routledge, 1950), 18-25, follows Durkheim in evaluating magic from a social and moral standpoint. Social prohibition forms the boundary between magic, seen by society as subversive, and religion, sanctioned by society. Therefore religious practices are predictable, prescribed and official while magical practices are considered unauthorised and abnormal. The anthropologist Bronislaw Malinowski, *Magic, Science and Religion* (New York:

Doubleday, 1954), 87-90, argued that we should distinguish magic from religion based upon their intention: magic is employed to achieve concrete, mostly individual goals. Religion is not primarily purpose-motivated, or at most focuses on long-term goals which concern collective issues of society. Most of these discussions of the nature of magic and religion are motivated by the desire to provide a definition of the notion of magic which will hold for all cultures and explain what all procedures thought of as magical have in common, i.e. they are based on the assumption that magic is a universal notion and not one that is culturally specific. Cf. the discussion in Matthew W. Dickie, *Magic and Magicians in the Greco-Roman World* (London: Routledge, 2001), 18-20. The notion of magic as a universal concept has been questioned by various recent anthropological studies, which argue that 'magic' is a modern-western biased construct which does not fit representations of other cultures: M. and R. Wax, "The notion of magic" *Current Anthropology* 4 (1963): 495-513; Edmund Leach, *Social Anthropology* (Oxford: Oxford University Press), 133, states: "As for magic, which readers of Fraser's *The Golden Bough* might suppose to lie at the very centre of the anthropologist's interests, after a lifetime's career as a professional anthropologist, I have reached the conclusion that the word has no meaning whatsoever." On this basis some scholars have condemned the word magic as a 'semantic trap.' Cf. for example Dorothy Hammond, "Magic: A Problem in Semantics," *American Anthropologist* 72 (1970), 1349-1356. The Classicist Fritz Graf, *Magic in the Ancient World* (Cambridge, MA: Harvard University Press, 1997), has examined Greek and Roman magic, arguing that the opposition between magic and religion existed self-consciously in these cultures although at an earlier stage in their existence, they did not make any such distinction. He argues that two factors gave rise to the hiving off of magic from religion, of which it had been an integral part: on the one hand, self-conscious philosophical reflection on the nature of the divine had led to a purified conception of the gods completely at odds with the assumptions about the nature of the divine made by those who practised *mageia*. On the other side, natural science began to look at nature as a closed system within which changes were to be attributed to physical causes only. Currently Classicists often view magic as a manifestation of ritual power and as a subclass of religious ritual: cf. for example Marvin Meyer and Paul Mirecki, introduction to *Ancient Magic and Ritual Power*, ed Marvin Meyer and Paul Mirecki, 3-5 (Leiden: Brill, 1995); Einar Thomassen, "Is magic a subclass of ritual?" in *The world of ancient magic*, ed. David R. Jordan, Hugo Montgomery and Einar Thomassen, 55-66 (Bergen: The Norwegian Institute at Athens, 1999).

CHAPTER THREE

THE PHILOSOPHIC MIRROR IN THE YOUNGER SENECA'S *DE CLEMENTIA*

ROSS HULKES

The dearth of references to the mirror [*speculum*] in Roman antiquity might suggest an indifference to how the Romans saw themselves and how they appeared to others. However, little could be further from the truth: the famous Roman moralist of the second century BC, the elder Cato, wrote what was to become a profoundly influential work on the nature of Roman (self) identity, the *Origines*. Cato's work was a highly colourful attempt to assert that the Roman race and identity originated with the people of his own native Tusculum in the heart of provincial Italy. One might, therefore, suggest that Cato was less concerned with the search for what he thought was the reality of Roman ethnicity than with promoting his own highly selective and imagined vision of Roman culture. The notion that Cato negotiated how he appeared to himself and others in the *Origines* could go some way to explaining why a culture such as his resisted abundant reference to the mirror, a medium which in the modern imagination at least, is centred around the concerns of accurate self-representation.

In fact, when a discussion of the mirror does appear in the ancient sources, it serves a relatively prosaic purpose. The first century AD natural historian, the elder Pliny, in his monumental *Natural History* gives a cursory mention to the mirror in a couple of books, but most markedly to give us an account of the particular effects of its physical properties and how they affect the clarity of the image it produces.[1] In the same century, the rhetorician Quintilian tells us that the Greek declaimer Demosthenes used to practice the physical gestures intrinsic to declamation in front of a large mirror [*grande speculum*]. In the context of a lively discussion concerning Roman declamation, Quintilian informs us that although the mirror reversed the images that Demosthenes saw, Demosthenes believed that his reflection offered an accurate representation of himself.[2]

One significant function of the mirror, then, was that it was believed to offer faithful representations of the images it reflected. Within the context of a culture which demanded that its literature be both figurative and persuasive, the distinct absence of references to the mirror points to the redundancy of "accuracy" in a literary context which favoured more colourful literary techniques such as *inuentio* [lit. invention], the exaggeration or inflation of one's language to persuade another of a particular argument.[3] However, in spite of the apparent incongruence of this facet of Latin literature and the inclination to describe the mirror in contexts where its practical value as a reflective object is emphasized, the mirror is not entirely devoid of figurative or metaphorical value in Roman thought. [4]

In the mid-first century AD, the philosopher Seneca wrote a treatise called the *De Clementia* [lit. *On Mercy*], a work of political philosophy designed to instruct the Roman emperor Nero on the nature of leniency in political adjudication. Seneca was tutor and moral guide to Nero, but his background as a philosopher gives his work a distinctive flavour.[5] Seneca was a prolific writer of moral essays which varied in content, but frequently demanded of the reader a critical and introspective look at inward character and virtue ethics. Seneca was an adherent of Stoicism which judged the virtue of one's character not on actions but on the motivation behind such actions. Hence, for Seneca, actions have no stable moral value but are regarded as morally indifferent insofar as they are not reliable indicators of someone's moral worth.[6] Crucially, however, Seneca begins the *De Clementia* with an obscure reference to how he will serve as a mirror for emperor Nero who, according to Seneca is poised to realise and embody the quality of mercy. He begins:

> Scribere de clementia, Nero Caesar, institui, ut quodam modo speculi uice fungerer et te tibi ostenderem peruenturum ad uoluptatem maximam omnium.

> [I have resolved to write to you, Nero Caesar, in order that I might function as a sort of mirror and reveal you to yourself, you who are poised to achieve the most prized of all possessions.] [7]

Seneca's evocation of the mirror here as a means by which he will reveal [*ostenderem*] Nero to himself suggests another way in which the mirror is a medium through which something (in this case Nero) can be accurately represented. Yet, in juxtaposition to the way in which Demosthenes uses the mirror quite literally as a means of reflecting his physical appearance, Seneca in his role as mirror does not seem to be implying that he will offer Nero a physical representation of himself, since Seneca is invoking a discussion about the abstract quality of clemency, "the most prized of all possessions". Seneca continues after this passage by remarking to Nero that it is good "to inspect and examine a good conscience" in spite of one's apparently virtuous disposition, and then punctuates his opening remarks by a hypothetical discourse in the first person, which represents an introspective self-address by Nero himself, attempting not only to examine his own good conscience, but also his role as head of state:[8]

> Egone ex omnibus mortalibus placui electusque sum, qui in terris deorum uice fungerer?

> [Have I been chosen and selected from all mankind to function as the gods' divine representative on earth?][9]

Nero begins, aptly mirroring Seneca's function as the mirror here, with the linguistic parallel of his own function as divine viceroy ["uice fungerer"].

Nero's hypothetical but introspective self-address is significant for informing upon Seneca's metaphorical role as a mirror because Seneca seems to be indicating that in reflecting Nero or revealing Nero to himself, he will be presenting Nero with the particular facets of Nero's good conscience. In other words, by writing the *De Clementia*, Seneca would appear to be revealing to Nero facets of his inward character in accordance with his disposition as a philosopher who is concerned with inner states of virtue, or lack thereof. Yet, in spite of Stoicism's emphasis upon the value of mental states as the only true measure of one's virtue, it does not entirely disregard the correlation of external circumstance to psychic states. Indeed, in Seneca's most comprehensive tract on and denunciation of human emotion, the *De Ira,* [lit. *On Anger*], Seneca's prefatory remarks inform us that there is no emotion more capable than anger at manifesting itself in one's physical appearance.[10] Among conspicuous and maladaptive traits of the angry man, according to Seneca, are his blazing and sparkling eyes, a blood red countenance, pronounced breathing and an inability to articulate effective speech.[11] Yet, for all of Seneca's allowances that physiognomy may be *some* kind of psychic indicator, he hardly sees physical characteristics as a comprehensive substitute for direct access to the human psyche. In another crucial passage from the *De Ira*, Seneca offers a hypothetical description of the angry man undergoing self-examination:

> Quibusdam, ut ait Sextius, iratis profuit aspexisse speculum; perturbauit illos tanta mutatio sui; uelut in rem praesentem adducti non agnouerunt se. Et quantulum ex uera deformitate imago illa speculo repercussa reddebat. Animus si ostendi et si in ulla materia perlucere posset, intuentis nos confunderet ater maculosusque et aestuans et distortus et tumidus. Nunc quoque tanta deformitas eius est per ossa carnesque et tot impedimenta effluentis; quid si nudus ostenderetur?

[As Sextus remarked, it was good for some angry people to look at themselves in a mirror. Such a profound change in their appearance frightened them. As if presented with stark reality, they did not recognise themselves. And how little of the true ugliness did that reflection present. If the soul could be revealed and it was able to shine through all matter, black, mottled, broiling, distorted and swollen, it would confound us. As it is, such ugliness is only mediated by bone, flesh, and so many other corporeal impediments. What if the soul could be laid bare?][12]

In a text which pre-dates the *De Clementia*, [13] Seneca offers both an important and seminal image of the mirror. Following on from his prefatory remarks in the *De Ira* concerning the appearance of the angry man, Seneca suggests that it might be useful for him to see himself in the mirror so that the full terror of his appearance might deter him from his irascible disposition. However, directly after this passage, Seneca negates the need for such therapeutic action.[14] Indeed, the man who voluntarily came to the mirror for such counsel would be redeemed anyway since such a move constitutes recognition of and insight into one's own pathology.[15] In Seneca's mind, then, recognition of one's own pathology is tantamount to a complete cure. More importantly, though, Seneca's evocation of the mirror leads him onto a discussion about how little of the ugliness of the angry man would actually be revealed in his reflection, since the soul, the source of human consciousness is mediated through and filtered by our physical being. Finally, Seneca ends here with a rhetorical question, inquiring about the possibilities of a potential mirror for the human soul, a mirror which would reveal to us all of the inward horrors and distortions of the angry man.

Seneca's inquiry here is of critical importance because it would seem to be a significant stimulus for his role as mirror to the psyche of emperor Nero. Seneca's context for offering up himself as a mirror for Nero is, as we have seen, a psychological one. Seneca invokes Nero to embark upon a course of introspection and an examination of his own conscience with Seneca as his moral guide. In the above passage from the *De Ira*, Seneca is hinting at the possibility of revealing the soul, but in the context of a passage which seeks to highlight the mirror as a means by which the angry man might view the ugliness of his physical being. What Seneca seems to seek, then, is a mirror by which the soul could be revealed to us in all its unadulterated horror, and it is here that the seeds of Seneca's role as Nero's psychological mirror are sown. In fact in a verbal repetition of his offer to reveal [*ostenderem*] Nero to himself in the opening lines of the *De Clementia*, Seneca speculates on the possibilities for human psycho-pathology if the soul could be revealed [*ostendi*]: "What if the soul could be laid bare?" ["quid si nudus ostenderetur?"].

In both the *De Ira* and *De Clementia*, then, we have two images of the mirror as a means by which the human psyche may be viewed. In the *De Ira*, Seneca's invocation of a mirror for revealing psychic activity is followed up by his own self- appointment as the mirror for Nero's own character in the *De Clementia*. Yet, we should not read Seneca's desire to offer Nero a nude image of his soul as one which should be taken too literally. In fact Seneca admits that the soul is necessarily mediated through the constraints of corporeal matter, a statement which leads us to view body and soul as inextricably bound up. This is an assertion which accords with Stoicism's wider philosophy of (meta)physical theory. As a Stoic, Seneca had a belief in the idea of a human soul which was notionally separate from material existence. Yet, this idea should be placed in the wider Stoic belief about a world which is governed by a perpetual abstract force or metaphysical energy called *ratio* [lit. reason] which was thought to keep the universe in motion and in a constant state of pneumatic tension. Seneca's proposition about the existence of a human soul should therefore be set against a wider belief about a collective force which the human soul tapped into. Hence in the Stoic view, all human activity is driven by the idea of metaphysical reason which keeps all physical aspects of the cosmos in a state of perpetual motion.[16]

The notion that Seneca might draw upon a philosophy which is underpinned by a belief in a collective metaphysical energy is, in fact, fundamental to the manner in which we should understand Seneca's decision to use the metaphor of the mirror in both the *De Ira* and the *De Clementia*. We have already examined how both texts are linked by this metaphor. However, in relation to Seneca's belief that the world was bound by a concept of reason, it is important to recognise that not only does Seneca regard the emotion anger as antithetical to reason and rationality,[17] but that in both the *De Ira* and *De Clementia*, Seneca regards anger as antithetical to his wider moral aims. More specifically, both texts converge in the sense that they regard anger as the primary obstacle to the rational administration of justice and political leniency.[18]

In the *De Clementia*, for example, Seneca says that in his youth the first Roman emperor Augustus was prone to anger, a fact which would apparently be the source of some regret for Nero's predecessor in light of his future acts of political leniency.[19] Such imperatives concerning the discouragement of anger in sovereign rulers have already been reinforced earlier on in the *De Clementia*, when Seneca says that cruel and inexorable anger does not befit a king who, by using anger, does not extol himself much above his subjects.[20] Seneca concludes that it is far better for the king to curb his own power and subject none to his own anger.[21] The importance of political leniency in such psychological terms becomes apparent when similar appeals surface in the *De Ira*: in the process of managing anger against those who have offended us,

Seneca informs us that a more corrective measure than repulsion should be employed with those who we deem to transgress. Seneca tells us that we all offend against moral propriety and that, if we grow angry with those who act immorally, then we stand open to a charge of hypocrisy since none of us can find ourselves innocent in respect of our tendency to transgress.[22] Rhetorically, Seneca asks us to consider by self-inspection whether the crimes we have been guilty of are the crimes we rebuke others for,[23] and advises that we would do well to look back on our own conduct and consider how often we were, for whatever reason, careless and indiscreet since no-one is born wise but only becomes so.[24]

Seneca's appeal to a judicial and politically-minded empathy is interesting here because his justification for the remission of punishment is echoed in the *De Clementia*: Seneca concurs with earlier statements in the *De Ira* by declaring that if anyone could attain a state of moral rectitude, then it would be through a process of moral erring and informs us that we have all committed moral wrong ["peccauimus omnes"].[25] Such a convergence of ideas in both texts by Seneca may be explained by the fact that his philosophy is preoccupied with ultimately aligning itself with the idea of a metaphysical reason; the fact that clemency is apparently perfectly congruous with such a notion of philosophic reason implies that Seneca's opposition between anger and rationality in the *De Ira* makes anger the perfect counterpart to clemency, if we are to see Seneca as trying to form a coherent philosophy.[26] Furthermore, in the third book of the *De Ira,* Seneca presents us with a catalogue of abusive and cruel antique kings; given that Seneca's *De Clementia* is an attempt not only to offer instruction to a Roman emperor, but to justify the notion of one-man rule as a political system, it is no surprise that Seneca decides to write a more positive counterpart to his earlier ideas on kingship in the *De Ira.*[27]

Seneca's desire to base his justification of clemency as a political tool upon an appeal to human empathy is of great importance, however, if we consider the image of the mirror which Seneca details in the opening lines of the *De Clementia*. Indeed, if we are to read Seneca's philosophic justification of his interpretation of the nature of clemency here, then we should understand that not only anger, but excessively harsh use of punishment in judicial matters is contrary to being true to our own (collective) sense of self. In fact, what Seneca is asking us to do when examining whether or not punishment is necessary in the reprimand of someone else is to paradoxically peer inside ourselves and to consider whether or not a potential charge of hypocrisy will allow us to exercise corrective measures. In other words, what Seneca is asking us to do is to actually consider the examination of another's behaviour as a potential reflection of ourselves, to consider the fact that what we see we when we scrutinise others for their faults is the mirror image of ourselves.

However, when Seneca evokes the image of the mirror he is appointing himself the looking glass for Nero's soul, and as a mirror which will rather flatteringly reveal its more salubrious form, which Seneca dubs Nero's *naturalis bonitas*, or "innate goodness". [28] Seneca's mirroring function is therefore problematised by the fact that Seneca's *De Clementia* is not just a didactic tract informing Nero of what type of ruler he should be but an encomium of a prince who as Seneca puts it, already possesses innate goodness, an innate goodness without which Nero would not have been able to surpass the achievements of his predecessors. [29] Yet, based upon Seneca's broader moral framework in both the *De Ira* and *De Clementia* in which morality is largely contingent upon a humanstic philosophy in which one remits punishment based upon collective empathy, Seneca's image of the mirror is a powerful metaphor. Indeed, one function of a mirror is to reflect back to us our own image so that in the mirror we must inevitably and clearly see ourselves. Seneca's role as Nero's tutor and political advisor is to reveal Nero to himself. Yet, Seneca's moral message appears to be one in which he can guide Nero on the correct moral path via human empathy. If Nero can "see" himself in Seneca with Seneca as his looking glass, then Seneca can demonstrate to Nero the virtue of clemency proper, that is, to be the clement ruler by observing in Seneca the traits which he himself exhibits.

What we should observe in such a mirror image is the importance of the fact that not only will Nero see himself in Seneca, but that Seneca will in a sense become Nero by "assuming" the form of Nero's reflection. In this way, Seneca's role as Nero's mirror does not just serve the purpose of guiding a Roman emperor via the basic tenet of Senecan political philosophy. Significantly, there is a strong implication that Seneca, by "becoming" the image of Nero himself will be imbued with the innate goodness characteristic of his political superior. Seneca will, then, not just serve as human being through whom Nero can identify any of his own potential moral flaws, moral flaws which would be a human commonplace, but he will also form the image of Nero himself and reflect back to Nero, the image of moral superiority which Seneca prophesises that Nero will become. In short, Seneca seems to be the mirror recipient of a political philosophy, a political philosophy disseminated by Nero through Seneca.

In appointing Nero the moral authority and image which Seneca assumes as the recipient of Nero's innate goodness, Seneca may seem to negotiate the tensions that exist within his role both as political subordinate and as a moral guide. Such a tension might be diffused further by the fact that a mirror gives an accurate reflection of the image it assumes. Under such conditions, one would imagine that Seneca's role as mirror is simply to offer Nero a moral portrait of what objectively exists, that true to the task of the philosopher, Seneca is fulfilling his promise to offer his readership a series of moral truths including the "fact" that Nero is an inherently and naturally good person.

Furthermore Seneca's role as a moral reflection of Nero is more than hinted at in the way that Seneca exploits language in the *De Clementia*, as we have seen. In the opening lines of the *De Clementia*, Seneca explains to us that he will "function as a mirror" ["speculi uice fungerer"], but in a close parallel of the Latin phraseology in the opening lines Seneca then goes on to appoint Nero in his ghost-written oration to divine representative on earth, Nero who will "function as a god" ["deorum uice fungerer"]. The linguistic "reflection" here intimates the close relationship which Nero and Seneca will have, but it also alludes to the fact that in some senses Nero and Seneca will be as one; Seneca will reflect Nero both metaphorically and ideologically.

The notion that an emperor is supposed to represent some kind of divine emissary is an important idea in the *De Clementia*, given all we have considered regarding Seneca's attempts to make the text a reflection of his wider philosophic purpose. In our examination of the passage of the *De Ira* in which Seneca made a rhetorical appeal to a vision of the human soul, we established not only how the human soul consisted of a cosmic life force, called *ratio*, but that it was necessarily mediated through the human body in such a way that body and soul were inextricably bound up. Therefore, Seneca's metaphysical stance negated any possibility that the human soul could be seen in the reflection of any looking glass in its abstract form independent of the body's mediation.

However, if we consider that what Seneca is talking about when he conceives of metaphysical energy is an abstract force with no corporeal form which only becomes manifest when certain physical bodies are imbued with its force, then Seneca's image of the mirror ultimately becomes a much more seductive and contentious metaphor: mirrors form a reflection of any stimulus image with which they comes into contact. Yet, the mirror surface in itself is not visible in the sense that it cannot be viewed apart from the images it forms, a notion reflected in Roman culture by the fact that Latin does not always distinguish between the mirror's actual surface and the mirror itself. This implies that the mirror's function as a reflective surface, and not the mirror itself as an independent entity is a potent focus for its existence in the Roman imagination - a fact supported by Quintilian's qualification of the mirror as a "fulgor speculi" or "mirror image" in his discussion of the Greek orator Demosthenes.[30] In the sense that the mirror can only be made manifest by the images it assumes, then, the mirror becomes a rather appropriate metaphor for the Senecan position on the nature of body and soul in the *De Clementia;* just as the mirror is inextricably bound up with its image, so the soul is inextricably bound up with the body. Crucially, though, just as the soul is an abstract idea without the mediation of the body, so the mirror is an abstract form without the corresponding image it becomes. In short, therefore, the mirror, in its abstract form could be viewed as a metaphor for Seneca's concept of the abstract human soul and a divine metaphysics.[31]

If Seneca has conceived of the mirror as a metaphor for the soul or a metaphysical force, then he is rather presumptuously appointing himself to such a role. Such associations would be very difficult to negotiate for the philosopher who was only supposed to be Nero's tutor. Indeed, if body and soul, mirror and image are to be viewed as inextricably co-dependent, then by implication, so are Seneca and Nero. However, we should not view the relationship of the tutor to his emperor as uncomplicatedly "equal". As mentioned earlier, Seneca's role as tutor is also to be a moral guide, to provide Nero with the appropriate moral instruction such that he may be a just emperor. In spite of Seneca's rather utopian image of Nero's innate goodness, the emphasis of the *De Clementia* is still one of didacticism, an emphasis which suggests that it is Seneca who will be the ultimate source of moral wisdom which will necessarily enable Nero to rule the Roman empire. In a sense, it is only a short step to realising that, if Seneca is aligning himself with the notion of a metaphysical force then he would undoubtedly possess the trait of omniscience. Furthermore, that Seneca can be regarded as the ultimate source of moral wisdom for the emperor only re-emphasises the notion of divinity as a question of a "first cause" or divine telos, since the Christian religion, for example, has been powerfully critiqued in terms of metaphysical origins.[32]

Seneca's appointment of himself as Nero's mirror is now explicable given the potential associations the metaphor holds for Seneca's own image. Direct attempts to pronounce himself more than the emperor who is himself acting on god's behalf, would have been problematic. As a result, Seneca does not actually pronounce himself a mirror but as someone *functioning* as a mirror. The implied distance from a divine metaphysics could have been enough to prevent Seneca from placing himself in too presumptuous a position. But Seneca's role as moral authoritarian for the emperor who not only rules an empire, but is innately good, means that Seneca must (obliquely at least) assert his role as moral authority. Indeed, that metaphysics was the domain of philosophers in this epoch is, in a sense, complicated for Seneca. Seneca pronounces himself the mirror for Nero most probably to assert his authority in the sphere of a moral knowledge which Nero would evidently need for just governance; Seneca was willing to bestow upon Nero the role of divine emissary and god's *political* representative on earth, but the domain of the requisite *moral* knowledge for this task appeared to remain the property of the omniscient but benevolent philosopher.[33]

Notes and References

I would like to take this opportunity to thank the editor and my supervisor, Dr. Ellen O'Gorman, for all their helpful and constructive comments in the drafting of this paper. Most of all, though, I would like to thank my wife for all her gentle motions which proved indispensable to the end result.

[1] See, in particular, Pliny's assessment of the mirror at *Natural History* 33.128

[2] Quintilian *Institutes* 11.3.68.

[3] The first century BC orator and politician Cicero defines *inuentio* as "the devising of truths or things similar to truths which render argumentation more plausible" (*De Inuentione* 1.7). The notion of *inuentio* has its roots in rhetorical argumentation, although as Tony Woodman has pointed out in his *Rhetoric in Classical Historiography: Four Studies* (Portland: Areopagatica, 1988), it was a highly important facet of historical writing as well.

[4] For the mirror's value as a reflective object, the Perseus online resource offers a dictionary which includes some interesting statistics on the relative (in)frequency of the Latin term *speculum*. The entry for *speculum* (which is derived from an edition of Charlton T. Lewis' and Charles Short's *A Latin Dictionary*), can be found at www.perseus.tufts.edu/cgi-bin/resolveform?lang=la, by inputting *speculum* to the Latin word search and opening the link to the Lewis and Short entry. Aside from the metaphorical use of the mirror which constitutes the subject of this paper, poetic or metaphorical contexts in which the mirror appears in Roman literature are few. For references to the mirror in Latin literature, one might again consult the entry for *speculum* in the Perseus edition of Charlton T. Lewis' and Charles Short's *A Latin dictionary* by using the web page given above (esp. entry B and II).

[5] Biographical information on the life of the Roman emperor Nero and his tutor Seneca is superabundant. Nero himself was only a teenager when Seneca was given charge of his moral education by Nero's mother, the elder Agrippina. Nero has been regarded as one of the stereotypically "bad" Roman emperors, but for an introductory survey of the tyrant's reign (54-68AD), one might consult David Shotter's *Nero* (London: Blackwell Press, 1996). Seneca himself, was a complicated historical figure, but for a survey of his turbulent political years before his appointment as Nero's tutor, one should consult Miriam T. Griffin's *Seneca: A Philosopher in Politics*, 2nd ed. (Oxford: Oxford Clarendon Press, 1992), 29-66. For a more recent survey of the philosopher's life, one might consult Paul Veyne's *Seneca: The Life of a Stoic* (New York: Routledge, 2003).

[6] For a good overview of Stoicism's inception, a philosophic sect which began in ancient Greece under its figurehead Zeno in the Hellenistic era, one should consult A.A Long's *Hellenistic Philosophy: Stoics, Epicureans, Sceptics*, 2nd ed. (London: Duckworth, 1986), 109-18, and 118-21 for an overview of the philosophy itself. For a more complete account of Stoic philosophy F.H. Sandbach's *The Stoics*, 2nd ed. (Bristol: Bristol Classical Press, 1989) is a good guide. Most recently, however, Brad Inwood's edition of *the Cambridge Companion to the Stoics* (Cambridge: Cambridge University Press, 2003)

provides the non-specialised reader a good overview of the range and influence of Stoic philosophy. The same author also provides an excellent analysis of Stoic ethics in *Ethics and Human Action in Early Stoicism* (Oxford: Oxford Clarendon Press, 1985).

[7] *De Clementia* 1.1. Probably the best and most contemporary edition of the Latin text, the *De Clementia*, can be found in the Loeb edition of J.W. Basore's revised translation of *Seneca: Moral Essays*, vol. 1, (London: Heinemann, 1998), 356-447. For the purpose of this essay, I am following Basore's analysis of the Latin manuscripts, but the text is badly in need of a modern independent commentary. All translations are based on those of the Loeb edition with amendments.

[8] *De Clem.* 1.1.1

[9] Ibid., 1.1.2.

[10] *De Ira* 1.1.5: "...other emotions are kept hidden and thrive by stealth. Anger is more brazen and visible in the countenance and the greater it is, the more openly it shows itself." For the purposes of this paper, I shall be using the Latin text of the *De Ira* from Basore, 106-355. Seneca's essay represents a significant utilitarian denunciation of the need for anger in human life, although the text again has no modern independent commentary.

[11] *De Ira* 1.1.4.

[12] Ibid., 2.36.1-3.

[13] As Basore, IX, states. The date of composition for the *De Ira* is almost impossible to date with any degree of accuracy except to say that it was written some time after the death of emperor Caligula in 41AD.

[14] For a practical and therapeutic approach to Stoic ethics and the ethics of Hellenistic philosophy more generally, see Martha C. Nussbaum's *The Therapy of Desire: Theory and Practice of Hellenistic Ethics* (New Jersey: Princeton, 1994). Even more recently, one could also consult Richard Sorabji's *Emotion and Peace of Mind: From Stoic Agitation to Christian Temptation* (Oxford: Oxford University Press, 2000).

[15] *De Ira* 2.36.3.

[16] For a good survey of the principles of Stoic physics, see A.A. Long, 147-78, and A.A. Long's and D.N. Sedley's edition of *The Hellenistic Philosophers*, vol. 1, (Cambridge: Cambridge University Press), 266-343.

[17] See, for example, *De Ira* 1.7.2, 1.8ff, 1.10.1-2, 1.17.3-5 and 1.19.1-2.

[18] See the *De Clementia* where Seneca tells us that "clemency exists in accordance with reason" (*"clementia rationi accedit"* (2.5.1)).

[19] *De Clem.* 1.11.1. C.f. Augustus' later act of clemency in respect of his political subject, Lucius Cinna's attempt on his life in which Augustus' anger (1.9.5) is abated by the counsel of his wife Livia (1.9.6) which leads to Cinna's acquittal (1.9.11).

[20] *De Clem.* 1.5.6.

[21] Ibid., 1.17.3.

[22] *De Ira* 1.14.2-3. Also see 2.28.1 and 3.4.4.

[23] Ibid., 2.28.8. It is worth pointing out that here Seneca invokes a series of rhetorical but introspective appeals to the conscience in this passage similar in flavour to the discourse which Seneca puts into the mouth of Nero in the opening passages of the *De Clementia*.

[24] *De Ira* 3.25.2 and 2.10.6 respectively.

[25] *De Clem.* 1.6.3-4.

[26] See note 18 above.

[27] See, for example, Seneca's assertion that kingship exists in accordance with the idea of natural law at *De Clem.* 1.16.2 and 1.19.2-4.

[28] *De Clem.* 1.1.6.

[29] Ibid.

[30] See note 2 above. Latin often qualifies the mirror as a *fulgor speculi(orum)*, or literally the "image of the mirror(s)". By using the Perseus web page quoted in note 4, inputting *fulgor* and referring to the Lewis and Short dictionary entry at IIA, one can find instances of this beyond the authorship of Quintilian.

[31] Appropriately, Seneca does not qualify his evocation of the *speculum* in the opening lines of the *De Clementia,* suggesting that his focus in employing the image of the mirror is more concerned with its abstract existence, and not its functional existence, that is its role as a reflective surface, not as an object which forms images.

[32] That divinity or belief in god can be associated with the concept of a metaphysical origin is a claim discussed by Bertrand Russell in his essay "Why I am not a Christian" in *Bertrand Russell on God and Religion*, ed. Al Seckel, 57-71 (New York: Prometheus, 1986). Seneca himself in his work of natural philosophy the *Quaestiones Naturales* or "Natural Questions" offers many synonyms for the Stoic notion of a divine metaphysics (2.45.2-3) including a *causa causarum* or "cause of causes".

[33] Seneca's personal association with the metaphysical operates in direct contradiction to passages in the *De Clementia* where Seneca likens Nero to the metaphysical spirit or cosmic bond of the political state (see, for example 1.4 and 1.5.1). Yet, given that Nero's metaphorical role takes place per analogem within the political arena, Seneca's more literal approximation to divine omniscience through his possession of moral wisdom, remains unchallenged.

Part II:

Mirrors of God

CHAPTER FOUR

SEEING THROUGH A GLASS DARKLY: THE INTERPRETATION OF A BIBLICAL VERSE IN AUGUSTINE OF HIPPO

MARK KAUNTZE

The words are only speculation (From the Latin *speculum*, mirror):
They seek and cannot find the meaning of the music.
—John Ashbery, "Self-Portrait in a Convex Mirror"

The thirteenth chapter of the First Epistle to the Corinthians contains one of the best known passages of the New Testament, in which St Paul insists on the pre-eminence of love [*agape*] as a way of knowing God. Unlike the knowledge of prophecy, which comes to an end with death, love persists and facilitates the perfect vision of God in the life to come. In a famous and beautiful passage, in which Paul expresses this contrast, he writes that "now we see through a glass, darkly; but afterwards, face to face" (1 Corinthians 13:12). Modern commentators have long recognised the centrality of this passage in Paul's mystical teachings. The verse was also a perennial favourite of medieval writers, and it appears as a recurring motif in a great number of theological and philosophical treatises from the fifth to the fifteenth century. In this essay I shall look at just one interpretation of Paul's verse, arguably the most striking and certainly the most influential, in the writings of Augustine, the North African bishop of Hippo, around the turn of the fifth century. Before turning to Augustine though, and in order to bring out the peculiarities of his reading, let us first ask what Paul may have meant by this image, and what purpose he intended it to serve in the argument of his Epistle.

To begin with, we need to be clear about the meaning of the words themselves.[1] The King James Version suggests something like seeing through a tinted window. This is not though what Paul or his translators had in mind. Paul uses the Greek word "eisoptron" [$\acute{\varepsilon}\iota\sigma o\pi\tau\rho o\nu$], which the sixteenth-century English renders as "glass", as in looking glass or mirror. The suggestion that one is looking "through" something is also deceptive, for again this is an archaism derived from the Greek and Latin use of the preposition "through" in connection with mirrors, where we would more naturally say "in." To look "through a glass", then, is to look "in a mirror" – and it is this archaic expression, incidentally, that Lewis Carroll plays on in the title of his *Alice Through the Looking Glass*. What though of the manner in which we are said to see through a glass "darkly"? Here again there is room for confusion. The words used are "en aenigmati", and *aenigma* is a rhetorical term for a kind of allegory, or more generally, for riddling or obscure speech. The image in Paul's mirror, then, is one that is riddled with ambiguity.

What did Paul mean by this? The verse occurs in the context of a discussion of what the sayings of the prophets can add to our knowledge of God in this life. Paul's contention is that even with the insights attained by the inspired prophets of the Old Testament our picture of God can never amount to more than an obscure reflection. It seems likely that Paul chose this analogy because the Corinthians to whom he was preaching are known to have specialised in the production of mirrors.[2] Two points are important here. Firstly, these mirrors were sheets of polished bronze, not the metal-backed glass variety more familiar to us. According to glass historians Macfarlane and Martin, the Romans, although expert in glass technology and capable of making mirrors from the material, preferred to use metal.[3] The metal of the mirror here may explain something about the obscurity of the image to which Paul alludes. Although it would be anachronistic to suggest that the reflections produced by metal surfaces would have appeared obscure in comparison to a technology that was probably not widely known, it must nonetheless have been apparent that these images did not have the same level of resolution as those produced by reflective surfaces in nature, such as still water. Secondly, the role played by the mirror here is not what a modern reader might take it to be. For in ancient Greek literature mirrors are often depicted as magical objects, in which one would look not primarily to see oneself but rather something that is invisible to others.[4] In a similar way, the point here appears to be not about self-perception but a simple contrast between the indirectness of even the best knowledge of God available in this life (that of the prophets) and the direct knowledge of a face-to-face encounter in the afterlife.

It is in this sense of a contrast between prophecy and the beatific vision that Paul's verse appears to have been understood in Greek and Latin theology over the next three hundred years.[5] Then came Augustine or, to be more precise, late Augustine. For although the bishop of Hippo referred to Paul's verse often in his early work, for example the *Confessions*, there it is always used to suggest the limitations of human knowledge of God. Specifically, the verse functions in the *Confessions* as a reminder that although Augustine may have progressed from the sinfulness of his early life, his progress towards knowledge of God is necessarily restricted. In a prayer to God at the beginning of the eighth book, for example, he recalls his state of mind in the period following his conversion: "Concerning your eternal life I was now certain, although I saw it only enigmatically and as if in a mirror."[6] Here and elsewhere in the *Confessions* Augustine tends to employ Paul's words simply as an authoritative confirmation of a conclusion that he has already reached, rather than using the verse creatively as an integral part of his argument. Such a distinctive treatment had to await the final book of his work on the Trinity, *De trinitate*.[7]

By the time Augustine completed *De trinitate*, not long before his death, he had been at work on this ambitious treatise of speculative theology for around twenty-five years. The first seven books of the work lay out the Church's teachings on the Trinity as defined at the Council of Nicea in 325 (namely that the Trinity is three persons but one substance), and books eight to fifteen attempt to see how analogies for understanding the Trinity might be developed out of human experience. A important premise of the *Confessions* had been the idea that to study man was a way of studying God, and that insight is developed in *De trinitate* into an argument that the human mind is akin to the Trinity in the sense that the operation of the three powers of the mind, namely memory, intellect and will, bears formal similarity to the unity of Father, Son and Sprit in the Trinity. The central assumption of the work is that any understanding by analogy, however limited, of the supreme mystery of the Christian faith is a spiritual therapy, which will help restore the image of God in our souls so that we can more fully share in the experience of the divine presence in this life. *De trinitate* is a massive work and it is beyond the scope of this essay to examine the statements of doctrine in the early books or to look in detail at the trinitarian analogies with man, which Augustine develops in the second half of the work. It is the final, fifteenth book that is of particular interest to us, for it is there that Augustine considers the value of these various analogies by asking how faithful a reflection is the image of God apparent in the human mind. It is in this context that he provides a fascinating interpretation of 1 Corinthians 13:12.

Near the beginning of Book 15, Augustine sums up the direction that his work has so far taken. He explains that in his desire to understand the Trinity, he has sought out certain aspects of humanity worthy of analogy with that mystery. This search led him from certain outer human characteristics, such as sight, which requires a trinity of the beholder, the object beheld and the act of beholding, gradually towards more inner human trinities, and the discovery, in the perfection of the soul's highest faculties, of the most accurate image of its perfect creator.[8] These highest faculties are reason and understanding, which are activities of the mind. Minds are unique to humans – although, according to Augustine, their operation is not fully enjoyed by women (*De trin.*, XII.7-8) – and they mark man out above the rest of creation as having been made in the image of God. It is to the mind, then, that one must look to study the image of God. Those characteristics of the mind that Augustine finds most analogous to the Trinity are the three powers of memory, intellect and will. In answer to the question of how it is that Father, Son and Spirit can simultaneously be both three and one Augustine argues, very roughly, that it is rather like the way in which memory, intellect and will are distinct yet interdependent faculties of the mind.

The details of this analogy do not concern us at present.[9] What is significant in terms of Augustine's reading of the Corinthian Epistle is his assessment in the final book of the strengths and weaknesses of the various analogies developed throughout the work, and of how closely they map that to which they purport to correspond. Their value, according to Augustine, is that they allow us to see as if through a mirror in an enigma. Separating these two Pauline terms, he first considers the meaning of the mirror:

> Quale sit et quod sit hoc speculum si quaeramus, profecto illud occurrit quod in speculo nisi imago non cernitur. Hoc ergo facere conati sumus ut per hanc imaginem quod nos sumus videremus utcumque a quo facti sumus tamquam per speculum. (*De trin.*, XV.8.14)

> [If we ask what this mirror is, and of what sort it is, the first thing that comes to mind is that nothing else is discerned in a mirror except an image. We have, therefore, tried to do this [that is, the project of *De trinitate*] in order that through this image, which we are, we might see him by whom we were made, just as if through a mirror.]

Immediately it is obvious here that Augustine is up to something altogether different from what Paul appears to have had in mind in 1 Corinthians 13:12. What he has done is to frame Paul's words in the context of another famous Biblical verse, in which man is said to be made in the image of God (Genesis 1:26), with the effect of suggesting that if man's mind is an image of the Trinity then it will also be the mirror that reflects that image. Augustine abstracts Paul's words from the discussion of prophecy of which they were once part and, by so doing, he is able, as it were, to relocate the mirror. For Augustine this mirror is not a metaphor for the indirect witnesses to God's nature that come from outside ourselves in the form of a prophet's sayings, but rather a metaphor for the contemplative resources made available to each of us by the possession of a mind.

What was it, we might ask, that prompted Augustine into this novel interpretation of the Corinthian verse? Partly, as he tells us himself, it is the natural association between mirror and image. Augustine is also, however, drawing on another Biblical verse, this time from Paul's second Epistle to the

Corinthians (2 Corinthians 3:18), which again makes use of mirror imagery.[10]
He continues (from the previous quotation):

> Hoc significant etiam illud quod ait idem apostolus: "Nos autem revelata facie
> gloriam domini speculantes in eandem imaginem transformamur de gloria in
> gloriam tamquam a domini spiritu." (*De trin.*, XV.8.14)

> [Such is also the meaning of the words spoken by the same Apostle: "But we,
> with face unveiled, reflecting the glory of God, are transformed into the same
> image, from glory to glory, as through the spirit of the Lord."]

In this second passage Paul refers to the veil through which the Old Testament
prophets beheld God, by which he means their restricted knowledge before the
Incarnation, and he comments that this veil has been disposed of by Christ.
Whereas before, man's face had to be protected from the blinding light of God
(Exodus 34:33), now, with the knowledge of the Gospels, his face may shine
with the rays of directly reflected divinity.

What does Augustine take this to mean? The word used here for "reflecting"
is the present participle "speculantes", and Augustine goes on to insist on this
word's etymological connection with the Latin word for mirror, *speculum*,
rather than with *specula*, the word for watch-tower.[11] This is important because
he wants to establish a connection at this point between *speculum* and
speculatio, meaning abstract thought – an association absent from the original
Greek of the New Testament, where ἔσοπτρον, the word Paul uses for mirror,
has no etymological relationship with any Greek words for thinking.
Augustine's interest in making this link between reflection in its visual and
cognitive senses is perhaps to establish a biblical rationale for his trinitarian
theology. Given his method of analysing the thought processes of his own mind
in order to discern the best possible image of the Trinity, and thereby participate
more fully in that mystery, the appeal of these two Pauline verses is clear. The
mirror of the First Epistle, in which we see the image of God, must, for
Augustine, be the human mind. It follows, then, that the reflecting referred to in
the Second Epistle must be the process of thinking about the image of the
Trinity in our minds, a process that will lead us to the kind of spiritual
transformation described by Paul.

In order to assess the status of this reflection of the Trinity in the human
mind, it is useful to think about optical theory in this context. According to
Plato's theory of optics, which prevailed in Latin Christendom until the
translation in the early thirteenth century of the treatise *On Vision* by the Arabic
philosopher Alhazen (*c.* 1041), a reflection is formed when the fire that
emanates from an object meets the fire that emanates from the eye on the
reflective surface. There, the two fires coalesce to form an image and this image

is transmitted back to the eye along the trail of fire.[12] The significance of this lies in the fact that, in contrast with modern theories of reflection, the reflected image is something that actually forms on the mirror's surface. So in Augustine's analogy the Trinity is imprinted on the mind rather than being, as we might imagine, passingly mirrored in it. And indeed Augustine says as much when he equates reflection with painting, by remarking that man is the panel on which the image of the Trinity is painted.[13]

But how good a painting is it? Augustine obviously did not believe that the image of God in the mind's mirror was entirely clear. As he goes on to remind us in the next chapter, it is also an enigma. Ironically, the meaning of 1 Corinthians 13:12 remains unknown to those who do not understand what an enigma is. Enigma has been mistaken by some commentators, he complains, as a synonym for allegory, whereas allegory is in fact a genus, which contains enigma as one of its species. Following classical rhetoricians, such as Quintillian and Cicero, Augustine writes that, "every enigma is an allegory, but not every allegory is an enigma... [and] to explain it briefly, an enigma is an obscure allegory, such as: 'The horseleech has three daughters' (Proverbs 30:15), and whatever expressions are similar to this."[14] As a whole, then, Augustine takes Paul's verse to mean that the image of God reflected in the thought processes of the human mind is not as faithful as a normal mirror image: it is only a likeness; and so too are the analogies between the mind and the Trinity that he has constructed. Paul's words, 'we see now in a mirror in an enigma', perfectly capture Augustine's sense of the strengths and weaknesses of his analogies: they reflect an image of God, but this image is no more than a likeness.

By defining mirror in terms of image, and enigma in terms of likeness, Augustine returns again to that key text of philosophical theology, the Genesis verse in which God describes man as made in his image and likeness, in his *imago* and *similitudo* (Genesis 1:26). This echo of Genesis is significant because it reinforces the idea that it is due to the way in which man is created that he can see God in himself. According to Bernard McGinn, Augustine "distinguished between *similitudo* as any form of likeness between things, and *imago* as a particular kind of likeness by which something both relates to and is expressive of its source."[15] This distinction helps to show why Augustine equated mirror with image, and enigma with likeness. Man is created in the image of God in the sense that man, and most especially the mind of man into which Augustine is looking, both relates to and is expressive of God. Equally though, man's mind is but a likeness of God, and thus shares in all that likeness contains of unlikeness. So although man is made in the image of God, there is a dissimilarity between creator and created; and Augustine's reason for introducing this echo of Genesis was perhaps to imply that if we look into our minds hoping to see the image of

God reflected, we should expect difficulties in recognising that image. Augustine dwells on the paradox inherent in this situation at the end of this chapter on enigma:

> Et hoc est grandius aenigma ut non videamus quod non videre non possumus. Quis enim non videt cogitationem suam? Et quis videt cogitationem suam (non oculis carnalibus dico sed ipso interiore conspectus)? (*De trin.*, XV.9.16)

> [And this is a greater enigma, that we do not see what it is impossible for us not to see. For who does not see his own thought? And who does see it, not, I say, with the eyes of the flesh but with the interior gaze itself?]

The causes of these difficulties and the ways in which they might be overcome are part of another story, and one that Augustine tells from personal experience in his *Confessions*. For the purpose of this essay, it remains for us to summarise what Augustine has done with Paul's verse in the final book of *De trinitate*. Augustine's understanding of the view of God through a mirror and in an enigma differed markedly from what Paul appears to have intended in the Corinthian verse. Whereas the Apostle used the mirror as a metaphor for the sayings of the prophets, Augustine uses it as a metaphor for the human mind. A verse that had, by Augustine's time, become a platitude for the indirectness of human knowledge of God, is transformed in the closing pages of *De trinitate* into a keystone of the whole structure of Augustine's trinitarian theology. The tools used in this transformation appear to have been partly the natural association of mirrors with images, and thus with the image of God in which man is made, and partly the wide semantic range of the Latin vocabulary of reflection (*speculum/ speculatio*). The product is a verse which, in its juxtaposition of mirror and enigma, characterises respectively the successes and failures of Augustine's trinitarian analogies.

It was perhaps because of this, and in spite of its neglect of the prophetic context of the thirteenth chapter of the First Epistle, that Augustine's reading of this Pauline verse proved so influential. It surfaces, for example, in Anselm of Canterbury's late eleventh-century trinitarian work, the *Monologion*, where Anselm was clearly thinking of Augustine when he wrote that the mind "might most appropriately be called its own mirror – the mirror in which it sees the face of that which, famously, it cannot see face to face." [16] Less predictably, Augustine's mirror seems to have caught the imagination of medieval readers of classical mythology, as can be seen from a twelfth-century commentary on the late antique allegorist, Martianus Capella, where Psyche, who receives a mirror as a birthday present from the goddess Urania, is interpreted as representing the image and likeness of God, and the image of the Trinity. [17] In addition, the inclusion of Augustine's reading as the sole interpretation in the standard set of glosses on the Bible that was codified in the twelfth century, suggests both that it had become the primary interpretation and that its influence on later medieval readings of Paul's Epistle was guaranteed.[18]

In the few pages devoted to the Middle Ages in Arthur Koestler's history of cosmology, Koestler wrote that "the brighter elements [of Augustine's thought] were ignored by the generations after him, and the shadow he cast was dark and oppressive."[19] To my mind though, these passages of Augustine that we have been looking at, and which appear to have been taken up and adapted with enthusiasm by medieval thinkers, are anything but dark and oppressive. These exercises in Biblical exegesis are not the stuff of a stale tradition, which Koestler perhaps imagined being handed down unquestioningly from one generation of benighted monks to the next. They are interpretations capable of leading the reader into unexpected territory; away from the platitude of man's indirect knowledge of God in this life, and into difficult thinking about the correlation between our moral characters and our ability to see God where we should not be able to miss him – in our every thought. It is these kinds of challenging elements that appealed and continue to appeal to readers of Augustine.

Notes and References

I would like to thank Gillian Clark and Jimmy Doyle for their comments on a draft of this paper.

[1] The fundamental study of this verse in the context of the Corinthian Epistles is Norbert Hugédé, *La Métaphore du miroir dans les epîtres de Saint Paul aux Corinthiens* (Paris: Delachaux Niestlé, 1957).

[2] James Moffat, *The First Epistle of Paul to the Corinthians* (London: Hodder Stroughton, 1959), 200-2.

[3] A. Macfarlane and G. Martin, *The Glass Bathyscaphe: How Glass Changed the World* (London: Profile Books, 2002), 13-16.

[4] For an extensive review of ancient Greek and Hellenistic texts that deal with mirrors see Hugédé, 48-137, and for the use of mirrors in divination in the ancient world see the essay by Crystal Addey in this volume.

[5] Examples include Tertullian, *Adversus Praxean*, XIV; Origen, *De principiis*, II.3; Ambrose of Milan, *De Abraham*, II.9; and Rufinus, *De benedictionibus patriarcharum*, II.30.

[6] "De vita tua aeterna certus eram, quamvis eam in aenigmate et quasi per speculum videram..." Augustine, *Confessiones*, ed. with commentary, James J. O'Donnell, 3 vols. (Oxford: Clarendon Press, 1992), I: VIII.1.1. See also *Confessiones*, X.5.7, XII.13.16 and XIII.15.18.

[7] All references are to *De trinitate libri xv*, ed. W. J. Mountain, 2 vols., Corpus Christianorum, Series Latina, L–LA (Turnhout: Brepols, 1968).

[8] *De trin.*, XV.2.3: " . . . in creatura prius per quasdam sui generis trinitates quodam modo gradatim donec ad mentem hominis pervenirem quaesisse indicia summae illius trinitatis quam quaerimus cum deum quaerimus." [" . . . in my search for that highest Trinity, which we seek when we seek God, I first sought traces of it in the creature, and proceeded, as it were, step by step through certain trinities of its own kind until I arrived at the mind of man."]

[9] For a clear summary see Bernard McGinn, *The Presence of God: A History of Western Mysticism, I: The Foundations of Mysticism* (London: SCM, 1991), 243-8.

[10] Besides these two Corinthian verses there are only two other metaphorical uses of mirror imagery in the Bible: Wisdom 7:26 and James 1:23. Mirrors also appear at Exodus 38:8 and Job 37:18.

[11] In fact, this is a textual crux in the Second Epistle. To translate κατοπτρίξεσθαι as *speculantes* or "reflecting" is to give the word a sense rarely attested in Greek literature. Although Jerome's Vulgate translates it in this way, the more frequently attested sense of κατοπτρίξεσθαι is "beholding as in a mirror", and this is favoured by other Latin theologians, such as Tertullian, who translate it as *contemplantes*. This second translation alleviates an apparent inconsistency with 1 Corinthians 13:12; for the idea of Christians, with their faces unveiled by the Incarnation, beholding the glory of God as in a mirror, that is, in the example of the life of Christ, is still compatible with the human knowledge/beatific vision dichotomy established in the First Epistle; whereas the impression created by the translation "reflecting" [*speculantes*] is that of a direct reflection of God's glory in the faces of the believers, an idea at odds with the insistence in 1 Corinthians 13:12 on the obscurity of all human reflection on the divine. Liddell and Scott's Greek-English Lexicon (q.v. κατοπτρ-ίζω) cites 2 Cor 3:18 and offers both alternatives. For a historical review of the exegesis see Hugédé, 20-36.

[12] Plato, *Timaeus*, 46a-b, trans. & discussed by Francis M. Cornford, *Plato's Cosmology: The Timaeus of Plato* (London: Routledge, 1937), 154-6.

[13] *De trin.* XV.22.43: "Aliud est itaque trinitas res ipsa, aliud imago trinitatis in re alia. Propter quam imaginem simul et illud in quo sunt haec tria imago dicitur, sicut imago dicitur simul et tabula et quod in ea pictum est, sed propter picturam quae in ea est simul et tabula nomine imaginis appellatur." ["A thing, therefore, which is a trinity is not the same as an image of a trinity in another thing; on account of which image that, too, in which these three are, is at the same time called an image; just as the panel and the picture painted on it together are called an image, but on account of the picture painted on it."]

[14] *De trin.*, XV.9.15: "omne aenigma allegoria est, non omne allegoria aenigma est... Aenigma est autem breviter explicem obscura alegoria sicuti est: 'Sanguisugae tres errant filiae' (Proverbs 30:15), et quaecumque similia." Compare Cicero's definition of *aenigma* in *De oratore*, trans. H. Rackham, 2 vols. (Cambridge, Mass.: Loeb, 1942), II: III.41: "Something resembling the real thing is taken, and the words that properly belong to it are then applied metaphorically to the other thing."

[15] McGinn, 243. For further discussion of these terms, see Peter Dronke, *Fabula: Explorations into the Uses of Myth in Medieval Platonism* (Leiden-Köln: Brill, 1974), 32-47, which does not, however, discuss *De trinitate*.

[16] Anselm of Canterbury, *The Major Woks*, ed. Brian Davies and Gillian R. Evans (Oxford: Oxford University Press, 1998), 73.

[17] *The Commentary on Martianus Capella's* De nuptiis Philologiae et Mercurii *Attributed to Bernardus Silvestris*, ed. Haijo J. Westra (Toronto: Pontifical Institute of Medieval Studies, 1986), 145.

[18] *Biblia Latina cum glossa ordinaria*, Facsimile reprint of the editio princeps, Adolf Rusch of Strasburg, 1480/81, 4 vols. (Turnhout: Brepols, 1992), IV: 329-30, where enigma is glossed as "obscura allegoria", and the mirror as showing "creaturas in quibus aliqua similitudo dei relucet." For the twelfth century see also Robert Javelet, *Image et resemblance au douzième siècle, de Saint Anselme à Alain de Lille*, 2 vols. (Paris: Letouzé, 1967), vol. I, 379-90.

[19] Arthur Koestler, *Sleepwalkers: A History of Man's Changing Vision of the Universe* (Harmondsworth: Penguin Books, 1959), 89.

Chapter Five

Chaucer and the Subject of the Mirror

Miranda Anderson

This essay begins with a general discussion about the mirror as a metaphor before focusing in on the way in which Chaucer's use of mirror metaphors relates to various interpretations of the nature of man which were circulating in the medieval period. What is particular about the form and meaning of mirror metaphors? The physical properties of a mirror relate to the figurative properties of a metaphor, which is based on notions of transfer: an image of the beholder is transferred onto a reflection, which is at once analogous to and yet different from the observing self, playing with the co-existence of similitude and dissimilitude, and the mutual formation of each other by the original and the image. The complexity of the mirror as a literary motif arises from the liminal space which it inhabits, being neither entirely subject nor entirely object: the mirror is potentially revelatory of the interior world of the self and yet conversely figures the objectified self within the external world. For this double reason, and for demonstrating their interrelation, the physical properties of the mirror have led to its figurative employment to explicate the functioning of the human mind and the construction of subjectivity.

Within the wider discourses of Chaucer's context, the tradition of anxiety over the human mind's inability to encompass itself, is dressed up in the transcendental garb of Christian theology. Thus as in the Augustinian paradox, the closest likeness of man to God is in the mind, but because it is the image of God we can't understand it. In *De Symbolo*, Augustine neatly describes the enigma of the self:

> It is in the mind that God has made man to His image and likeness, there it is that His image is stamped. If the mind is not to be fathomed even by itself that is because it is the image of God.[1]

In the Wycliffe Bible the dual nature of man, as an image of God and as fallen, are illustrated by the use of firstly an explicit and secondly an implicit mirror metaphor. The partialness of human understanding and the indirectness of our vision of God within the temporal world, will be transformed into a fullness of human understanding arising out of an end point which is a return to our origin "we seen now bi a myrrour in derknesse: but than face to face, now I knowe of parti, but thane I shal know as I am knowen".[2] Man as the synecdochical subject is teleologically fulfilled through his metamorphosis into the image of God. In his exposition of Genesis, Aquinas privileges intellectual discernment as "the closest likeness to God in creation" because the mind can attend indirectly to God, "as to an object seen in a mirror", when "it remembers and understands and loves itself".[3] Thus self-knowledge and intellectual understanding are linked to the imaging of God by man. However, there is a second imaging of God by man in which women do not participate and this is prelapsarian because men are "by nature more reasonable and discerning", while intellectually inferior women less closely resemble God and are more closely associated with the material world and passivity.[4] Moreover, because the human mind's comprehension of itself, of the internal, is only reflectively known through the abstraction of sense images, that is of the external, a chasm is evident in man's understanding through which he may fall.

The new stress by Aquinas on the imaging of God by man as entailing the active participation of the individual implicates man in the creation of his existential experience. The onus is placed on the recipient for the deception his internal faculties cause him to undergo as while the senses rarely misrepresent what they perceive, by taking the imaginary for real we can deceive ourselves, or by making false connections the mind makes false concepts.[5] Aquinas's theory of individual deception being caused by man's internal faculties is followed by the perspectival theorist Witelo in terms of vision. Witelo, along with Alhazen, is referred to by Chaucer in his *Squire's Tale*. Smith explains that Witelo showed that "visual deceptions are not, strictly speaking, visual; on the contrary, they are due to errors of estimation" during the act of contemplation.[6] In Books 5 to 10 of *Perspectiva*, Witelo focuses on the various ways in which mirrors contribute to visual deception. This contemporary interest in the field of optics upon the mirror as an instrument related to specular misjudgement, corresponds with Chaucer's use of mirrors which are figured as deceitful or misleading. Moreover, Witelo's theory also provides evidence of the new stress being placed on the subject as an active participant in the internal creation of his own reality.

This stress is also evident in the movement in literary texts from the use of Latin to the vernacular, in that the adoption of the latter reflects the idea of a nobility, in language and in man, not restricted to historical ancestry but as cultivatable through its origin in reason, as is described by Dante:

...the nobility of man and the nobility of his language lie in their natural origins, and just as natural human virtue can be fostered and can bring forth its fruits and aspire to greater perfection, so can the natural vernacular be trained and cultivated by art.[7]

In relation to the period's literary use of mirror metaphors, Herbert Grabes provides a historical survey of conventions. The twelfth century had primarily seen the use of the term *speculum* (lat. mirror) in sermons and with the increasing number of manuscripts, there had been a correlative increase in the number of mirror-titles. The thirteenth century saw the continuing popularity of *speculum* in Latin mirror-titles and, with the first appearance of the word *mirror* in John of Garland's *Dictionarius* (c.1225),[8] the beginning of its use in vernacular lyric poetry and in vernacular mirror-titles. Then in the fourteenth century an increase in vernacular mirror-titles and widespread use of mirror metaphors in Romances. Chaucer uses the word *mirour* in a variety of works, although following the general trend, it appears most dominantly in vernacular works of a purportedly romantic nature.

The following examples from Chaucer that we are going to look at relate to Aquinas's analysis of biblical mirror metaphors in two ways. Firstly in terms of Aquinas's conception of mirroring God as being an active process and secondly to his association of the feminine with temporality. *Fortune* is subtitled *Balades de Visage sanz Peinture*, which figuratively suggests the illusionary nature of that which is valued in worldly Fortune and associates her with the feminine; good fortune is a painted face, whose true face when revealed is but misfortune. The ballade recounts a trial of Fortune, who is constant only in her inconstancy. In the second verse, the plaintiff against Fortune speaks, depicting a stereotypical image of her wheel incessantly turning and, more unusually, using a mirror metaphor; "Yit is left me the light of my resoun/ to knowen frend fro fo in thy mirour."[9] The rhetoric employed creates an allegorical reading of the ballade, revolving around an inconstant lover. This interpretation of the mirror metaphor in *Fortune* is supported by Chaucer's use of a mirror metaphor to in *Balade against Women Unconstant*:

> Right as a mirour nothing may impresse,
> But, lightly as it cometh, so mot it pace,
> So fareth your love, youre werkes beren witnesse.[10]

Thus, the accused here is comparable to Fortune in her inconstancy, and the mirror metaphor again functions to suggest transitoriness. Indeed Chaucer's description of the woman later in the poem might equally serve as a pithy description of Fortune; "For ever in changing stant your sikernesse"[11] Thus the mirror metaphor in *Balade Against Women Unconstant* acts as a microcosm of the mirror metaphor in *Fortune*, such analogical thinking being invited by the idea of a hierarchical gradated cosmos and by the reflexive and reductive qualities of the convex mirror, commonly in use in the fourteenth century. The concern with the passive qualities of the mirror relate to Aquinas's understanding of self-knowledge as arising through mental activity. The emphasis upon the transience of that which is reflected, especially when contrasted in *Fortune* with the light of reason, may also be linked to the privileging of reason as mirroring God. The association of negative qualities with the feminine within these works echoes the misogynist conception of Aquinas that women are more closely connected with passivity and the transitoriness of the material world.

My next example relates to Aquinas's description of passion as a potential pitfall which may transform man into the image of subhuman bestiality rather than the image of God. Aquinas says that if "passion is so great that a man loses all reason, then he becomes like the other animals, deprived of all will."[12] In *The Knight's Tale* Arcite demonstrates the partialness of human vision and illustrates how *amor* can negatively transform an individual. Arcite is in a state of madness and melancholy caused by his lovesick state: "lyk manye,/ Engendered of humor malencolik/ Biforen, in his celle fantastic".[13] The functions of Arcite's rational soul have been impeded by his imagination's fixation upon a particular object: by his self-internment within his fantasy. Catching sight of himself in a mirror, he realises that his lovesick state has so disfigured his outward appearance that he is unrecognisable:

> And with that word he caughte a greet mirour,
> And saugh that chaunged was al his colour,
> And saugh his visage al in another kynde.[14]

This external disfigurement is caused by Arcite's internal state: it is a symptom of his psychological malady and reflects the intimate interrelation of the physical and psychological realms.[15] What is figuratively implied by Arcite's inability to recognise himself in the mirror is the lack of his resemblance to his own image and this in turn signifies his distance from a likeness to God.

Chaucer's use of mirror metaphors to explore the nature of the human mind depicts it as viewing external images in an internal mirror, again reflecting a blurring between outer and inner, and here between the operation of introspection and perception in the human subject, as the inner processes are explained through the external phenomenon. Grabes suggests that the mind mirror metaphor only became popular with the Elizabethans and has found no direct parallel for the use of the mirror metaphor in *The Merchant's Tale* [16], in which Januarie views prospective marriage candidates in the mirror of his thoughts. But in Chaucer's translation of the *Roman de la Rose*, the source of this is evident. The God of Love describes 'Swete-Thought' as one of the remedies to a lovestruck state:

> For Thought anoon thanne shall bygynne,
> As fer God wot, as he can fynde,
> To make a mirrour of his mynde;
> For to biholde he wole not lette.
> Hir persone he shall afore hym sette.[17]

This metaphor also features in *Troilus and Criseyde*, where Troilus impaled through his eyes by love's arrow, begins to consider Criseyde anew:

> Thus gan he make a mirour of his mynde
> In which he saugh al holly hire figure,
> And that he wel koulde in his herte fynde.[18]

These mind mirror metaphors function as an inversion of the mind mirroring God and physical desire functions as an impediment rather than as a mode of access to truth. Instead of approaching God with the mind through the abstraction of sense images in order to come to self understanding and so hereafter an eternity imaging God, the protagonists submit their reason to their senses and their will to bodily desire through their imprinting of their beloved's image within themselves. The mirror of their mind which should reflect God, becomes a mirror which only reflects the Fall.

Aquinas refers to the Fall as the inaugurator of *concupiscence*; "which consists in the disordered turning to temporal goods". Also he describes the libido as "a habitual state in which our sense-appetites are not subject to reason as they were in the original integrated state of man." Miller relates how the Fall was regarded as the dissolution of *virilitas* into *mulierbritas*, that is "effeminacy", whether the story was interpreted literally or allegorically; "Literally, Adam the first husband abrogated his responsibility when he allowed his moral authority to be swayed by Eve. Allegorically, Reason consented to the seductions of the Flesh."[19] The protagonists exemplify man's fallen state while re-enacting the Fall in microcosm, as the phallic arrow of desire impales the male lover and masculine reason submits to the feminine senses. Thus their individual re-enactments of the Fall relate to Aquinas's conception of the feminine as being at a double remove from God and serve to explore the problematics of fallen man imaging God.

Chaucer develops similar concerns through various other mirror metaphors in *Troilus and Criseyde*. The surface level of the text is an exploration of courtly love's joys and woes and a depiction of the psychological effects upon the soul and mind of being in love. The beloved is described as the mirror of excellence and the origin and end of all pleasure; "As he that is the welle of worthynesse,/ Of trouthe grownd, mirour of goodlihed," [20] Here is illustrated the slippage occurring between the vocabulary and imagery of secular and spiritual love, while the medieval reader would yet be aware Who is truly worthy of such devotion. Pandarus in persuading Criseyde to love considers her outward appearance:

> And with that word he gan right inwardly
> Byholden hire and loken on hire face,
> And seyde, "On swich a mirour goode grace!"[21]

In a contrasting use of the metaphor, he warns her that she shall too late regret her disdain of love, as youth and beauty quickly fade:

> The kynges fool is wont to crien loude,
> Whan that hym thinketh a woman berth hire hye,
> "So longe mote ye lyve, and alle proude,
> Til crowes feet be growe under youre ye,
> And sende yow than a myrour in to prye,
> In which that ye may se youre face a morwe!"
> I bidde wisshe yow namore sorwe.[22]

On one level these can be related to the *carpe diem* of Medieval and Renaissance love poetry, yet on a higher level this tradition is subverted to transmit a deeper meaning. Both these metaphorical applications are inversions of the conventional didactic use outlined by theologians. Outer beauty should lead the subject to reform his inner self to equal it by inner virtue; outer deformity or the threat of mortality, should lead the subject to compensate by inner virtue. [23] However, Criseyde's beauty is used as a reason for her suitability for earthly love, rather than as a perfection her soul should seek to imitate. Then, the transience of her beauty serves not as a warning that she should consider hereafter, but conversely that she should seize worldly pleasure while she can. Thus, as with the description of the lover as the "mirour of goodlihed", dual interpretations of the metaphors are possible.

Lee Patterson interprets *Troilus and Criseyde* as an investigation by Chaucer into the dilemma of the recursiveness of the historical process, which only at the end is forced to accept its lack of meaning, resulting in the narrator's final desperate response in sending up a prayer for release.[24] Patterson's argument that in Troilus and Criseyde "Chaucer manages to suggest the ultimate impotence, even irrelevance of Boethianism"[25] arises from his synchronisation of the two different levels of Boethius's theory on the nature of man. Patterson describes Boethianism as follows: "Boethianism offers to its believers the

knowledge of a *fons et origo*, [source and origin], that is not only itself
unmediated but identical with the 'oon ende of blisfulnesse' to which man's
intentio naturalis, or natural intention, instinctively converts him."[26] However,
according to Boethius the *intentio naturalis* is the natural urge towards life and
an inversion of the will of the soul. [27] Although they both arise from the same
desire for stability and unity, the natural intention involves a misunderstanding
as to where the *summum bonum*, the greatest good, lies; it is a divergent effect
of the primordial desire for union.[28] Thus man's natural intention does not
instinctively convert him to a knowledge of his origin and end, but rather an
understanding of the latter is something which the subject has to strive to
remember. Troilus's lack of this knowledge, which is made evident by his
imaging of Criseyde in his mind, is what makes him fated. Boethianism is not
"philosophically antithetical" to Troilus and Criseyde:[29] Chaucer explores in
literature the problematics of the limitations of human reason and desire, which
were acknowledged in Boethius's philosophy. Thus the predicament of the
Medieval subject is caused by the type of mistake Patterson has made:
confusing the workings of natural intention with the will of the soul. The duality
of the nature of man is explored in Chaucer's mind mirror metaphors and while
the surface level of the text is an exploration of the realm of natural intention,
the anagogical level refers the reader to the realm of the will of the soul. Thus
the figural level anticipates the epilogue, in which Chaucer directs the reader as
to the moral of his story and reminds us of whom we should be the image:

> O yonge, fresshe folks, he or she,
> In which that love up groweth with youre age,
> Repeyreth hom fro worldly vanyte,
> And of youre herte up casteth the visage
> To thilke God that after his ymage
> Yow made, and thynketh al nys but a faire,
> This world that passeth soone as flouris faire.[30]

This reading of *Troilus and Criseyde* suggests that Cultural Materialism's
conception of dual meanings co-existing in a text, could validly be applied here,
where the dominant Christian didactic ideology only emerges to contain other
possible interpretations at the end; mirroring Christianity's teleological
structure. Boccacio's *Il Filostrato*, a source used by Chaucer, ends only with the
moral of warning ladies not to cruelly reject lovers, and the fact that previously
the story had been used as an instigation to persuade women to love would have
heightened the transformation of it by Chaucer into finally a reminder that
caritas is the superior form of love. The fact that the gullible narrator ironically
celebrates Troilus's conversion to *amor*: "Blissed be Love, that kan thus folk
converte!"[31] highlights Chaucer's technique of drawing the reader in and

implicating the reader in his and Troilus's folly, which as Huppé argues heightens the shock of recognition at the ultimate meaning at the end of the story.[32]

Richard Hillman describes "the discursive focus of most formal tragedy" as the "individual's struggle to achieve meaning within the duplicity of signification".[33] *Troilus and Criseyde* is a tragedy because Troilus fails to ascend to the realm beyond duplicitous signification. Thus the romance, already twisted out of an epic is transformed by Chaucer into a tragedy. If Boethian philosophy is problematised it is in terms of the subject's difficulty in rising from within its entanglement in the worldly realm to an understanding of the deeper meaning and circularity that lies behind it. However, this problematisation is mediated by the fact that Boethius himself acknowledged the difficulty in fallen man's finding his way home to the "wonderful circle of simplicity of God".[34] The heightened stress on this difficulty, which forms the theme of Chaucer's mirror metaphors examined in this paper, relates to the new emphasis in theological and perspectival theories on the implication of the subject in their perception of reality and in their spiritual progress. Thus the paradox of man's nature as fallen and divinely imprinted, as self-motivated and as seemingly controlled by external and internal compulsions, is the location of Chaucer's exploration of being a subject. In Chaucer's works, as in Aquinas's theories, the individual must actively exert himself to realise the theological underpinning and the ultimate aim of the subject: to become a mirror of God.

Notes and References

[1] St. Augustine quoted in Etienne Gilson, *The Spirit of Medieval Philosophy* (London: University of Notre Dame Press, 1991), 220 and compare with St. Bernard quoted on 215: "Begin by considering thyself and, better still, end with that." Also see Aquinas, *An Aquinas Reader*, ed. M. T. Clark (London: Hodder and Staughton, 1972), 277: "So in the order of love, after God man should love himself more than all others."

[2] "Videmus nunc per speculum in aenigmate, tunc autem facie ad faciem; nunc cognosco ex parte, tunc autem cognoscam sicut et cognitus sum." ["For now we see through a glass, darkly; but then face to face: now I know in part; but then shall I know even as also I am known"], 1 Cor. 13:12.

[3] Aquinas, *Summa Theologiae* (Texas: Christian Classics, 1991), 144-5.

[4] Ibid., 143.

[5] Ibid., 47-8.

[6] A. Mark Smith, in Introduction to *Witelonis Perspectivae*, Studia Copernica 23. ed. & trans. A. Mark Smith (Warsaw: The Polish Academy of Sciences Press, 1983), 63.

[7] Dante quoted in A. J. Minnis and A.B. Scott (eds.), Medieval Literary Criticism, c. 1100-1375 (Oxford, Clarendon Press: 1988), 381.

[8] C.O.E.D.: "Willelmus vicinus noster, habet…specula (myrrys [? read myrurys])", 1089 (839).

[9] Chaucer, The Riverside Chaucer, ll. 9-10. ed. by A.D. Benson (Oxford: OUP, 1987), 652.

[10] Ibid., ll. 8-10, 657.

[11] Ibid., l. 17, 657.

[12] Aquinas, Summa Theologiae, 187.

[13] Chaucer, ll. 1260-8, 44. See Arnaldus of Villanova quoted in D. W. Robertson, A Preface to Chaucer (New Jersey: Princeton University Press, 1962), 109: The "humor malencolik" was thought to affect the "celle fantastik" or imagination, which is the middle chamber of the brain, and thus one is divested of the powers of reason and judgement, as Arnaldus of Villanova describes, because the sufferer "making a memory of it [that is the object of their desire] thinks of the thing continuously".

[14] Chaucer, ll. 1398-401, 44.

[15] The pagan setting here, as in Troilus and Criseyde, provides a distanced setting for the exploration of conflicting aspects in the ideologies of Courtly Love and Christianity.

[16] Herbert Grabes, The Mutable Glass: Mirror-imagery in titles and texts of the Middle Ages and English Renaissance, trans. Gordon Collier. (Cambridge: Cambridge University Press, 1982), 170 & 89.

[17] Chaucer, ll. 2804-5, 716.

[18] Chaucer, Bk.I, ll. 365-7, 478. Similarly the cuckolded Januarie in The Merchant"s Tale l.1600, 158: "purtreyed [Mayus] in his herte and in his thought."

[19] Robert P. Miller, Chaucer: Sources and Backgrounds (Oxford, Oxford University Press, 1977), 400.

[20] Chaucer, Bk.II, ll. 842-2, 500.

[21] Ibid., Bk.II, ll. 264-6, 493

[22] Ibid., Bk. II, ll. 400-6, 495 & compare with Henryson"s use of the mirror metaphor in The Testament of Cresseid, in The Mercat Anthology of English Literature, 1375-1870, ed. R. D. S. Jack & P. A. T. Rozendaal (Edinburgh: Mercat Press, 1997): in v. 50, where a real mirror serves to make Cresseid turn from worldly goods; in v. 64, Cresseid offers herself as a corrective mirror to other women through reminding them of the transitoriness of beauty and fickleness of Fortune; and in v.80 she compares her own instability to the fragility of glass.

[23] Grabes, 122: The mirroring of imperfection or depravity in the mirror, Grabes convincingly cites as evidence that the exemplary mirror did not function within a Neo-Platonic framework. Also, as an instance of this kind of idea, see Chaucer, The Parson's Tale, 321: "It is a greet folye, a womman to have a fair array outward and in hirself be foul inward." Also, compare with Gower, Bk. VIII, l. 2821, Confessio Amantis, ed. Russell A. Peck (London: Holt, Rhinehart & Winston, 1968), 483: in which the dreamer is given a mirror by Venus in which he sees himself grow old; his wits and reason return to him and he is freed from love.

[24] Lee Patterson. Chaucer and the Subject of History, (London: Routledge, 1991), 84 & 166.

[25] Ibid., 153.

[26] Ibid., 152.

[27] Boethius. *The Consolation of Philosophy*, Bk.III, Pr. 11, in *Boethius: Tractates & Consolation*, ed. H.F. Stewart & E.K. Rand. (London: William Heinemann, 1918), 28 "For even in living creatures the love of life proceedeth not from the will of the soul, but from the principles of nature. For the will many times embraceth death."

[28] Patterson, 282-5.

[29] Patterson, 115.

[30] Chaucer, Bk.V, ll.1835-41, 584. Chaucer transformation of *Il Filostrato*, is nowhere more apparent: while Boccaccio misogynistically warns youths to beware of a young inconstant woman, who "rates her beauty more highly than does a mirror", Chaucer expands the moral of his story to include all worldly *Vanitas*. Boccaccio, *Il Filostrato*, in *The Story of Troilus*, Canto VIII, ed. & trans. R.K. Gordon, (Dutton: New York, 1978), 124.

[31] Chaucer, Bk. I, l.308, 477.

[32] Huppe, Bernard. "The Unlikely Narrator: The Narrative Strategy of the Troilus", *Signs and Symbols in Chaucer"s Poetry*, ed. John P. Hermann & John J. Burke, Jr., 179-94 (Alabama: University of Alabama Press, 1981).

[33] Richard Hillman, *Self-speaking in Medieval and Early Modern Drama* (London: Macmillan Press, 1997), 205.

[34] Boethius, Bk. III, Pr. 12, 292-3.

CHAPTER SIX

MIRRORS AS TRANSMITTERS OF DIVINE HARMONY IN MARSILIO FICINO'S *COMPENDIUM IN TIMAEUM*

JACOMIEN PRINS

In 1438, the famous Byzantine scholar, Gemisthus Pletho, visited the Council of Ferrara in Florence, and whilst there he inspired Cosimo de'Medici to start a centre of Greek learning. When Cosimo's project was realized in 1462, Marsilio Ficino (1433-1499), the son of Cosimo's physician, was selected to lead the group of scholars that later generations have referred to as the Platonic Academy. By 1462 Marsilio Ficino had already been schooled in Platonic studies for several years and had written the first draft of his *Timaeus*-commentary.[1] His lifelong interest in Plato's *Timaeus* resulted in the first version of his *Compendium in Timaeum* in 1481, the mature version of this commentary was published in 1484 and then reissued in an expanded form in 1496. This fascinating commentary represents a new episode both in the commentary-tradition on Plato's *Timaeus* and in the tradition of the harmony of the spheres. This essay concentrates on two important concepts in Ficino's *Timaeus-commentary*: the idea of cosmic harmony and the metaphor of the mirror. I argue that the way in which Ficino combines these two concepts in his *Compendium in Timaeum* is vital for a significant transformation of the tradition of the harmony of the spheres. In addition to this, I try to prove that Ficino uses the metaphor of the mirror to clarify ambiguities or to fill in gaps in the explanation of certain phenomena within the tradition of the harmony of the spheres, which till then remained obscure and unexplained.

Harmony and mirrors in Ficino's theory of cosmogenesis

Ficino's *Timaeus-commentary* presents us with the unique possibility of examining the influence of Plato's ideas about cosmic harmony upon the Italian Renaissance.[2] Plato's *Timaeus* is based on the Pythagorean belief that numbers and proportions are the basic principles of the cosmos. The *Timaeus* presents a scientific model of the cosmos by means of a myth about the creation of Things in nature and the World Soul and about the creation of man; along with a description of their structure and functioning. Creation is described as the imposition by the divine Demiurge of a mathematical order on matter, which previously existed in a state of chaos, but is now transformed into a perfect harmonic order.[3]

Scattered throughout his philosophy are Ficino's use of a complex of ideas about mirror reflection, shadow and imprint structures to explain how harmonic order is installed in the whole cosmos. Traces of his Neoplatonic orientation as well as his Aristotelean education can be found in this complex of ideas. In his *Timaeus-commentary*, Ficino begins his discussion on harmonic cosmic order by stating that all matter is dependent on God and that prior to the act of creation everything was a kind of dark stuff containing a divine spark in need of illumination by divine light.[4] For Ficino, Plato's divine Demiurge was an adumbration of the Christian God and the myth of creation in the *Timaeus* and the biblical account of the creation of the cosmos are simply two variations of the one and only true story of the beginning of the world. Therefore, the best way to acquire knowledge of the master seal of the cosmos is, in his opinion, to juxtapose the Mosaic and the Platonic truth.[5]

Like many of his predecessors and contemporaries, Ficino is convinced that the *Timaeus* offers important clues for the interpretation of the book of Genesis and that Genesis similarly holds clues to the *Timaeus*. With regard to knowledge of cosmic harmony, these clues have to be looked for in the Pythagorean truths that Plato incorporated in his dialogue. This conviction can be understood against the background of Ficino's belief in the existence of a *prisca theologia*, a pagan tradition of divine knowledge, which Ficino believed paralleled and confirmed the revealed truth of the Holy Scriptures.[6] In order to bridge the gap between pagan and Christian thinkers, Ficino took up the position that the greatest of the ancient pagan thinkers, including Pythagoras and Plato, were initiated in the secrets of the harmonic structure of the cosmos. Ficino also believed that Timaeus Locrus was a ring in the chain of eternal wisdom and that Plato had used Timaeus Locrus' *De natura mundi et animae*[7] as his most important source: all these wise men knew that the cosmos was created harmonically and that this structure was presented in the form of images that have to be interpreted in the right way.

Quemadmodum in Parmenide cuncta divinorum genera pro viribus comprehendit, sic omnia in Timaeo complectitur naturalia; et utrobique plurimum Pythagoricus est, sub persona Pythagorica disputans . . . In Timaeo autem, Timaeum Locrum Pythagoricum, qui librum de universi natura composuit, sequitur. Ita tamen, ut his non eloquentiam solum adiungat, sed mysteria. Quoniam vero divina quidem naturalium principia et exemplaria sunt, naturalia vero divinorum effectus atque imagines...

[Just as Plato includes in the *Parmenides*, as much as possible, all the classes of things divine, so he embraces in the *Timaeus* everything in the realm of nature; and in each dialogue he is principally a Pythagorean speaking a Pythagorean part . . . In the *Timaeus* [Plato] however follows Timaeus Locrus, a Pythagorean who composed a book about the nature of the universe. In such a way, however, that he added to these things not only eloquence, but also mystery. Since in fact things divine are the principles and exemplars of things natural, and things natural are the effects and images of those things divine . . .][8]

On the basis of a mistake about the age and authenticity of the work of Timaeus Locrus, which actually is an early to mid-first century B.C. work, Ficino grounded much of his explanation of the harmonic principles of the cosmos on this source. Following Pythagoras, Plato and Timaeus Locrus, Ficino contends that the universe has two causes: Mind, which governs rational beings, and Necessity, which governs things in nature and all irrational beings. In imitation of his predecessors Ficino assigns numerical values to the various proportions produced by the mixture of the Same and the Different, which are the two opposing forces in Plato's *Timaeus*, that produce all motion, growth, and change in the cosmos.[9] Ficino combines the Timaean idea, given in the quotation above, that divine things are the principles and exemplars of things in nature, with the biblical idea that the image of God is mirrored in the whole cosmos (Genesis 1:26), in such a way that things in nature become the effects and images of the divine Mind, which is the first and most perfect image of God.

Ficino follows the *Timaeus* and Timaeus Locrus in their account of the geometrical proportions on which the harmonic cosmos is founded, finally declaring that the image of God is perfectly mirrored in the shape of the dodecahedron, one of the five Platonic solids, since that is the closest approximation to the perfect sphere, which is the image of a purely intellectual realm.[10] Ficino beliefs that everything within this perfect sphere can be classified into three ontological entities: Mind, the World Soul and Things in nature, all of which Ficino equates with mirrors.[11] During creation these mirrors become imprinted with the image of God, and are made capable of reflecting and transmitting the harmonic order, which is synonymous with God's image.[12] Although in a weaker form, harmonic order is certainly also present in nature, as can be seen, for example in the movements of the planets.

In Ficino's *Timaeus-commentary* the incorporeal substances of Mind and the World Soul are the first things to be created. Firstly, God called Mind into being. Subsequently the World Soul came into being by way of illumination by the divine Mind. Thereafter, Ficino deals with the way in which the fertile Mind of God imbues Things in nature, such as the planets, which he considers to be the most perfect elements of the cosmos, because their incorruptible circular movement becomes close to the eternal and static divine Mind. Ficino associates with the Platonists in his assertion that every planet reflects a different aspect of the divine Mind:

> Forte vero nec fuerit a Platonicis alienum dicere firmamento referri mentem, Saturno secretissimam rationem, Mercurio vero communem; sed utroque speculativam. Iove practicam, sole sensum et ipsam iracundiae animositatem pro ratione pugnantem. Marte iracundiam quoque, sed sensibus suffragantem. Venere atque luna concupiscendi naturam, Venere quidem concupiscentiam ad speciem propagandam, luna vero ad individuum conservandum.

> [As it happens the Platonists would not actually be strangers to saying that the [divine] Mind is mirrored in the firmament, [and] that Saturn reflects the most mysterious consideration, Mercury reflects the common sense; but both reflect speculative [aspects of the divine Mind]. Jupiter reflects the active [aspect of Mind], the Sun reflects intelligence and courage of the heated temper fighting for reason. Mars also reflects irascibility, but one sustaining the senses. Venus and the Moon reflect the nature of lust. Venus, on the one hand reflects the desire to conserve the human species, the Moon, on the other hand, reflects the desire to conserve the individual.][13]

The way in which Ficino attributes certain aspects of the divine Mind to the different planets can be related to the biblical account of how the image of God is mirrored in His creation (1 Corinthians 13:12), as well as to the account of the construction of the World Soul in *Timaeus* 34b-36d, where the mathematical relations between its parts are represented as identical with those of a musical scale.[14] In this passage Plato explains that the harmonious movements of the World Soul and its cosmic body cannot be heard by our external ears, but are made perceptible in the visible rotations of the stars and planets, whose movements are expressions of different aspects of the World Soul. The orderly rationality imbued in the planets by means of the divine Mind and the World Soul can be presented indirectly to our hearing through the music man makes on earth, since the principles underlying the mathematical structure of the World Soul are the same as those governing the structure of a musical scale and these are also the same principles that govern our human soul. Thus, in Ficino's *Timaeus-commentary* the orderly rationality inherent in the planets mirrors both certain aspects of the divine Mind and the tones of a musical scale. The planets together are able to express in their spiritual and musical diversity the unity of the Mind of their Creator, which can be grasped as the most perfect harmony.

This theory results in my schematic representation of the Ficinian harmonic cosmos as follows:

Mind	Place in cosmos	Inhabitant	Musical mode[15]
Pure divine Mind	highest heaven	God	Inaudible Harmony
Angelic Mind	1st ethereal heaven	Angels	Angelic song
Angelic Mind	2nd heaven	Fixed stars	Hypermixolydian
Speculative Mind	3rd heaven	Saturn	Mixolydian
Active Mind	4th heaven	Jupiter	Lydian
Senses and Emotions	5th heaven	Mars	Phrygian
Desire for procreation	6th heaven	Venus	Hypolydian
Speculative Mind	7th heaven	Mercury	Hypophrygian
Insight, Reason & Emotion	8th heaven	Sun[16]	Dorian
Self-centred Desire	9th heaven	Moon	Hypodorian

Through an analysis of the quotation above it becomes entirely clear, that the way the planets reflect aspects of the divine Mind in Ficino's *Timaeus-commentary*, is not simply a matter of reflecting like a normal image in a mirror, but a more complicated kind of reflection, because something of the reflected image of God remains in the mirror. This is possible, because Ficino uses the concepts of reflection and imprint as interchangeable. The fusion of the three ideas dates back to at least the turn of the fifth century, the period in which Augustine formulated a kind of theology in which mirrors, images and the image of God are linked together in such a way that they can be used for the purpose of acquiring knowledge of God and His creation.[17] In spite of Plato's attempts to distinguish between the two different concepts of shadow and mirror image, the Platonic tradition, of which Augustine was a part, had a tendency not only to blur them with one another, but also to link them to Aristotelian ideas of imprinting higher forms onto matter.[18] The Aristotelian theory that knowledge is acquired by means of a process of imprinting was integrated in the Platonic tradition in such a way that images, shadows and imprints became subcategories of a kind of reflection that never met a mirror other than in a complex metaphor.

Harmony and mirrors in Ficino's theory of the creation of man

The biblical verse recounting that man is made in the image of God (Genesis 1:26) is integrated into Ficino's *Timaeus-commentary* in such a way that every human being is able to come in contact with cosmic harmony by means of the divine spark with which all parts of the human mind, soul and body are endowed. Ficino states that, as concerns the subject of the creation of man, there exist no fundamental differences between the Bible and the philosophy of Plato:

Rursus in medio disputationis cursu diis a patre praecipitur exornare hominem, dominum animalium, quem ad imaginem et similitudinem suam esse velit, atque praeesse. Deinde paucis interiectis reditur ad hominem . . . Atque in cunctis mosaico more probatur, hominem in divino hoc opificio et in primis proponi et postremus fieri quasi finem.

[Again, in the midst of the disputation, the Father ordained the gods to equip man, the lord of the animals, whom he wanted to be made in His image and likeness, and that he would rule over [all creation]. Next, [in the *Timaeus*], after a short interval, [Plato] turns to the human being . . . And in all these topics [Plato] demonstrates, as you find in Moses, that the human being is intended in this creative work of God from the very beginning to become finally, as it were, the goal [of it].][19]

Ficino is convinced that whilst God initiated the creation of individual souls, he handed over completion of this task to His sons or angels, who introduced them into the cosmos, some by way of the sun or the moon, and others by way of the planets that wander according to the principle of the Different, which is the source of the irrational part of the soul. Each soul, however, received a portion of the principle of Sameness, which Ficino equates with an imprint of the image of God, and which became the rational part of the soul. A soul who received more of this principle would have a happier fate than one receiving less, but because Ficino strongly believes in the Christian doctrine of free will, and therefore does not believe that human fate is completely determined by the position of the stars and planets at the moment of his birth, he pays a lot of attention to the way in which man is able to change his destiny. Human beings can influence their fate in a positive way by trying to reach a state of harmony and spiritual enlightenment, and the sense of hearing functions as an instrument on this spiritual path.

Through his ingenious way of combining the biblical truth of the creation of man in the image and likeness of God with Platonic wisdom about cosmic harmony, the liver comes to serve in Ficino's *Timaeus-commentary* as a mirror capable of reflecting the image of God's perfect harmony. In this context Ficino adopts an idea that Plato developed in the *Timaeus*: Plato claims in this dialogue that the principal function of sight is to allow us to observe the revolutions of the divine Mind in the heavens, and to apply them to the cycles of our own intelligence, which are akin to them, so that we can come to imitate the absolutely unwavering cycles of the Platonic god, by stabilizing our own wandering ones.[20] Plato contends that both sight and hearing are equally given for this purpose, but Ficino is of the opinion that the sense of hearing is more appropriate for this goal than the sense of seeing.[21]

Ficino's preference for the sense of hearing is based on the fact that the sense of seeing uses static visual images, while the sense of hearing uses dynamic aural images. Ficino beliefs that hearing puts us in more direct contact with external reality than seeing, since sound consists of aerial movements, which can actually occur in our *spiritus*, a substance in between body and soul, whereas sight merely the reproduces surface-images of things.[22] Thus, music is able to dynamically affect the whole human being. Therefore, Ficino comes to the conclusion that the whole moral and emotional life of a human being consists of the actions of the body and the motions of the *spiritus* and soul, and that these can be imitated in music and transmitted by it.[23] It is necessary to analyse the processes by which music moves the human body, *spiritus* and soul, in order to be able to understand how man can reach a state of harmony and spiritual enlightenment by means of listening to music.

Sound is created, according to Ficino, by banging two objects against each other.[24] Like when you throw a pebble in a pond, the sound source produces circular sound waves that first of all reach the human ear, and immediately afterwards the brain. When sound passes through the brain it is affected by the rational soul, and it is the consequent movement of the rational soul combined with the spirited air of the sound waves that reaches the ears, which is passed on through the heart to the liver and which is experienced as hearing. The movement constituting hearing runs from the head to the liver, and although Ficino is not explicit about this, we may presuppose that this movement is accompanied by a converse flow of movement in the opposite direction in order to make knowledge of the harmonic structure of the cosmos possible.

In Plato's *Timaeus* the lowest part of the soul is housed in the abdomen, as far as possible from the head, the seat of rational thought.[25] It has no understanding of reason, but is influenced by images and phantasms, and therefore the Creator placed it in close contact with the liver. By making the liver smooth and shiny, God enabled it to serve as a mirror that reflects rational thoughts, transmitted from the divine as well as the human mind. Gentle thoughts activate the liver's sweetness, making everything harmonious, producing pleasing images and making the irrational part of the soul happy.[26] Ficino elaborates on this passage in Chapter XXXXV of his *Compendium in Timaeum*, where he subscribes to the Pythagorean viewpoint that the liver functions as a mirror:[27]

> Verum de hoc ipso iecore miram Pythagoricorum notabis opinionem, videlicet id membrum ex certa soliditate et clara pariter lenitate, sic esse contemperatum, ut speculi modo imagines rerum accipiat, facile admodum atque reddat.

> [In fact concerning the liver you have to observe the miraculous opinion of the Pythagoreans, obviously the one according to which this organ, made of a certain consistency and an equally shining softness, is harmoniously tuned, in such a way that it receives easily the images of things in the way of a mirror and reflects them.][28]

Ficino's account of the miraculous opinion of the Pythagoreans on the mirroring function of the liver is third-hand, and we cannot be absolutely sure if he only mentioned this view that was handed down through Plato's *Timaeus* or entirely adopted it. In my opinion it is extremely probable that Ficino adopted it, because he could thus use the mirror in his explanation of the way in which God bestowed His creatures with knowledge of divine harmony.

This chapter of Ficino's *Timaeus-commentary* provides the principal clue to the manner in which music presents itself to the part of the soul responsible for perception and emotion. Hearing, like thought, is transmitted as a movement between the head and the liver. Because the liver is connected with the perceptive lower soul, this part of the soul can act as a receptor for anything that is reflected from the liver's smooth surface. From Ficino's explanation it is possible to argue that the movements of hearing impinges on the liver as unprocessed images which are then reflected from it to the lower soul as processed images.[29] The unprocessed images are a kind of impression made by one thing on another through pressure or impact, as for example the impression of a seal-stone in wax. Hearing has been defined as a set of movements, whose musical characteristics consist in the various speeds of these movements and the relations between the movements. It is the pattern formed by this system of movements that impresses itself on the liver as an unprocessed image while one is listening to music. Ficino combines the *Timaeus* with Genesis in such a way, that God becomes the designer of the liver as a mirror imprinted with His image and likeness in order to offer man the possibility to come in contact with His perfect harmony. What is reflected from the liver in the process of listening to music is a processed image, which can carry a powerful emotive and spiritual charge. If a human being has reached a state of inner peace, for example by visually studying the orbits of the planets, God is able to imprint the human soul directly with a moving harmonic image, in the same way as he directs images of future events to the liver:

> Ubi vero rationis imaginationisque vacat prudens et continuata et laboriosa discursio, saepe imagines futurorum a superis in speculum nostrum prosilientes, inde in indicium manifeste resiliunt.

> [Where, however, the alert, continuous and laborious movement of the reason and of the imagination becomes less, often the images of future events that are sent by superior [creatures], present themselves in our mirror [i.e. the liver], and from there they are clearly reflected to our sense of judgement.][30]

God has imprinted man in such a way with His image that He is able to communicate with His creature in a direct way. Because His image is expressed in the principles underlying the cosmos, which are the same as those governing the structure of a musical scale and the human soul, He can be presented directly to us through music. Ficino does not explain in detail how by means of the liver the magical transformation of aural images into human knowledge of the harmonic principles of the cosmos is achieved, but I think that an explanation has to be looked for in Ficino's theory of the role of *spiritus* in the process of hearing, which, as we have seen before, is another theoretical concept that Ficino uses to bridge the gap between body and soul. The *spiritus* accompanying the sound waves inside the human body, is assigned with the task of transferring harmonic images to the liver, projecting these unprocessed images onto its surface and then transferring the processed images to the human brain. If we accept that in being captivated by music we are taken out of our minds in the literal way Ficino requires, we shall conclude that the experience of earthly music can produce shadowy musical images of higher harmonic principles in human souls. These musical images, which are reflected from the liver, travel back to the head where they call for interpretation. Since God imprinted these musical images with His harmonic image, the rational soul is presented thereby which materials in which it can discover divine harmony. Finally Ficino warns the reader that only if the listener is trained in the science of harmony and mathematics, he will be able to read in the mirror images of the liver the harmonic principles of the cosmos:

> Verum quidnam portendant discernere illius est officium, qui ab antecedentibus in consequentia prudenter sagaciterque discurrere consuevit.

> [To observe what they portend, that is the task of him who is accustomed to move himself with cleverness and wisdom from the antecedents to the consequence.][31]

Conclusion

It is tentatively concluded that everywhere the mirror appears in Ficino's *Compendium in Timaeum* it functions as a passive medium of transmission of divine order and, at the same time, as an active device to propagate the harmonic image of God in all different parts of His creation. The way in which Ficino tried to reconcile the *Timaeus* with the book of Genesis resulted in a complex network of ideas in which the harmonic image of God was mirrored in the various hierarchical levels of divine Mind that corresponded both with the planets and the tones of a musical scale. Thus, in Ficino's cosmology the mirror became an omnipresent medium for the propagation of harmony throughout the whole cosmos.

It is not only within the theory of cosmogenesis, that the mirror was an important metaphor for Ficino. He also used it in his explanation of the creation of man. Within this context Ficino combined the *Timaeus* with Genesis in such a way, that God became the designer of the liver as a mirror imprinted with His image and likeness, in order to offer man the possibility to come into contact with His perfect harmony through spiritual enlightenment. It is highly probable that Ficino adopted the account on the miraculous opinion of the Pythagoreans on the mirroring function of the liver, because he could use it to bridge gaps in his explanation of the way in which God bestowed His creatures with divine harmony and of the way they could obtain knowledge of it.

Previously, within the commentary tradition on Plato's *Timaeus*, celestial music amounted to static descriptions of the cosmos meant to praise God and His creation, but almost completely averse to human involvement. Ficino, conversely, saw in the opinion of the Pythagoreans on the mirroring function of the liver possibilities for a theory in which man was given the opportunity to open his mind actively to the harmonic voice of God. With this, he integrated the doctrine of the miraculous power of music on the human soul successfully into his theory of cosmic harmony. Because of this, for the first time in Christian history certain knowledge of the harmonic structure of the cosmos was made to appear possible.

Notes and References

Intellectually this essay is most indebted to Sergius Kodera's "Narcissus, divine gazes and bloody mirrors: the concept of matter in Ficino", *Marsilio Ficino: his theology, his philosophy, his legacy*, ed. Michael J.B. Allen, (Leiden: Brill, 2002) 285-306, and Andrew Barker's, "Timaeus on music and the liver", *Reason and Necessity: Essays on Plato's Timaeus*, ed. M.R. Wright, (London: Duckworth, 2000) 85-99. I wish to thank Miranda Anderson, Luuk Huitink and Mark Kauntze for their corrections and reading of the first draft.

[1] See for the history of the development of Ficino's *Timaeus*-commentaries: Allen, Michael J.B., "Ficino's interpretation of Plato's *Timaeus* and its myth of the demiurge", *Plato's Third Eye: studies in Marsilio Ficino's metaphysics and its sources,* (Aldershot [etc.]: Variorum, 1995), 402-403.
[2] See for the reception and transmission of Plato's *Timaeus* in the Italian Renaissance: James Hankins, "The study of the *Timaeus* in early Renaissance Italy", *Natural Particulars: Nature and the Disciplines in Renaissance Europe*, ed. Anthony Grafton & Nancy Siraisi, (Cambridge, Mass., 1999), 77-119.
[3] *Timaeus* 29d-31a, in Francis M. Cornford, F.M., *Plato's cosmology: The Timaeus of Plato*, (London: Routledge & Kegan Paul, 1966 [repr.], 33-41.
[4] Marsilio Ficino, *CiT*, Cap. XII, [1443], <62^v>, 16,17 and Cap. VIIII, [1441-1442], <61^v>, 12-15. The page numbers refer to the following editions of Ficino's *Timaeus*-

commentary: Marsilio Ficino *Compendium in Timaeum,* in Marsilio Ficino, *Opera Omnia,* II, Basel 1576 (facsimile edition: Kristeller, P.O., Torino: Bottega d'Erasmo, 1962) 1438-1485; Marsilio Ficino *Compendium in Timaeum,* in Marsilio Ficino, *Commentaria in Platonem, Firenze* 1496 <59^r-80^v>; Alexandre Etienne, *Visages d'un interprète: Marsile Ficin et le Timée: De la dècouverte à la reception de la <<physique>> platonicienne:* Une etude historique et thématique du *Compendium in Timaeum,* Tome II (unpublished dissertation) (Lausanne, 1998) 3-89.

[5] Marsilio Ficino, *CiT,* Cap. XXIIII, [1449], <66^v>, 33.

[6] Schmidt-Biggemann, W., *Philosophia perennis: Historische Umrisse abendländischer Spiritualität in Antike, Mittelalter und Frühe Neuzeit,* (Frankfurt am Main: Suhrkamp, 1998) 259-268. English edition: *Philosophia perennis: Historical Outlines of Western Spirituality in Ancient, Medieval and Early Modern Thought,* series: *International Archives of the History of Ideas/Archives internationals d'histoire des idées,* vol. 189, (Dordrecht [etc.]: Springer, 2004.

[7] Timaeus Locrus, *De natura mundi et animae:* Überlieferung, Testimonia, Text und Übers. Von Walter Marg, *Philosophia antiqua* vol. 24 (Leiden: Brill, 1972; For an English translation see: Timaeus Locrus, *On the nature of the world and the soul by Timaios of Locri*; text, transl. and notes by Thomas H. Tobin, (Chico, California: Scholars Press, 1985).

[8] Marsilio Ficino, *CiT,* Cap. I, [1438], <59^r>, 3. The translations of the quotations and the italics used in the translations are my own.

[9] *Timaeus* 35a, in Francis M. Cornford, *op.cit.,* 59-66.

[10] *Timaeus* 57c-d, in: Francis M. Cornford, *op. cit,* 230-239; Marsilio Ficino, *CiT,* Cap. XXIII, [1447, 1448], <65^v, 66^r>, 28-31.

[11] In this respect Ficino's use of the metaphor of the mirror in his *Timaeus*-commentary is equal to his uses of this metaphor in his *Theologia Platonica, Philebus*-commentary, and *De amore.* See for an analysis of matter and mirrors in these sources: Sergius Kodera, *op cit,* 285-306.

[12] See, for example: Marsilio Ficino, *CiT,* Cap. X, [1442], <61^v, 62^r>, 14-15.

[13] Marsilio Ficino, *CiT,* Cap. XXXVIII, [1462], <75^v, 76^r>, 70.

[14] In Francis M. Cornford, *op. cit,* 77-93.

[15] Marsilio Ficino, *CiT,* Cap. XXXV, [1461], <74^r>, 63-64. Although Ficino does not explicitly mention here the link between planets and musical modes, it is possible to infer from this Chapter of his *Timaeus*-commentary that according to him the relationships presented in this diagram exist. See for an analysis of this theme: James Haar, *Musica Mundana: variations on a Pythagorean theme,* (unpublished dissertation, Harvard University: Cambridge MA, 1960) 351-362.

[16] In his *Timaeus*-commentary Ficino adopts the order of the planets as formulated by Jabir ibn Aflah (± 1100-1160). Marsilio Ficino, *CiT,* Cap. XXXV, [1461], <74^r>, 63-64.

[17] Sergius Kodera, *op cit,* 296. An investigation of Augustine's use of the metaphor of the mirror is contained in this volume in the essay of Mark Kauntze.

[18] The interchangeable use of the concepts of reflection and shadow is Aristotelian in origin. See Aristotle, *De anima,* 419b.

[19] Marsilio Ficino, *CiT,* Cap. XXXXV, [1464] <79^r>, 83.

[20] *Timaeus* 46c-47e. *Accessory causes contrasted with the purpose of sight and hearing* in Francis M. Cornford, *op. cit*, 156-159, especially 47b-d, 158.

[21] Marsilio Ficino, *CiT*, Cap. XXVIIII, [1453], <69^r>, 43.

[22] Ficino's concept of *spiritus* and its relationship to sound and reasoning have been described in the following classic article: Daniel P. Walker, "Ficino's *Spiritus* and Music", *Annales musicologiques*, 1 (1953), 131-150, reprinted in his *Music, Spirit and Language in the Renaissance*, ed. P.M. Gouk (London: Variorum Reprints, 1985), Chapter VIII.

[23] Marsilio Ficino, *CiT*, Cap. XXVIIII, [1453], <69^v>, 44.

[24] See for Ficino's early theory of musical sound: Marsilio Ficino, 1944, *De sono*, in Paul O. Kristeller, "The Scholastic Background of Marsilio Ficino with edition of unpublished texts", in: *Traditio: studies in ancient and medieval history, thought and religion*, II, 1944, 257-318.

[25] *Timaeus* 70d-72b. *Belly, liver, spleen*, in Francis M. Cornford, *op. cit*, 286-290.

[26] Andrew Barker, *op. cit*, 93.

[27] Although Ficino is clearly following Plato in this chapter, it could be possible that he also used Iamblichus as his source. Ficino's copy of *Iamblici Calcidei libri de Pythagorica secta* is now in Rome in the Biblioteca Apostolica Vaticana, *Vat.Lat.* 4530. See: Sebastiano Gentile, "Sulle prime traduzioni dal Greco di Marsilio Ficino", *Rinascimento*, XXX (1990), 74-75; C.S. Celenza, "Pythagoras in the Renaissance: The case of Marsilio Ficino", *Renaissance Quarterly* 52 (1999), 667-711.

[28] Marsilio Ficino, *CiT*, Cap. XXXXV, [1465], <79^r>, 84.

[29] In his *Timaeus*-commentary Ficino has adopted Plato's application of the Pythagorean idea of the mirroring function of the liver in divination, but he does not mention or solve the problem of ambiguity this idea causes for a Timaean epistemology, about which Cornford wrote: "Commentators who do not believe in divination have exaggerated what Archer-Hind calls 'the keen irony pervading the whole' of the passage describing it as the gift of heaven to human unreason." Francis M. Cornford, *op. cit*, 289.

[30] Marsilio Ficino, *CiT*, Cap. XXXXV, [1465], <79^r>, 84.

[31] Marsilio Ficino, *CiT*, Cap. XXXXV, [1465], <79^r>, 84.

PART III:

MIRRORS OF PERCEPTION

Chapter Seven

Shaving in a Mirror with Ockham's Razor

Richard L. Gregory

Reflections in a simple looking glass are extraordinarily puzzling. The extensive literature, over millennia, of the philosophy and science of mirrors continues to be confused and confusing, especially over why reflections are horizontally but not vertically reversed when the optics are symmetrical. The difficulty for seeing what is happening may be the seductive temptations of many plausible kinds of explanations – optical, physiological, verbal – which are familiar and useful in other contexts. Optical ray diagrams are especially tempting, but they cannot distinguish horizontal from vertical – any more than a map can tell north without a compass – so although they are generally useful, they cannot answer this mirror question. Here we explore in detail one simple hypothesis for a complete explanation of a variety of such phenomena: only physical rotation is relevant. This may be rotation of the reflected object (from direct view of the back of objects) or rotation of the eyes of the observer (from direct view behind). All other considerations are excised by Ockham's razor, which accepts the simplest hypothesis while rejecting unnecessary postulates, even though based on truths. The special, indeed the unique case of one's own face is considered in detail for the first time. It is likely that mirror images are so puzzling because they cannot be explored by touch. This is evidence that interactive hands on experience is important for young children discovering the object world, and for enriching understanding of the principles of science in practical classes in schools and universities. This applies also to exploratory science centres attempting to introduce science to the public, for without initial guiding touch we see darkly.

The Puzzle

Mirrors have intrigued and puzzled the curious through recorded history and no doubt from much earlier – from reflections in prehistoric sacred lakes, to Alice's looking glass, to today's buildings of mirror walls. Mirrors of gold or copper, and most treasured silver, were made as early as 3000BC by Egyptians of the First Dynasty.

One's image through the mirror is one's double – the doppelgänger of horror – which haunts us by mocking our passing time from its shadow world. Very possibly images in mirrors suggested mind-brain dualism; associated with Descartes, but really far older as embalmed in religions. What the looking glass reveals is biologically extraordinary; for one's own face is invisible without the mirror, so though hidden from its owner it is open to public view, for the secrets of one's mind to be read by all and sundry.

Why light reflects the way it does was discussed by the Greeks, who studied mirrors as a branch of science. This became even more mysterious when the ancient notion that light bounces off shiny surfaces like a ball had to be abandoned, as it was found that Brewster's angle of maximum polarisation depends on the refractive index; so light 'sees' into the material of the mirror, rather than bouncing off its surface. The obvious (as it seems at school) 'angle of reflection equals angle of incidence' has only recently been explained by the dance of electrons in the mirror, choreographed by principles of quantum electrodynamics.[1] I have discussed the history, science, and myths of mirrors in 'Mirrors in mind';[2] this does not however consider the special puzzle of one's own face, which will be considered here.

That a virtual image depends on the focusing of the eye (or a camera), and so is quite different from a real image, was appreciated by Newton in his 'Opticks' (1704). Newton also realised that it depends psychologically on lack of cognition. We see objects as through the mirror, though we know they are in front, because visual perception falsely accepts that light always comes directly from objects. Thus we see ourselves through the looking glass though we know we are in front of it. So paradoxically we have two selves, one being an insubstantial ghost.

Mirrors are surely the most puzzling objects we possess. Mirror images fool the eye – and so are conjurors' friends – and especially by image reversal, they confuse the mind. Perhaps mirrors puzzle and are puzzling as they give sight without testing touch: the opposite of blindness. I learned this from the rare case of Sidney Bradford, who was released from a life of blindness with corneal transplants at the age of 52. Following the operations, he found mirrors so fascinating he would spend the evening with his back to his friends while watching them in the long mirror of his local bar, every now and again putting out his hands to try to touch them through the glass.[3] I still share his amazement at the discovery of the sight without touch of the mirror world.

Especially confusing, for almost everyone, is the sideways reversal of reflected objects. Why, though the mirror is symmetrical, are objects in a looking glass reversed right-left yet not up-down? This has confused practically everyone since Plato, and he got it wrong.[4] The philosopher Immanuel Kant, in his "Prolegomena to any future metaphysics" (1783), said that it is a problem too hard for the human mind to grasp. To me it seems, rather, very simple, though surprisingly puzzling, for it appears to violate Curie's Principle: systematic asymmetry cannot be produced from symmetry. So how can a flat vertical looking glass, viewed straight on, reverse sideways yet not up-down? That there is any problem is sometimes denied. But writing, for example, certainly looks very different in a mirror: an E looks reversed, but an M looks normal.

Suggested explanations of 'mirror reversal' have involved: physics (of space); anatomy (horizontal separation of the eyes, also the near lateral symmetry of the human body); physiology (neural reversal in eye or brain); psychology (mental rotation, in perception or imagination); linguistics (ambiguity of the words 'right' and 'left' – as advocated by the philosopher Jonathan Bennett and critically explored by Block).[5] Of course optics is often invoked – especially crossings of light paths at the mirror or in the eyes – yet there is no crossing in plane mirrors and for the eyes there are both vertical and horizontal crossing; so the asymmetry is not explained in either case. It may be noted that for a vertical mirror a ray diagram does not tell us why horizontal reversal is general, because the diagram has no special orientation. (Similarly a map cannot tell us where north is, or east or west or south, without a compass.) Does the explanation lie in optics, anatomy, psychology, language – what? All these and more have claimed the answer and yet all are wrong – this is just too interdisciplinary!

There is also a very different kind of mirror reversal – of depth. This is, however, sometimes invoked to explain lateral reversal (Martin Gardner tried this),[6] though the reversal in depth is orthogonal both to up-down and to right-left, and cannot favour either. Martin Gardner also introduces mental rotation, saying that we rotate ourselves mentally this way because it is easiest, as our bodies are more nearly symmetrical right-left than up-down. But mental rotation is far too slow and inaccurate.[7] And we see the mirror reversal even when there is no information to alert the brain that a mirror is involved; as when there is no frame, or in a photograph of a reflection. Indeed, the fact that photographs show the reversal precludes any such psychological cause.

Ockham's razor

It is essential to cut away misleading concepts and irrelevant (even though true) facts that are accepted in the false hypotheses for explaining mirror reversal. Cutting out the irrelevant and false would leave the truth – if any are true. This is the principle of Ockham's razor. If all existing explanations are rejected, the field is clear for some new hypothesis.

The English philosopher William of Ockham (c. 1285-1347), known as the 'more than subtle doctor' believed only in particulars, so he was not a Platonist but generally defended Aristotle. He rejected the reality of universals as 'the worst error of philosophy'. He has been called 'the father of nominalism' – that universal ideas are captured by words, but do not exist outside the speaking mind. But most famously, he is credited with the strategy that explanations should be as simple as possible, with all extraneous axioms and assumptions and facts sliced off, by 'Ockham's razor'. Although this is the theme of much of his thinking he does not seem to have formulated it explicitly.[8] It is, indeed, important that the simpler the hypothesis the more power it has to explain clearly and be useful. This is now the heart of science.

All the hypotheses mentioned above can be cut away as irrelevant, even though each does have some truth in its own right. It is true that the eyes are (usually) horizontally separated. There is (cognitive) mental rotation. The words 'right' and 'left' are particularly ambiguous (thus for actors and audience they switch meanings). These kinds of explanations appeal to those who have trusted them and found them useful; but here they are seductive attractors – because none is relevant to the question. So they can be sliced off with Ockham's razor.

The answer

The one essential principle is that: mirror reversals are caused by physical rotations. It is this that will be explored here. Though simple this is not a familiar kind of explanation. It is not within trusted optics, psychology, linguistics, or any of the other hypotheses drawn from familiar sciences – so it may not be attractive. Conversely, the familiar and trusted explanations that are inappropriate, are seductively attractive and draw us away from the true answer.

The full story

Mirrors allow hidden backs of objects to be seen. A particularly clear example is given by writing on an opaque card. The reversal in the mirror is caused by the card having to be rotated, from the front direct view, for the writing to be visible in the mirror behind it. It must be behind to show the card. So we see the writing that is hidden at the back of the card made visible in the mirror, but reversed by the rotation of the card to present the writing to the mirror. Why is the writing on the opaque card right-left reversed but not upside down? Small objects are generally rotated around the vertical axis, as because of gravity this is the easiest rotation – giving right-left reversal. But the object can be rotated around its horizontal axis. Then the writing, or whatever, will appear in the mirror upside down (as it is) and not right-left reversed. What we see depends simply on how the object has been rotated, from direct view, to face the mirror behind it.

It is worth noting that writing on a transparent sheet need not be reversed – because it does not have to be rotated to be visible in the mirror. It appears the same on the transparent sheet and in the mirror. This explanation of mirror reversal is fine for objects that we pick up and turn around; but what about fixed objects? The mirror must be located behind the object for its back to be visible in the mirror, so it is already rotated.

Why, though, are whole rooms or landscapes mirror reversed? The most familiar example is the driving mirror of a car. This allows us to see things behind us while we are looking forward into the mirror. When we turn our head around, to see the cars behind directly with no mirror, there is no reversal. Their number plates look normal. By looking in the driving mirror we see behind though the eyes and head are aimed to the front of the car, so the head is rotated 180° from the direct view of the scene behind. As we turn our heads around the vertical axis, this gives horizontal, not vertical reversal. There is either right-left or up-down reversal but never both, for rotation is only possible around one axis at a time.

As number plates of the cars behind appear mirror reversed, it is useful for AMBULANCE to be printed ƎƆИA⅃UꓭMA to cancel the reversal of looking behind without turning the head. It is also a simple matter to reverse the whole scene behind optically, with a pair of mirrors forming a vertical corner. As the pair of mirrors is not optically symmetrical this does not challenge Curie's Principle, and it is entirely different from the lateral reversal in a plane mirror. The corner mirror should be useful for artists painting their self-portraits. Rembrandt came out left handed in a self portrait (now at Kenwood House in Hampstead) which, as established by X-rays, he later corrected. It just might be useful for cars, though we do get used to the reversal in the driving mirror.

Face to face

One's own face is invisible without a mirror, so one's face is a uniquely strange object for reflection. The image is like another person looking at you, yet it is yourself. When you wink your right eye you *feel* it is your right eye but *see* it as the left eye of your double. Your double winks its left eye, which is opposite your right eye, just as for another person facing you. But how does one see oneself 'mirror reversed' – reversed from what? For as one's own face is invisible without a mirror there is no direct view of one's face for comparison. This makes one's face an especially puzzling mirror object.

To see yourself in a mirror you have to turn around – normally rotating vertically as your feet are on the ground – so you become right-left reversed from how others see you face on. You can't see your own face without a mirror, because you can't take your eyes out and turn them around to see your face from in front. If you could take your eyes out they would have to turn around to see your face – then it would not appear reversed. The looking glass allows you to see your face without taking your eyes out and turning them around to look at yourself. So, the mirror view is 180°° rotated from what would be the direct view of your invisible face.

Here we are only considering viewing plane mirrors normally, at right angles. For the general case of angled plane mirrors, the eyes are effectively in the mirror – viewing from its position – but not rotated to aim at the object. They have to aim at the mirror to see the object, wherever this may be; so eye positions and eye rotations are decoupled by mirrors.

To appreciate just what is happening for one's own face, we need a clear criterion for what is or is not reversed. The clearest and most straightforward is the appearance of writing. Provided we ignore symmetrical letters (especially O and X) writing is immediately recognised as normal, or up-down or right-left reversed. Taking the word MIRRORS (noting especially the order of the letters and the orientations of M, R, and S) we immediately recognise the possible reversals.

Let's use this for checking what happens to your own face in a looking glass. Ask someone to place writing (such as the word MIRRORS) on your forehead. It will look normal from in front to the experimenter. In the mirror, it will appear right-left reversed. The writing and your face are reversed in the mirror by comparison with the experimenter's view, looking directly at your face, because the experimenter is rotated 180° from your direction of viewing.

Let's change the experiment slightly. Try writing MIRRORS on a transparent sheet (such as used for overhead projectors) and ask the experimenter to place this on your forehead so it looks normal for him. Then lift it off, and move it without rotation towards the mirror. This is rather like lifting off your face. Now look at the writing on the transparent sheet directly and also reflected in the mirror. Both appear to you right-left reversed. This is because you see them from behind, and neither has been rotated; yet both are reversed for the experimenter looking from in front – whose head is rotated 180° from the direction you are looking. It is this difference of direction of viewing that gives the rotation, and so the reversal.

But why do you look reversed to yourself? This is a puzzle, because you do not see your face without the mirror. But you do know your face – by touch. In fact there are two touch faces: your private inner face, which you experience by pursing the lips or screwing up the eyes; and your invisible to you public outer face, which you can touch from outside as with a razor. In the mirror you are reversed from your public outer face, but not from your inner private face. So you are both reversed and not reversed! This is because you have two touch faces: one within and the other without. You are mirror reversed from your public outer touch face but not from your private inner touch face. Both, however, are depth reversed.

To understand depth reversal, we need to appreciate the curious status of virtual images. The virtual images of plane mirrors are nothing without the optical focusing of an eye, or a camera. The image is the reflected object shifted in space, and seen from a different viewpoint. Real images (such as slide projections on a screen) are entirely different from virtual images. They persist even though there is no observer (except for Bishop Berkeley!), while virtual images in a mirror are nothing without an eye. Shut the eyes and they go away; but real images remain, though unseen

No psychology is involved for virtual images – except for *lack* of visual cognition. This ensures that we see the reflected objects in wrong and sometimes impossible places even though we know where they are. Objects, including oneself, are perceptually through the mirror, because the visual system 'assumes' that the light entering the eyes comes directly from objects, though we appreciate conceptually that the light has been reflected back from a mirror. This was demonstrated by Sir Isaac Newton as is shown in Figure 7.1, on the following page.

Ins and outs of a close shave

You know your private touch face without reference to your reversed *doppelgänger* reflection; but this is not what William shaves – he shaves your public face (preferably without confusion from looking in the glass). The barber shaving you while looking in the mirror is also bothered by this depth reversal, and he has to learn to correct for it. The reversals are particularly bothering when tying a tie. Many of us avoid looking in the mirror, and no doubt there are equivalent problems for ladies making up their faces.

Shaving oneself, one is faced with the problem that the mirror image is sideways reversed from one's outer public touch face, though not from one's private touch face, and it is depth reversed from both touch faces. A man shaves his outer face as seen in the mirror reversed. But the movements of hand and razor are not reversed, and the same is true for ladies wielding lipstick or eyebrow pencil. The movements are not reversed; but what is seen of the hand, the razor, and so on is different. You see the front of hand and razor directly, but their far sides or backs in the mirror. (This is like the writing on the transparent sheet.) As direction of movement is not reversed, the near and far sides of hand and razor move together – or shaving would be even more dangerous than it is!

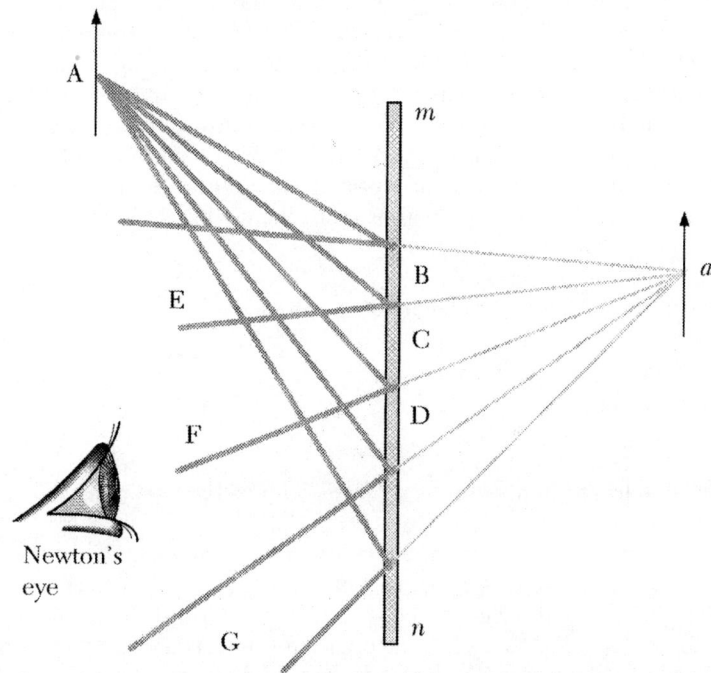

Figure 7.1. Sir Isaac Newton's diagram of how virtual images are seen (from 'Opticks'): the brain assumes the light comes directly from the objects though we know it is reflected. Newton does not consider lateral mirror reversal. Kindly provided by Richard L. Gregory and reproduced with permission from Maney and the Institute of Materials, Minerals and Mining.

The cutting edge

It turns out that one's own face is a very special object. It is special because it is only visible to oneself in a mirror though it is public property for anyone else. As it is not visible to oneself without a mirror, its reversal cannot be seen by comparison with the direct view. Evidently it is compared with one's private touch face. So when you see your own face and also the back of the room in a looking glass, both are reversed for the same reason, but your reasons for knowing they are reversed are different, for you can feel your invisible face from inside but not the visible room.

We started with the proposition that sideways (or up-down) reversals seen in a plane mirror are due to object rotation. It turns out that there are two kinds of objects to consider: small objects whose far sides are visible in the mirror, and the scene behind the observer – who sees behind while looking at the mirror in front. Thus his or her eyes (and head) are rotated from the direct view behind, as in a driving mirror. One's own face is a unique mirror object, being invisible without the mirror; yet seen reversed, and almost as someone else – one's double – through it. We arrive at three principles of mirror reversal; the first two being by rotation, the third by increasing path length with object distance:

First Principle – object reversal
Object rotated so its back is visible in the mirror

Second Principle – observer reversal
Observer rotated from the scene behind

Third Principle – depth reversal
Increased path length from observer or object with increased distance.

Perhaps most puzzling is why mirrors are so puzzling. This might be because their images are ghosts that cannot be explored by touch. This suggests that practical classes in schools and universities, and also hands on science centres for the public, are very important for understanding the world of material objects.[9] However this may be, mirrors show how hard it is to think appropriately without being misled by seductive irrelevancies. We may conclude that through his cutting ways, William of Ockham invented a very useful eclectic razor.

Final reflections

If in experimental mood William traced the outline of his reflected head on the mirror, while the glass was steamy or with a little soap, he would have discovered that the tracing was exactly half the size of his head. Even more surprising: his head would continue to fill the tracing from whatever distance he viewed himself in the mirror. He would have realised, no doubt, that this is because the glass is half way between his head and his (non-existing!) virtual image, seen through the mirror. So mirrors behave very differently from windows though they look similar, which warned William that analogies based on surface similarities can be deeply misleading.

While still in experimental mood, William might have tried varying the angle of the 90° corner mirror that showed his face not reversed, but as others saw him from in front. This was so when the corner was vertical. But when he rotated the corner mirror, around the line of sight, he would see himself and the reflected room rotating at twice the speed of the of the mirrors' rotation. He would be upside down when the edge of the corner mirror was horizontal. This he would explain correctly with an optical ray diagram – though it failed for the simple looking glass. It failed for the looking glass because the diagram could not tell vertical from horizontal. The corner mirror is different because it is optically asymmetrical. Unlike the looking glass its image reversals, and the rotations, can be described by its optical properties. It is confusing that such different kinds of explanations apply to what appear to be very similar things.

William was no doubt surprised when he set the angle of the vertical corner mirrors not at 90° but at 60°. For with the 60° corner mirrors, his face and writing or whatever appeared reversed exactly as in the looking glass. And when he rotated the 60° around the line of sight the image did not rotate. Entirely unlike the 90° corner, the 60° mirrors were exactly like the simple looking glass.

Surprisingly, although the 60° pair of corner mirrors is physically asymmetrical the mirrors behave as though they are a single (symmetrical) plane mirror. Reducing the angle still further produces an infinite sequence – reversing to non-reversing, with corresponding rotation to non-rotation – when the mirrors are rotated around the line of sight. This optical phenomenon must be known, though I have not seen it described. What happens is: rays from each mirror meet the other at 90°. So it is functionally a single normal mirror though two angled mirrors are involved. So although they form an asymmetrical structure they are optically symmetrical, like a normal mirror. Again we see that appearance without hands on experimenting is deceptive.

It must be tempting to explain the 'mirror reversal' of a looking glass in similar optical terms; but rotation of objects, or of the observer, is hardly optical – and the same reversals occur without a mirror, in printing. This is because the paper is rotated from the typeface; so type is in 'mirror writing'.

Another surprise is that the single mirror is so different from the 90° corner mirrors – though identical with 60° mirrors. It is even more surprising that the object rotation reversal of a simple looking glass is conceptually entirely different from the optical reversal of the 90° corner mirror. These surprises show our (though the reader may be an exception!) lack of understanding from appearances alone, without hands on experiments.

No new concepts are involved here. Getting on for 700 years ago, William of Ockham would have known the necessary concepts. Yet William had to sharpen his razor to separate these cases, and cut away seductive irrelevancies, to arrive at the simple answer. No doubt this 'more than subtle doctor' – and of course barbers were the doctors of that time – was stroppy with customers who disagreed with his account.

Notes and References

[1] R.P. Feynman. *QED. The strange theory of light and matter.* (1988, NJ: Princeton University Press, 1988).

[2] R.L. Gregory. *Mirrors in mind.* (London: Penguin, 1997).

[3] R.L. Gregory & J.G. Wallace. "Recovery from early blindness". *Experimental Psychology Monograph* 2. (Cambridge: Heffers, 1963). Reprinted in R. L. Gregory. *Concepts and mechanisms of perception.* (London: Duckworth, 1974).

[4] Plato. Timaeus, trans. D. Lee. (London: Penguin, 1977).

[5] J. Bennett. "The difference between right and left", *American Philosophy Quarterly,* 1970, VIII, (3), 175-191. N. Block. "Why do mirrors reverse left/right but not up/down?", *Journal of Philosophy,* 1974, IXX, 259-277.

[6] M. Gardner. *The ambidextrous universe.* (London, Penguin, 1965).

[7] R. N. Shephard and J. Metzler. "Mental rotation of three-dimensional objects". *Cognitive Psychology,* 1971, 3, 701-703.

[8] R. Audi (ed.). *The Cambridge dictionary of philosophy.* (Cambridge: Cambdridge University Press, 1995).

[9] R.L. Gregory. "First hand science: the Exploratory in Bristol", *Science and Public Affairs,* 1983, 3, 13-24. H. Hein. "The museum as teacher of theory: a case study of the Exploratorium vision section". *Journal of Museum Studies,* 1987, 2, (4), 30-39. R.A. Hodgkin. *Playing and exploring.* (New York: Methuen, 1985).

CHAPTER EIGHT

EARLY MODERN MIRRORS

MIRANDA ANDERSON

I dare speak it to myself, for it is not vainglory for a man and his glass to confer
in his own chamber.
—Cloten, *Cymbeline* (4.1.5)

A piece of glass and metal: a mirror. Behind it the blank solid wall. But
through it I see what everyone finds there, my own reflection, and I find what
only I see there, my own reflection. The more transparent the surface of the
mirror the more effectively it becomes invisible as an object, as you appear in it
as an interactive *doppelgänger* of yourself in real time: gazing back at you, you
are gazing back at you, gazing. This essay begins by exploring the longer term
ways in which the mirror has acted as an interactive prop in the formation of
cognitive processes and of subjectivity; partly through considering how our gaze
into the mirror might be compared with the use of language as an extension of
ourselves. My suggestion is, that like language, a mirror acts as a "mind tool"
that enables human subjects to stretch beyond our brain and body boundaries.[1]
In addition, it is argued here that our relation to the mirror as a tool is formed in
correlation to the technological, sociocultural, and psychophysiological context
of any particular time and place, so that when we look in the mirror, we are and
are not performing the same process as another person in another time or
another place; with variations operating along a spectrum (in relative
accordance to the extent of differentiations existing between one and another).

Next, the discussion focuses in on particulars about mirrors and their motifs
that pertain specifically to the early modern period, in particular concentrating
on a few Shakespearean mirror motifs to help unpack early modern
understanding of mirrors. Beginning with a look at the diverse types of mirrors
around due to the technological developments in mirror manufacture leads into a
consideration of how this affected who used mirrors and what mirror were used
for. Also discussed is the effect of technological developments upon the
production of glass objects in general; of interest here because of the common
early modern use of the word "glass" for both transparent "glass" and a

reflective "mirror". Turning next to literary conventions of mirror motif usage, the combined effects of technological development and sociocultural context is reflected in the deployment by certain writers of ethical distinctions between the old and new types of mirrors. The essay closes with a summing up of the early modern understanding of the mirror in relation to the extrospective and introspective types of social and psychological mirroring that preceded and continued alongside the popular spread of the object itself. Throughout, there is an investigation into the intimate relation of the mirror motif to both visual and verbal reflexivity, which similarly move fluidly between outward and inward, with boundaries shown variously as permeable and impermeable.

Mirror Mind Tools

The philosopher Andy Clark has described writing as a cognitive tool that by enabling the offloading and concretisation of initial thoughts allows more complex thoughts to develop: the brain through using the external tools of pen and paper, or perhaps computer, can externalise its thoughts in a stable form which allows for further reflection, and so hopefully further clearer and higher level thoughts upon the original murky and mundane ones.[2] This idea that cognition and subjectivity are extended into the world is popularly known in cognitive science as the "extended mind" hypothesis. Following this structure but reapplying it to the mirror and the viewing subject, in a similar way the subject through using the external tool of the mirror offloads aspects of itself onto the visual form it views in the mirror, at the same time as internalizing the perceived reflection as itself. Clark's description of artists' use of a sketchbook is also a useful comparison: "the iterated process of externalizing and re-perceiving turns out to be integral to the process".[3] This mirror-image allows for further reflection upon an aspect of ourselves that otherwise remains invisible to us, our physicality as a whole being, our face and its expressions, and a double view into our own eyes looking out and in simultaneously. Thus, the mirror allows more complex and clearer thoughts about our nebulous self, by providing us with a form with which to interact.

As Richard Gregory discusses in the previous essay, through the mirror we can experience a parallel of the outsider's view of the expressions we make that both consciously and nonconsciously act as representatives of our thoughts and feelings. These facial expressions enable others to "read" what we think and feel, and exposure to our own and our mirroring of others facial expressions develop our skills in reading other minds and in representing our own.[4] As writing has been shown to fundamentally alter a subject's cognitive processes and social relations: so through our adaptation to the many mirrored surfaces of the modern world, we have learned to think of ourselves in a fundamental way in relation to what we see reflected in a mirror. This heightens our sense of ourselves as an embodied object of vision and as the subject that is looking; this doubly intensified sense of self produces more conscious interaction between subjects. Cognitively the use of the mirror enables the construction of our subjectivity by means of a technological instrument, instead of through other intermediaries or through reflective capabilities within our own mind. Whilst the mirror is a tool that requires the understanding that the image viewed is inverted, it can relatively quickly become "transparent in use", [5] since unlike writing or reading it is unnecessary to acquire more complex skills. This is evidenced by the Biami Tribe's introduction to them, as explained by Mark Pendergrast in the introduction: a few days of awe was followed by their quick adaptation to using them as practical tools for the application of their own tribal make up, instead of helping one another as before, [6] with the implication that a collective sense of ourselves through practical social mirroring is supplemented by the mirror as an independent means of "making-up" a subject. In practical terms, our everyday cycle of preening and looking is repeated until, more or less quickly, a groomed subject is formed by these loops out into the mirror into someone ready to venture out into the public eye. Moreover, in epistemological terms the self-reflection acts as a form of "mind tool", which fundamentally affects the evolution of ideas of yourself as a subject, both within and without the brain.

Multiplicity of Mirrors

Having briefly considered how mirrors in general work, the remainder of this essay will consider in more detail how the particularities of early modern mirrors interacted with the sociocultural and literary context, beginning with a look at what early modern mirrors were. Mirrors nowadays though they come in all shapes and sizes tend to be of a fairly uniform quality and made of transparent glass backed with an alloy that gives a bright and clear reflection. Whereas then, as with the gradual spread of literacy and print technology, which resulted in the co-existence of residual forms of oral culture with written and printed forms of using language, [7] the gradual spread of new types of mirror technology resulted in diverse forms and shapes of mirrors co-existing, plus the use of social mirroring and meditative self-reflection continuing alongside.

From the mid-sixteenth century, Melchior-Bonnet describes that "mirrors could be had at any price and quality", although of course the price would generally reflect the quality. [8] Even the oldest type of reflection in still water, common due to the rivers, pools, lakes, dew and puddles of our landscape, is drawn upon by mirror motifs of the early modern period. Thus, for example, in a *Midsummer Night's Dream*, Lysander describes the moon lovingly examining herself in the dew: "Phoebe doth behold/ Her silver visage in the wat'ry glass,/ Decking with liquid pearl the bladed grass".[9] Small convex mirrors, familiar to us from medieval and early modern art (and featured in essays in the last section of this book), were made of a thick glass with a greenish tint that had been blown into globes, lined with a heavy lead tain, and then subdivided. These were distorting both on account of their shape, which compressed and reduced the reflection, and on account of the thickness and irregularities of the glass and the darkness and unevenness of the lead backing. Therefore even into the early seventeenth century many of the elite preferred to keep using metal speculums of gold, silver, bronze or steel, or less commonly mirrors of polished black obsidian or jet, although these required regular polishing to keep their reflections unclouded. Thus the description of the latter type: "Stones so well polisht, that they equall for brightnesse a steele mirrour."[10] However, during the sixteenth century gradually becoming more available in England, were imported flat clear shining glasses with lighter and brighter quicksilver and tin tains, although they were not produced in England until after 1624.[11] These new crystal mirrors were enabled by Flemish mirror makers' development of a quicksilver and tin alloy, which was later combined with the Venetian glass industry's ingenious production of a transparent flat clear thin glass, *cristallo*. These gradually were to transform both the number of mirrors in circulation and the way that mirrors were used. [12]

Mirror Use

Who were early modern mirrors used by? The new glass mirrors were very popular with the elite and were light enough that now small mirrors could be worn like jewellery or fashion accessories, tied round the waist by women and worn by men in their hats. In Jonson's *Cynthia's Revels*, the wittily named Amorphus, having warned that the face is an index of the mind, instructs his companion to "place your mirrour in your hat", but to "set" his face by him, notably juxtaposing the technological with the social means and making the former just decoration and the latter a practical tool.[13] Yet, the increasing urbanisation, social mobility, and centralised courtlife, which heightened concern over personal appearance, as Sabine Melchior-Bonnet notes, did increase practical mirror use:

> Situated at the crossroads of nature and culture, it educated the eye and assisted in relaying lessons in civility. From a glance in the mirror flowed not only a taste for ornament and an attention to social display and hierarchy, but also a new geography of the body, which made visible previously unfamiliar images (one's back and profile) and stirred up sensations of modesty and self-consciousness.[14]

Mirrorware was therefore also useful as a practical aesthetic and epistemological tool. Yet whilst the mirror was a tool equipped to combat concern it also potentially produced a circular dynamic in which these portable mirrors led to more frequent reappraisals and therefore more self-consciousness, or to its reverse face, vanity, and so back to the mirror. Like women, courtiers were particularly liable to be accused of "glass-gazing", on account of their effeminate concern with sartorial finery, an equivalent to their rhetorical displays; or inversely they were accused of being a "glass-faced flatterer", on account of their (to an extent necessary) visual and verbal mirroring of their superiors.[15]

However, as Laura Gowing suggests, mirrors were still relatively uncommon for ordinary people: for those who were not part of the elite or of their entourage of servants, and who were not actors, artists or artisans seeking patronage at court. To this general lack of mirrors in ordinary homes Gowing connects a more social type of self-consciousness:

> Seventeenth century bodies existed in a different conceptual world, where subjectivity was a more collective affair, a matter of belonging and embeddedness. After all, there were almost no mirrors in ordinary houses, and to study your reflection could suggest vanity and a sinful preoccupation with earthly things.[16]

Philippa Kelly has explored to what extent mirrors were available outside of urban and court circles by examining regional inventories: in one rural parish in the early seventeenth century she discovered that whilst only three of the wealthier members of town had bequeathed mirrors, their value would not have set them above general affordability. Therefore she deduces that they were just not seen as necessary.[17] Thus Kelly, like Bonnet, suggests that the central role of the mirror was for the personal grooming of society life.

Yet, there is evidence of a more intimate relation between these two types of mirroring, by a tool or by another subject. A dominant theme in Shakespeare's use of the mirror motif, as in the quote from Jonson earlier, is the role that another person can play through mirroring back, or else revealing their distance from, our perceptions of ourselves, of them or of the world. Mirrors, like language, are one of the ways in which we make the invisible visible, through looking at and into ourselves, courtesy of a cognitive prop. Shakespeare reveals the intersubjective mirroring of our words in discourse by a technique in which one character turns another's words against him, which in several cases is highlighted by the use of the image of a mirror or reflective surface, as in the following exchange in *The Taming of the Shrew*:

PETRUCCIO	Why, here's no crab, and therefore look not sour.
KATHERINE	There is, there is.
PETRUCCIO	Then show it me.
KATHERINE	Had I a glass I would.
PETRUCCIO	What, you mean my face?
KATHERINE	Well aimed, of such a young one.[18]

Thus, Kate refuses to passively play a flattering glass. Instead Kate subversively mimics the subjective perspective of Petruccio back at him revealing the lack of authority of his perspective over hers: just as the glass being figurally held up is not neutrally placed, so the biased position of the signifying subject is signalled by the mirror-like rebounding of Petruccio's words back at him. This highlights the potentially problematic lack of objectivity and phenomenological insight into another's mind in intersubjective forms of reflection. It also suggests that this participates in a continuing literary tradition about a social mode of human reflexivity that the mirror was understood in relation to and that in turn the mirror motif can be used to represent. Despite the ease with which mirrors can be assimilated by small communities, during the early modern period social mirroring would have continued to play a more dominant role in perceptions of mirrors as objects, due to their relative novelty and the partialness of more widespread mirror use, thus not yet absorbed into society as a common accessory used by all.

In addition, the religious and philosophical tradition of using the mirror motif to figure meditative contemplation, participates in early modern perceptions of mirrors. As evident from several of the essays within this book, the mirror has an introspective potential, which relates to the Augustinian or Socratic traditions of self-knowledge, wisdom and prudence; which in negative guise appears as our inheritance of fallen man's or of Narcissus's self-love, vanity and pride.[19] Francis Bacon describes the self-knowledge advised by the Delphic oracle in terms of a reflective beam: "*Radius Reflexus*, whereby Man beholdeth and contemplateth himselfe.[20] Yet, also in the works of Bacon, as Michael Kiernan notes, the injunction of the Delphic Oracle to "know thyself" is recorded as a colloquial rebuke: "A Nosce Teipsum", has become "a chiding" or a "disgrace".[21] A socialised and an externalised version of what is often thought of as the most famous instruction to turn inwards in contemplation of yourself makes a strong argument for the extent to which, what I will call, a concept of "extended reflexivity" was in operation.[22] This involved a blurring between the intrasubjective mode, occurring within a person, and the intersubjective mode, occurring between people.

The spread and the increased clarity of the mirror during the early modern period, by providing a surface, within which the subject could see itself reflected without intermediaries, offered up new means for a subject to reflect upon itself externalised and then to act upon what he saw there through an internalisation of the reflected image; suggesting that the most effective use of the mirror then as now was necessarily reflexive as well as transitive, providing an image of oneself as a subject, as well as, as an object. That the mirror provides a technological means of performing a similar function to social visual and verbal feedback, is reflected in the fact that the image viewed in the glass is described in Shakespeare's sonnets not only reflexively: "But when my glass shows me myself", but also moves between reflexivity and transitivity: "Look in thy glass, and tell the face thou viewest/ Now is the time that face should form another". In the second of these examples, the mirror-image is described first in third person terms, it is a bystander that the viewer must instil with knowledge, but next it appears as the active agent that must act.[23] That this conceit extends from the realm of the visual ("Look") to that of the verbal ("tell"), with the mirror used to demonstrate the concept of a cognitive prop in which words can act upon the mirror-image, works in part because words and mirroring both function intrasubjectively and intersubjectively. Besides, the lover's attempt to harness the beloved's narcissism, to turn him from his mirror-image to production of a child, suggests a similar blurring between technological and biological offspring.

Therefore for confirmation or evaluation of social bearing, the early modern subject may choose to turn to the world as his glass, or instead to the glass as the world. Whilst conversely for inward self-knowledge he may turn to his counter-reflection by the multiplicity of perspectives available within or through the entrance the mirror displays into his eyes and mind. Thus the glass operates as a social instrument for self-presentation and evaluation, and can visually represent and aid introspectiveness and increase self-consciousness. Furthermore, the link during the early modern period between social and psychophysiological processes of reflecting and mirroring were in turn strongly entwined with the understanding of mirrors as objects.

Glass Technology

Mirrors were just one type of product affected by the technological advances in the glassmaking industry, and the discussion here will now briefly consider how these other products affected perceptions of mirrors. Along with the industrialised production of improved mirrors the development of the industry resulted in new and improved magnifying glasses, spectacles, glass windows, and assisted in the development of telescopes and (not very precise) microscopes, which along with the continuing production of hour glasses,[24] indicates reasons why glass tools were associated with both spatial and temporal states and processes. Perspective glasses and mirrors were used in art and various types of these 'perspectives' had become newly fashionable as a form of visual entertainment and tricks. Reginald Scot suspiciously gives an inventory of the multiplicity of types of glasses around in the late sixteenth century:

> But the woonderous devises, and miraculous sights and conceipts made and conteined in glasse doo farre exceed all other; whereto the art perspective is verie necessarie. For it sheweth the illusions of them, whose experiments be seene in divers sorts of glasses; as in the hallowe, the plaine, the embossed, the columnaire, the pyramidate or piked, the turbinall, the bounched, the round, the cornered, the inversed, the eversed, the massie, the regular, the irregular, the coloured and cleare glasses: for you may have glasses so made, as what image or favour soever you print in your imagination, you shall thinke you see the same therein . . . There may be glasses also, wherein one may see another man's image and not his owne . . .[25]

This entry in his work on witchcraft results from the fact that glasses and mirrors were not only used for scientific observations but also for magic; and both to discover and reflect truth and to deceive. Theodore Ziolkowski relates the mirror's association with magic to its inherent mysteriousness: it can see what's happening behind the viewer's back, it doubles everything, and it contains in itself an inverted world.[26] In addition, the mirror was known to be able to cause fire by reflecting the sun's rays.[27] Perhaps the most famous early modern practitioner of scrying was John Dee, who used his 'shew-stones', an Aztec black obsidian stone mirror brought "by Angelicall Ministry" to contact spirits that the trickster Edmund Kelly convinced him were sent by "the Almighty" to provide the key to the underlying unity of the world.[28] Dee was not the only one fooled as Queen Elizabeth, amongst other dignitaries, had asked to see and expressed delight in the glass.[29] Thus the development of different types of mirrors and the widespread distribution of glass products during the early modern period further added to the original potential of the mirror to work as a fertile and polysemous literary motif.

Literary Conventions

How does all this relate to literary conventions? The social and literary fashion for mirrors between the late Middle Ages and the eighteenth century (though many would question this end point) is related by Herbert Grabes only secondarily to shifts in mode of thought, and primarily to technological change: "the improvement and cheap glass production of glass mirrors by the Venetians after the fourteenth century".[30] Grabes suggests that an apex in mirror use was reached between 1550 and 1650, with books, tracts and pamphlets widely using mirror-titles and the conceits of Elizabethan writers generating new forms of mirror metaphors.[31] He also relates the use of the encyclopaedic mirror-title during the medieval and early modern period to the fact that mirrors until the seventeenth century were often convex: "reflection and reduction, (re)presentation and compression formed here a double analogy between mirror and book".[32] The continuing concept and belief that knowledge could be encapsulated and encompassed in a book is therefore evident in the continuing use of mirror-titles and relates to the particular qualities of the convex glass, since (to adopt another commonplace analogy) like an eye it compresses that it reflects in a reduced but multidirectional form; as captured by Donne's distillation of the world into a pair of eyes in *The Canonization*:

Who did the whole world's soul extract, and drove
Into the glasses of your eyes
(So made such mirrors, and such spies,
That they did all to you epitomize).[33]

Thus, both the technological development of mirrors and the sociocultural context fuelled the literary deployment of mirror motifs.

The technological shift in mirror production was used by some writers for literary effect by employing the distinction between the material qualities of old and new types of mirrors. Rayna Kalas describes how Gascoigne in his verse satire *The Steele Glas*, along with various other writers, distinguished between the religious connotations of the earlier dimly reflective tools which required effort to see clearly in (like St. Paul's dark glass; discussed in Mark Kauntze's essay), and the vanity of the new mirrors as decorative and fashionable baubles. Kalas contends that the metaphor of the mirror is "calibrated to material changes in the physical object".[34] Whilst this is true, it is worth remembering that although Gascoigne took this opportunity to divest the negative connotations of mirroring onto the new instruments and so to preserve the positive ones for his metaphorical use of the old instruments in his work, and so also to create a contrast between the two types; nevertheless, both the positive and negative attributes had a long continuing relationship with mirrors and mirroring in general. As Kalas herself points out, other writers instead adopted the new crystal glass's brilliance and clarity to signify positive attributes, with Stephen Batman, for example, entitling his book of moral emblems *A Christall Glasse of Christian Reformation*.[35] This suggests that changes in any one area of influence may engender contradictory results.

However, there is not necessarily any consequence: the possibility of the moralistic distinction invited by the different material qualities of mirrors was not adopted by Shakespeare for contrastive means. His word of choice is predominantly "glass", but it is used almost interchangeably with "mirror": so without any difference implied in the representation of these ideal models, in *1*

Henry VI Salisbury is described as the "mirror of all martial men" and in *The Two Noble Kinsmen* Hippolyta as a "dear glass of ladies".[36] Therefore Grabes's argument that the use of the word mirror at this time was associated with "positive models of conduct and edification", while glass was used in association with moral satires and political tracts is not borne out by Shakespeare's interchangeable use.[37] The predominance of Shakespeare's use of "glass", likely reflects its richer ambiguities, as it could slip between denoting a mirror or the wide range of glass products mentioned earlier, and between signifying opaque reflectiveness and transparent penetrability. In fact, both mirror and glass motifs easily blur the boundaries between literal and figurative uses: suggestive of this is the OED's entitling of their first section for the noun "mirror": "Literally (or with obvious metaphor)".[38] Notably, whilst Shakespeare most frequently uses a noun form of "glass" or "mirror", the OED lists as the first verb form of "to mirror" Keats's use in 1820, when in fact in Shakespeare's *Troilus and Cressida* a passive verb form of mirror is used:

> For speculation turns not to itself
> Till it hath travelled and is mirrored there
> Where it may see itself.[39]

This suggests an addition is needed to this entry in the OED.

This quotation from *Troilus and Cressida* picks up on the relation between seeing and mirroring, which forms a continuing theme in the use of the mirror motif, with Luce Irigaray suggesting that Western use of mirror-imagery relates to "age-old oculocentrism".[40] The tradition of using mirror motifs to represent visual perception is a central theme in the medieval and early modern period, contributed to by that fact that the lens, that received and transmitted the visual information to the inner chambers of the brain, was thought of as a glass-like screen and named "crystalline" or "cristallinus".[41] Therefore, in *King Henry V* Pistol telling his wife to wipe her eyes, and enacting a mock up of a courtly farewell conveys it as: "Go, clear thy crystals".[42] An influential sixteenth century figure on the topic of optics and mirrors was Giambattista della Porta. Though the work he published in 1589 was on *Natural Magic*, the seventeenth chapter discusses trick mirrors, burning concave mirrors, telescopic-spectacles and he influentially explained that a camera obscura worked like an eye, with the pinhole as the equivalent of the pupil and the lens as a screen.[43] Thus della Porta helped to reinforce the existing parallels between mirrors and the eye that earlier theories had established.

Moreover, the eye-mirror motif was useful as an analogy for cognition because visual perception demonstrates the way in which an external material form can be translated into an internal immaterial image: demonstrating the permeability of the boundaries between the outward and inward and between materiality and immateriality. This was also contributed to by a figural understanding of being and knowing in visual terms. Bacon describes them as different forms of the same phenomenon: "for the truth of being, and the truth of knowing are one, differing no more than the direct beame, and the beame reflected."[44] Whether the cognitive process described were inward or outward the terminology used to describe visual functions could be usefully appropriated, as in the scene quoted above from *Troilus and Cressida*, where the reference to visual perception is used in order to explain how self-knowledge may in fact work via an extended reflexivity. This is made clearer in a passage closely following on from it:

> That no man is the lord of anything,
> Though in him there be much consisting,
> Till he communicate his parts to others
> Nor doth he of himself know them for aught
> Till he behold them formed in th' applause
> Where they're extended – who, like an arch reverb'rate
> The voice again; or like a gate of steel
> Fronting the sun, receives and renders back
> His figure and his heat. [45]

This passage also uses an analogy between visual reflexivity and verbal echoing. The interlinking of strands of thought concerning visual, verbal and cognitive processes encouraged early modern conceits use of them to knit together the pattern of the human subject, a design especially evident in mirror motifs. Bacon's reflected beam of knowing is described as operating through intersubjective reflection that precedes intrasubjective possession and understanding of oneself. The limits of physical perception, the face and the eyes inability to see themselves other than through the process of reflection, is used here to suggest the limits of introspection, of a parallel psychological inability of the subject to apprehend its own qualities, without a form of socially extended reflexivity. Here it is first person phenomenology rather than heterophenomenology that is brought into question as sufficient. Yet the context of manipulation within which this discussion takes place works to undermine the explicitly approved argument. All types of mirroring are interrelated but both outward and inward, and psychophysiological, social and technological mirrors are found to be not certainly reliable.

Critical Reflections

Literary critics have variously noted the relation of the early modern mirror metaphor to cognitive processes, to technology, and to subjectivity; however the focus has been directed at one or other of these connections, or at a one-way relation, rather than at their closely interwoven fabric. M.H. Abrams famous work *The Mirror and the Lamp* describes the mimetic medieval mirror and the lamp of the romantic period as heuristic devices involved in the forming of the modern critical tradition. Elaine Whitaker seeks to update Abrams by suggesting that in recent years the mirror and lamp as metaphorical vehicles "have given way to a postmodern halogen bulb".[46] Whitaker makes a strong argument for the effect of technological change upon the use and tenor of a metaphor:

> Just as thought is dependent on the properties of language, so it is dependent on objects furnished by technology.[47]

Her point regarding the dependence of thought on its technological environment is an important one except that it suggests one-way directionality rather than the dynamic recursive relationship that exists between cognitive processes and language and the technologies with which they interact. Meanwhile, Kalas restrictively argues that the effect of technology in the formation of subjectivity is not important, but only technology's effect on the mirror as a metaphor; another closure of interpretation too soon, a stopping short of the realisation of the complexity of the interactions that exist between technology, language and subjectivity.[48] My argument follows on from Andy Clark's proposal that the brain, the body and the world are interactive upon each other in a spiralling developmental relationship:

> What really matters is the complex reciprocal dance in which the brain tailors its activity to a technological and sociocultural environment, which – in concert with other brains – it simultaneously alters and amends. Human intelligence owes just about everything to this looping process of mutual accommodation.[49]

Arguably, in addition, what is suggested by the evidence here is just a few of the ways in which the early modern period also shared in a similar understanding of the boundaries between brain, body and world as leaky and negotiable.

Another slip by Whitaker is caused by her attributing distortions that occur only to the mirror, rather than realising the role of visual and cognitive processes therein, as she claims that it has always been the case that:

> Irregularities in the image reside in the imperfections of the mirror. The viewer's ability to see the image represented is presumed.[50]

Were we to put such trust in the viewer the mirror would be a vastly less interesting metaphor (and the world a place). The ambiguity about whether or not the flaw is in the perceiver or in the image presented by the mirror is creative of much dramatic tension in early modern literary works, and continues the tradition of medieval morality dramas, where a sinner does not necessarily initially realise that the darkened reflection he sees in a mirror is caused by his own flaws. Sarah Carpenter cites Chaundler's *Liber Apologeticus* (c. 1460) in which Man who has succumbed to Sensuality looking in the mirror questions first: "I wonder whether the mirror is sound?" before realising that it is he who is tainted.[51] Carpenter shows how this is later developed by Redford in *Wit and Science* (1530s), as Wit blames the dirtiness of the glass before turning it on the surprised audience, and thereby realises that it is his reflection alone that appears dirty by "measuring his view of himself against his perception of the outside world".[52] This is taken further in Shakespeare's use of mirror motifs in which perception of the self and the outside world are also compared and contrasted with other subjects' perceptions of them.

Early Modern Mind Tools

In the early modern period the mirror is often compared against the evolving technology of printed, written and spoken language, because of the parallel dynamic power of mirrors and mirroring to participate in our cognitive processes and inform our understanding of what we are. Earlier in this essay a few mirror motifs involving spoken language were considered, but before closing let us briefly consider the mirror's relation to the increasing use of texts. The closeness of the relationship between mirrors and texts is reflected by the fact that the printing press was invented by Johannes Gutenberg, a man who previously made mirrors and came up with the idea, from the way that they invert images.[53] Walter Ong explains that writing "structures knowledge at a distance from lived experience" and from the "familiar interaction of human beings".[54] Since the mirror, like a written or printed text, allows the offloading of cognitive processes and distance from them, it also creates a space between viewer and viewed that allows both for an increased familiarity of the subject to itself and inversely a space for reflections upon the images produced that allows the formation of a critical distance. In Shakespeare's *Sonnet 77*, there is a comparison of three objects through whose use it is suggested that the young man addressed may learn about himself physically, temporally and intellectually:

> Thy glass will show thee how thy beauties wear,
> Thy dial how thy precious minutes waste,
> The vacant leaves thy mind's imprint will bear,[55]

These external tools provide various didactic means whereby the young man may increase his knowledge about the world and himself; by making that which would otherwise be invisible visible: his face, time passing, and his thoughts.

The mirror, like the book, provides an extended reflexivity, and a more "thing-like" image,[56] as within it the subject can view itself unmediated by others directly.

To sum up, the mirror as an instrument is understood in relation to the use of other subjects or of a part of oneself as a mirror and within the early modern system of analogical thinking, the modes of understanding psychophysiological, sociocultural and technological processes are interwoven, as intimately as are inward and outward forms of reflexivity. Existing modes of understanding are reapplied in order to aid understanding of invisible, new or unexplained processes, such as imperceptible cognitive processes and the capacities and constraints of the mirror and of the human subject.

Notes

[1] Richard L. Gregory coined this term in his book *Mind in Science* (Cambridge: Cambridge University Press, 1981).

[2] Andy Clark, *Mindware* (Oxford: Oxford University Press, 2001), 142.

[3] Andy Clark, *Natural-Born Cyborgs* (Oxford: Oxford University Press, 2003), 77.

[4] See Paul Ekman, *Emotions Revealed: Understanding Faces and Feelings* (London: Phoenix, 2004).

[5] Clark, *Natural-Born Cyborgs*, 37-38.

[6] Mark Pendergrast, "Mirror Mirror: A Historical & Psychological Overview", in this book, 11-12. Also see Pendergrast's *Mirror Mirror: A History of the Human Love Affair with Reflection* (New York: Basic Books, 2004), 368-369.

[7] Walter Ong, *Orality to Literacy: The Technologizing of the Word* (London: Routledge Press, 1991), 113.

[8] Sabine Melchior-Bonnet. *The Mirror: A History*, trans. Katharine H. Jewett (London: Routledge, 2002), 23.

[9] Shakespeare, *A Misdsummer Night's Dream*, 1.1.209-211, in *The Collected Works of Shakespeare*. (London and New York: W. W. Norton and Company, 1997), 818. All further references to Shakespeare's works are to this Norton edition, unless otherwise stated.

[10] Sir T. Herbert Trav., 59 (1634) in OED 2002, "mirror", 1a.

[11] Rayna Kalas, "The Technology of Reflection: Renaissance Mirrors of Steel and Glass", *Journal of Medieval and Early Modern Studies*, Vol. 32, No. 3 (Fall 2002): 524.

[12] This summary of the technology of mirrors draws on Sabine Melchior-Bonnet, 9-69; Mark Pendergrast, *Mirror Mirror*, 1-27; and Rayna Kalas, 519-42.

[13] Jonson, *Cynthia's Revels*, 2.1 (1599), cited in OED 2002, "mirror", 2b.

[14] Melchior-Bonnet, 1.

[15] Shakespeare, *King Lear*, 2.2.13-21, 2364 and *Timon of Athens*, 1.1.59, 2254.

[16] Laura Gowing, *Common Bodies: Women, Touch and Power in Seventeenth Century England* (New Haven and London: Yale University Press, 2003), 5.

[17] Philippa Kelly, "Surpassing Glass", *Early Modern Literary Studies*, 8.1 (May 2002): 5. http://purl.oclc.org/emls/08-2/kellglas.htm. Kelly gives comparative evidence: one looking glass was valued at two shillings; a bed between two and six shillings; a mare and foal at four shillings; linen sheets between five and thirteen shillings and five bushels of wheat and rye at sixteen shillings.

[18] Shakespeare, *The Taming of the Shrew*, 2.1.226-230, 165. Shakespeare, *As You Like It*, 3.2.261-265, 1630: "JAQUES: By my troth, I was seeking for a fool when I found you./ ORLANDO: He is drown'd in the brook. Look but in, and you shall see him./ JAQUES: There shall I see mine own./ ORLANDO: Which I take to be either a fool or a cipher."

[19] Herbert Grabes, *The Mutable Glass: Mirror-imagery in titles and texts of the Middle Ages and English Renaissance*, trans. Gordon Collier (Cambridge: Cambridge University Press, 1982), 153-160. See also on the Narcissian theme Louise Vinge, *The Narcissus Theme in Western European Literature up to the Early Nineteenth Century*, trans. Robert Dewsnap, (Lund: Gleerups, 1967).

[20] Francis Bacon, *The Advancement of Learning*, 213^v-214^r, in *The Oxford Francis Bacon IV*, ed. Michael Kiernan (Oxford: Clarendon Press, 2000), 93.

[21] Bacon, *The Advancement of Learning*, 290, reference notes 8-11.

[22] I have coined this phrase as most aptly describing a reflexive process in consciouness, cognition or subjectivity that (although not necessarily occurring beyond the boundaries of the skull) is extended into the world.

[23] Shakespeare, *Sonnet 62*, l.9, and *Sonnet 3*, ll.1-2, in *Shakespeare's Sonnets*, ed. Katherine Duncan Jones (London: Arden Shakespeare, 2002), 117 & 62.

[24] H. J. Haden, Review of "The Development of English Glassmaking, 1560-1640", *Technology and Culture*, Vol. 17, No. 4 (October, 1976): 788-790. Also see Mason's *A History of the Sciences*, 208-9.

[25] From Reginald Scot's *Discoverie of Witchcraft* (1584) cited in Shickman, "The 'Perspective Glass' in Shakespeare's *Richard II*", *Studies in English Literature, 1500-1900*, Vol. 18, No. 2, Elizabethan and Jacobean Drama (Spring, 1978): 219. Also see Jonathan Miller's beautiful book of mirror images in art, *On Reflection*, (London: National Gallery Publications Limited, 1998), especially 56-7, for images of cylindrical glass that could be used to create 3D images.

[26] Ziolkowski, *Disenchanted Images: A Literary Iconology* (New Jersey: Princeton University Press, 1977), 162.

[27] John Webster's madmen to madden the Duchess in *The Duchess of Malfi* describe drawing doomday nearer by a perspective glass or by making a glass that will set the world on fire, and hell as a glass-house of fire that blows up women's souls. 4.2.71-8, *The Duchess of Malfi*, Six Plays by Contemporaries of Shakespeare, ed. C. B. Wheeler , (Oxford: Oxford University Press, 1961), 467.

[28] John Dee, *A true and faithful relation of what passed for many years betweene Dr. John Dee and...and some spirits tending...to a general alteration of most states and kingdoms in the world.* http://eebo.chadwyck.com., document images 2 and 30.

[29] Queen Elizabeth 'willed me to fetch my glass so famous, and to show unto her some of the properties of it, which I did to her Majesty's great contentment and delight', cited in Pendergrast, *Mirror Mirror*, 42.

[30] Grabes, 118.

[31] Grabes, 1-15.

[32] Grabes, 43.

[33] Donne, *The Canonization*, ll.40-43, in *John Donne's Poetry: Authoritative Texts and Criticism*, ed. A. L.Clements (New York: Norton & Company Inc., 1966), 7.

[34] Kalas, 536.

[35] Kalas, 536.

[36] Shakespeare, *1 Henry VI*, 1.6.50-52, 455 and *The Two Noble Kinsmen*, 1.1.90, 3208.

[37] Grabes, 1-11.

[38] OED 2002.

[39] Shakespeare, *Troilus and Cressida*, 3.3.104-6, 1876. OED 2002, first entry as Keats in *Lamia*: "He...bending to her open eyes, Where he was mirror'd small in paradise."

[40] Luce Irigaray, *Speculum of the Other Woman*, (New York: Cornell University Press, 1985), 48.

[41] Thomas Blount, *Glossographia* (1656). Although this comes from a mid-seventeenth century source Blount in defining the word "glass" still describes the Galenic concept of the lens, as the screen upon which pictures are shown. This dictionary is available online on The Early Modern English Dictionaries Database (EMEDD): http://www.chass.utoronto.ca/english/emed/emedd.html

[42] Shakespeare, *King Henry V*, 2.4.45, 1472.

[43] Pendergrast, *Mirror Mirror*, 75-77. Also discussed in Judit Varga's essay.

[44] Bacon, F2^r, 25-6.

[45] Shakespeare, *Troilus and Cressida*, 3.3.110-117, 1876.

[46] Elaine E. Whitaker, "The Mirror and the Halogen Bulb: A Review Essay", *South Atlantic Review*, Vol. 59, No. 2 (May, 1994): 113.

[47] Whitaker, 113.

[48] Kalas, 522.

[49] Clark, *Natural-Born Cyborgs*, 87.

[50] Whitaker, 114.

[51] Chaundler quoted by Sarah Carpenter, "Masks and Mirrors: Questions of Identity in Medieval Morality Drama", *Medieval English Theatre*, Vol. 13 (1991): 12.

[52] Carpenter, 15-16.

[53] Pendergrast, *Mirror Mirror*, 38.

[54] Ong, 42.

[55] Shakespeare, *Sonnet 77*, in *Shakespeare's Sonnets*, 265. (See my unpublished PhD thesis, Edinburgh University for a much fuller analysis of this sonnet).

[56] Ong, 98.

CHAPTER NINE

REFLECTIONS ON THE DOUBLE

LYNN HOLDEN

The double, or *doppelgänger*[1], is an ambiguous concept: both a visible phenomenon—a reflection, a shadow, a photograph, a portrait, a twin or a clone—and a metaphysical, philosophical or psychological construct— a god, or a subconscious or autoscopic hallucination. If the double can be described as an archetype, its significance is multivalent, while familiar expressions: *double-cross, double-dealing, double Dutch, double entendre, double agent, double talk, double-bind, double dyed, double vision* indicate a confusion, deliberate obscuration or "duplicity", attendant on its manifestations.

Both anthropologists and cultural historians have remarked upon the many taboos surrounding duplicates—twins in certain traditional societies were killed at birth and, more generally, shadows or reflections could be a source of danger if specific precautions were not taken. Superstitions such as covering the mirrors in the presence of a corpse and a belief in the misfortune incurred by a broken mirror have persisted until recent times. Underpinning such behaviour is a belief in an external soul and the concomitant idea of sympathetic or homeopathic magic; namely, that like affects like, and that what is inflicted on a replica affects the individual person. This is the motive behind sticking pins in effigies or, in a more technological era, tearing up a photo. In a similar way, knowledge of a person's name confers power, and hence there exist widespread taboos on naming. The name of a person, deity, spirit or other phenomenon is, in many traditions, believed to be linked to his very essence. Merely to mention the name is sufficient to evoke the presence, hence the common taboos on naming the dead (among the Malagasy of Madagasca, the Ilongot of northern Luzon in the Philippines and the Penan of Borneo, to name a few). Because names are so powerful, and the knowledge of a personal name allowed malevolent magic to be practised against its bearer, it was often kept secret. Similarly, in the tale of Rumpelstiltskin, collected by Jacob and Wilhelm Grimm in the 19th century and still told to children today, the evil plans of a dwarf are thwarted when his name is discovered.[2]

Mirrors were dangerous both for the dead and for the "undead" (vampires), as well as for demons and spirits and, most pertinently, for those who had not yet died. Either, as in Jean Cocteau's film, *Orphée*, Death enters and leaves through the mirror, carrying the soul away, or the soul of a corpse could be unintenionally trapped in the mirror and remain to haunt the living. Conversely it is possible that mirrors found in graves in China, Egypt, Madagascar, Serbia and Croatia were deliberate spirit-traps to retain the pernicious shade. Those without a soul, of course, cast no reflection although in Daoist tradition the mirror carried on the back of an adept as he climbs the sacred mountain will reveal the true form of demons.

As behaviour was adapted to circumvent peril so traditional narratives articulated the dangers of the double; long before Plato's philosophical allegory on the nature of truth—in which shadows cast by prisoners on a wall are mistaken for real things—myths located the dead as shadows in a barren or dusty underworld. As revenants, they would return to haunt the living: during the Japanese festival of *Obon*, the Mexican *Dias de los Muertos,* the Aztec commemoration of *Mictecacihuatl*, and in Europe, on *Walpurgisnacht* (also known as *Samhain* or Hallowe'en), or around Yuletide. For example, in the medieval Icelandic Eyrbryggja Saga the ghostly crew of a sunken fishing boat enter the steading at Yuletide to drink their own burial ale, and refuse to leave until they are put on trial (in a "door-doom", a local court or tribunal) and so expelled.

A fable on the insidious allure of the image is recorded by Ovid: the seer, Tiresias, is asked whether the beautiful youth, Narcissus, child of the water nymph, Liriope, can live long, given his exquisite looks. Tiresias replies, "Yes, unless he learns to know himself". The tale is familiar. In his overweening pride Narcissus rejects all advances, causing the smitten Echo to fade to an echo and a rejected suitor to appeal to the vengeful goddess, Nemesis. And so it is that Narcissus falls hopelessly in love with his own reflection in a forest pool, at first not recognising himself, "gazing into the eyes that were no eyes", only later realising whom he adores. What remains on the bank, after he has entered the underworld and sought his shadow on the Styx, is a single narcissus.

James George Frazer interpreted the Narcissus myth as a corruption of the earlier notion of death by reflection. The soul, resident in either the person's shadow or reflection on water, may be stolen away by water-spirits, a belief Frazer attributed to many traditional societies including the Greeks. [3] In psychoanalytic terms, an external soul is replaced by the idea of a divisible, multifaceted self, hence taboos on the double are related to concepts of the ego. In 1914, in a seminal study of the double, Otto Rank argued that Frazer's interpretation of the Narcissus tale did not explain why the story came to be an allegory against self-love, and that the logical deduction was that the awareness of mortality would be particularly damaging to a person's self-esteem. Drawing on Freud's theory of compensation, whereby one substitutes an acceptable meaning for inadmissible facts, Rank proposed that the fear of the double supplanted an original love of the double which was an insurance against the destruction of the ego, and a guarantee of immortality: since as a soul the double could exist after death.[4] Instigating these concepts was an inordinate self-love or narcissism, which obsessed the minds of both young children and early mankind. Once this stage had been "surmounted", as Freud put it, "the double reverses its aspect. From having been an insurance of immortality, it becomes the uncanny harbinger of death".[5]

But, as Freud perceived, the idea of the double does not necessarily disappear after a child has passed the stage of primary narcissism. It can be transformed into an independent observer who criticises and censors the ego in the form of a conscience, which, in the pathological condition involving delusions of observation, is totally dissociated from the ego. Self-criticism, replacing the earlier narcissism, is perceived as a pursuing double. Curiously, although Freud speaks of the pathological condition of "delusions of observation", autoscopy—in which someone encounters an hallucinatory image of his "double"—is rare and has no general pathological significance. The clinical psychiatrist, J.S. Grotstein, argues that the phenomenon is far more common as an intrapsychic (nonhallucinatory) experience.[6] Much more detailed clinical evidence exists for Capgras syndrome, named after its discoverer, Jean Marie Joseph Capgras, in which the sufferer's primary delusion is that a close friend or relative has been replaced by an impostor, an exact double. (This is similar to the Scottish folk belief in changelings, substitute spirit babies that fairies have left after stealing the human infant). Often the patient suffering from Capgras syndrome believes that the fraud must be murdered so that the real relation can be freed to return.

Probably because of the paucity of genuine case-studies of autoscopy, as opposed to Capras syndrome, Freud, like Rank, turned to anthropology, to religious practices and especially to fictional works of literature to demonstrate his thesis. In literature a character in a paranoid state is often portrayed as being pursued by a shadow, a mirrored image or a double. Certainly, in fiction, the theme of stalking by a replica is extensive. Rank speaks of the early film, *The Student of Prague*, with a screenplay by Hans Heinz Ewers,[7] a Faustian tale in which a destitute student sells his soul—in this case his mirrored reflection—to a stranger. The student is subsequently opposed and tormented by his own image until he shoots his double, only to realise that he has killed himself. The film is indebted to a tale by the German Romantic writer, E.T.A. Hoffmann, "The Story of the Lost Reflection", in which a respectable German husband and father, Erasmus Spikher, falls in love with the captivating Giulietta while in

Florence and, at her request, leaves his reflection behind in the mirror after murdering a rival. Hoffman is also the inspiration for Freud's influential essay on the uncanny, "Das Unheimliche". [8] In this paper, Freud focuses on Hoffmann's tale, "The Sandman" in which the ill-fated protagonist, Nathaniel, falls in love with a beautiful automaton, Olympia. Nathaniel is being pursued and watched by a sinister Sandman, who rips out the eyes of children and who is interchangeable both with the family lawyer, Coppelius, and with Coppola, the optician who fitted Olympia's eyes. Freud interprets the male characters as malign aspects of Nathaniel's father, upon whom he is fixated by his castration complex (the fear of blindness), while Olympia is a dissociated complex of the hero which confronts him as a person and is an incarnation of his narcissism. Denying unacceptable desires and fears, the narcissistic personality projects them onto another person to whom he attributes what Freud calls the "omnipotence of thoughts".

Hoffmann's work is replete with *doppelgängers*, *The Devil's Elixirs* and "The Doubles" being prime examples; but a fascination with the pursuing double, whether human, shadow, reflection or painted image, who undermines, and sometimes destroys, the hero, is a common theme from the time of the Romantics onwards. One thinks of Chamisso's *Wonderful story of Peter Schlemihl*, a tale of a doomed hero who sells not his reflection but his shadow in a Faustian pact, and of Hans Christian Anderson's "The Shadow", influenced by Chamisso, in which a shadow, carelessly lost, usurps its owner and takes his place. Edgar Allan Poe was another writer attracted to the *doppelgänger* theme; "William Wilson" depicts the eponymous protagonist haunted by someone with the same name. In Guy de Maupassant's "The Horla", the hero is tormented by an invisible spirit whose opaque body prevents him seeing his own reflection in the mirror. Like Fydor Dostoyevsky's novella, *The Double* and James Hogg's *The Private Memoirs and Confessions of a Justified Sinner,* "The Horla" is a consummate study of psychological disintegration in which the actual existence of a double is doubtful. In Oscar Wilde's *The Picture of Dorian Gray* the narcissistic youth hides a painted image of himself that is gradually transformed by his dissipation while he remains beautiful.[9] Film, too, has widely taken up the theme; *The Student of Prague* was the first in a long tradition that includes Kieślowski's *The Double Life of Véronique* and Maya Deren's seminal *Meshes of the Afternoon* (1943), in which a woman is driven to suicide after nightmarish confrontations with her doubles, mirrored images, and the knife which finally kills her.

It is a curious paradox that Rank and Freud found it necessary to draw on literary examples to illustrate their theories while subsequent literary critics have turned to Rank, Freud and other psychoanalysts to explain the same texts. Hélène Cixous revises Freud's reading of "The Sandman", finding a subversion of reality in the tale: the "uncanny" elements create a series of lacunae in the narrative structure through which, in a sense (because the "real" is deprived of meaning) death enters. In Cixous' reading, therefore, the double is not only symptomatic of displaced sexual anxiety but signifies death itself.[10] Jacques Lacan adopts Freud's paradigm and dwells on the mirror phase (the Imaginary) of an individual's development, which he places between primary narcissism (self-love) and attachment to the loved objects (others): looking at his image in the mirror or in the mother's face, a person begins to shape a sense of social identity, realising that the mirrored image is both "self" and "other". For Lacan, the ego is a cultural construction which he equates with Freud's super-ego, or conscience, an ideal self which watches and condemns the self as it tries to meet the demands of the social other.[11] Julia Kristeva speaks of the "imaginary realm" of undifferentiation which, at the time of ego formation, progresses towards a person's insertion in the "symbolic order", a social arena replete with language and "syntax". Disruption of the ego leads to a regression, a fragmentation of character and a corresponding loss of the "realistic" language of a unified self. As this reversal to a time of undifferentiation is untenable—"self" cannot be re-united to "other"—tales of the double tend to end in madness or death.[12]

But the double is not always a harbinger of disaster. A Chinese tale, "Scholar Chu", set during the mid-Autumn Chinese festival commemorating the dead, describes how a youth, Chu, offers to sit the civil service exams in the place of his friend, Chen, in order to repay an old debt. During the course of an examination, Chen is entertained by Chu's cousin, Liu, and taken to a painted barge where a famous courtesan sings a mournful funeral dirge. Later they walk through a covered walkway with poetic inscriptions on the wall and Chen inscribes the courtesan's lyrics on the stone. At dusk, they return home, and Chu appears to be coming through the door, but Chen realises it is not Chu and the stranger collapses. Chen finally understands that it is he himself who has collapsed. It turns out that both Chu and Liu were ghosts and that the courtesan on the barge had also died several days earlier. When Chen goes to look at his writing on the wall it is already fading. When Chu had switched identities with Chen to take the exam, Chu's soul had taken over Chen's body; only the disembodied soul of Chen was entertained during the Autumn festival and this soul wrote the lines of the ghost.

Also, in Krzysztof Kieślowski's film, *The Double Life of Véronique,* two identical girls, Veronika and Véronique are born on the same day in Poland and France. Both girls share a prodigious talent for music but while the Polish Veronika chooses to perform despite intimations of heart problems, Véronique decides to stop singing and teach music instead. The decision follows the death on stage of Veronika who dies of a heart attack, a death which Véronique intuits and to which she also could succumb as she too has heart problems. It would appear that the mishaps of Veronika somehow warn Véronique, just as in the story of a mysterious puppeteer which relates how, at the age of two, one girl had burnt her hand on a stove while the other, a few days later, instinctively withdrew her own. This idea of a shadow helper that is apparent in both these tales appeals to those interpreters who have looked to Jung, rather than Freud, as a mentor. Like Freud, Jung believed that there are aspects of the individual (and, Jung maintained, collective) psyche that are hidden from the conscious mind. These suppressed dimensions are revealed, at extreme moments, as frightening archetypes: sometimes a wise but fearful old man, an enigmatic anima or animus or, most fearful of all, the sinister dark shadow where the murderous potentialities of one's own psyche dwell. They become independent precisely because the conscious ego tries to deny them. The figure of the double embodies the dark, shadow side of the personality which must be recognised and integrated if one is to achieve one's full potential: "Good does not become better by being exaggerated, but worse, and a small evil becomes a big one through being disregarded and repressed. The shadow is very much a part of human nature, and it is only at night that no shadows exist."[13] Moreover he believed that the really creative thing in man always comes from the place where you least expect it, from the small thing, the shadow. Rank, too, in a later (posthumously published) essay, "The Double as Immortal Self", turned from the Freudian view of repressed sexual desire as a primal human instinct to the Jungian position where the desire for rebirth is the prime motivating factor. Modern man's misfortune, Rank lamented, was an inability to integrate ancient archetypes such as the Egyptian *ka* or the twin-tradition, manifest in religious and epic texts, into his psyche.

The limitation of a psychological paradigm for the *doppelgänger* motif lies in its reductionism. It ignores what it purports to explain: the flamboyant imagination prominent in dreams, psychotic illnesses or religious and literary texts. Symbols are multivalent. For example, whilst, as has been discussed, the lack of a shadow may indicate the presence of a spirit, it may also signify political persecution and dispossession. Thus, Paul Celan, victim of the Holocaust, writes of a Jew walking with his shadow, "his own and not his own – because the Jew, you know, what does he have that is really his own, that is not borrowed . . . how could he come with his own [shadow] when God had made him a Jew".[14] Or as another example, there is the multiplicity of themes arising just from the idea of a helpful double: a replica may help achieve academic merit, as in the tale of Chu, or mysteriously warn of danger, as in *Véronique*, or it may also enter a religious fable. In a famous thirteenth century Dutch poem, a nun, Beatrijs, forsakes her convent to live with her lover. After fourteen hard years, during which she is abandoned by her paramour and reduced to prostitution, she creeps back into the convent where she discovers that the Virgin Mary, acting as a surrogate nun, had dressed in her abandoned clothes and taken her place during her absence. A replica may also act as a sexual surrogate, whether to protect a virgin's purity or, in contradistinction to the legends of the Virgin Mary, for more licentious ends. This theme has inspired a book-length study, *The Bedtrick*, by Wendy Doniger.[15]

The double may be benign, fearful, or divine, it may be, as René Girard maintains,[16] the inner monster whom we cannot confront—the scapegoat—or it might be a comical narrative device; it can be ironic, a descent into psychosis or a hidden suppressed self that we need to keep alive. Playfully aware of all its attendant ambiguities, Angela Carter includes androgyny, dialectics, and parallel worlds in her short tale, "Reflections". The protagonist, a man who has been raped in the mirror world re-enters the glass: "Proud as a man, I once again advanced to meet my image in the mirror. Full of self-confidence, I held out my hands to embrace my self, my antiself, my self not-self, my assassin, my death, the world's death".[17] Carter is a writer who delights in paradox and ambiguity and she is also acutely aware of structuralism in linguistics and literary theory, of dialectics, and of the apparent contradictions within particle physics. In this story she skilfully intertwines these theories with literary references to androgynes, to doubles, and to the mirror which, by reflecting both sides, acts as the mediator and makes the impossible possible.

Yet, while usage and interpretation of the motif varies, there is one often recurring feature in this variety of *doppelgänger* narratives: a tension between the familiar and the strange. In his essay on the uncanny, Freud had noted the relationship between *Das Unheimliche*, the uncanny, and *Das Heimliche*, the homely, which is also the repository of the strange, the forbidden or repressed. It is an ambiguity which for Tzvetan Todorov defines the structure of fantastic literature: the uncanny or unreal takes place in the real world, a fact which underlines its unreality or impossibility.[18] The double blurs boundaries and distinctions; as Mary Douglas would say, it is an anomaly, out of place, in a liminal realm, and therefore dangerous and tabooed.[19] This makes it an ideal instrument for Gothic, surreal or post-modern literature which aim to deconstruct our perception of reality. Gothic literature represents a reaction against the rationality of the Enlightenment and revels in the breaking of taboos, as does surrealist writing, which is directly inspired by Freud, while post-modern literature endeavours to undermine the notions of author and narrative which define the self.

But it is also true that the human imagination is fascinated by the inconceivable. Rudolf Otto recognises this when he says that the "real attraction" of a ghostly apparition is "because it is a thing that 'doesn't really exist at all', the 'wholly other', something which has no place in our scheme of reality but belongs to an absolutely different one, and which at the same time arouses an irrepressible interest in the mind".[20] The double is like the ghost: a thing "that doesn't exist at all". While it is difficult to accept those analyses of Freud which relate to the double, dependent as they are on literary texts and tenuous case-notes, it is Freud's recognition of *homo ludens* which perhaps best explains the double:

> As people grow up . . . they cease to play and they seem to give up the yield of pleasure which they gained from playing. But whoever understands the human mind knows that hardly anything is harder for a man to give up than a pleasure which he has once experienced . . . instead of playing he now creates what are called 'day-dreams' . . . a piece of creative writing, like a day-dream, is a continuation of, and a substitution for, what was once the play of childhood.[21]

And just as the child has an imaginary playmate, the instigator of all its misdemeanours, the perpetrator of all its crimes, the one true friend, so the writer creates a *doppelgänger*, an instrument of subversion, a procurer of possibilities, an efficacious literary device. Narratives of the double may function as play but they are as serious in their concentration, as expansive in their themes and, sometimes, as deadly in their intent, as play.[22]

Notes and References

[1] The German term, *"doppelgänger"*, applied to people who see themselves, was introduced by Jean Paul Richter in 1796: Jean Paul Richter, "Siebenkäs" in *Werke* (München: Carl Hansen Verlag), 242.

[2] Lynn Holden, "Naming," in *Encyclopedia of Taboos* (Oxford, Santa Barbara: ABC-CLIO, 2000), 187-9.

[3] James G. Frazer, "The Soul as a Shadow and a Reflexion," in *The Golden Bough: Taboo and the Perils of the Soul,* (3rd ed.; London: Macmillan 1911-1915).

[4] Otto Rank, *The Double,* trans. Harry Tucker (New York: Meridian, 1971), 69-86.

[5] Sigmund Freud, "The Uncanny" in *Art and Literature*, trans. James Strachey (London: Penguin, 1990), 357.

[6] J.S. Grotstein, "Autoscopy: the experience of oneself as a double", *Hillside Journal of Clinical Psychiatry* 5, no. 2 (1983): 259-304. For information on individual case-studies related to Capgras syndrome, I am indebted to the forensic psychiatrist, Timucin Türker.

[7] I have referred to the English translations of foreign books and films.

[8] Freud, "The Uncanny", 348-358. The phrase "omnipotence of thoughts" appears in Freud, "Animism, Magic, Omnipotence of Thoughts" in *The Pelican Freud Library: 13. The Origins of Religion* (London: Penguin, 1985), 143.

[9] A few other notable examples are: Henry James' "The Jolly Corner", Heinrich Heine's poem "Silent is the Night", Osbert Sitwell's, "The Man Who Lost Himself", José Saramago's *The Double*, Joseph Conrad's "The Secret Sharer", Alain Robbe-Grillet's *Djinn* and Franz Werfel's *Mirror Man*.

[10] Hélène Cixous, "La fiction et ses fantômes: une lecture de l'*Unheimliche* de Freud" *Poétique* 10 (1973): 199-216. See also, Cixous, "The Character of 'Character'" trans. Keith Cohen *New Literary History*, 5, no. 2, (1974): 383-402. Also, readings of Freud in Cixous's *Prénoms de Personne* (Paris, Seuil, 1974).

[11] Jacques Lacan, "The mirror stage as formative of the I" in *Ecrits: A Selection*, trans. Alan Sheridan (London: Tavistock, 1977), 1-7.

[12] Julia Kristeva *La Révolution du langage poétique* (Paris: Seuil, 1974). Kristeva, *Desire in Language: A Semiotic Approach to Literature and Art*, ed. L. S. Roudiez, trans. T. Gora, et al. (Oxford: Blackwell, 1981), 83.

[13] C. G. Jung, "A Psychological Approach to the Dogma of the Trinity" in *Collected Writings* 11: Psychology and Religion: East and West (Princeton, New Jersey: Princeton University Press, 1970), 286.

[14] Paul Celan, *Collected Prose*, trans. Rosmarie Waldrop, (Manchester: Carcanet, 1986), 17-18.

[15] Wendy Doniger, *The Bedtrick: Tales of Sex and Masquerade* (Chicago and London: University of Chicago Press, 2000). See also Doniger's *Dreams, Illusions and Other Realities* (Chicago and London: University of Chicago Press, 1984), 98-103.

[16] Réne Girard, "From Mimetic Desire to the Monstrous Double," in *Violence and the Sacred*, trans. Patrick Gregory (Baltimore and London: John Hopkins University Press, 1977), 143-68.

[17] Angela Carter, "Reflections", in *Collected Short Stories (Fireworks)* (London: Vintage, 1996), 95.

[18] Tzvetan Todorov, *The Fantastic: A Structural Approach to a Literary Genre*, trans. Richard Howard (Cleveland and London: Press of Case Western Reserve University, 1973), 107-175. Todorov applies the paradox to writing itself and says that "Literature can become possible only insofar as it makes itself impossible", 175.

[19] Mary Douglas, *Purity and Danger: An Analysis of the Concepts of Pollution and Taboo* (London, Boston, Melbourne and Henley: Ark-Routledge and Kegan Paul, 1984), 38-40. Also relevant is my *Encyclopedia of Taboos* (Oxford, Santa Barbara, Denver: ABC-CLIO, 2000).

[20] Rudolf Otto, *The Idea of the Holy,* trans. John W. Harvey (London, Oxford, New York: Oxford University Press, 1979), 28.

[21] J. Huizinga, *Homo Ludens* (Groningen: Tjeenk Willink, 1974). Sigmund Freud, "Creative Writers and Daydreaming" in *Penguin Freud Library 14. Art and Literature* (London: Penguin, 1990) 133, 139.

[22] Other studies pertinent to the theme of the double include: Mark Pendergrast, *Mirror Mirror* (New York: Basic Books, 2004), 1-27; Andrew J. Webber, *The Doppelgänger* (Oxford: Clarendon Press, 1996); Carl Francis Keppler, *The Literature of the Second Self* (Tucson, Arizona: The University of Arizona Press, 1972); Victor I. Stoichita, *A Short History of the Shadow* (London: Reaktion Books, 1997), 123-152; Christof Forderer, *Ich-Eklipsen: Doppelgänger in der Literatur seit 1800* (Stuttgart: J.B. Metzler, 1999); Albert

J. Guerard, "Concepts of The Double" in *Stories of the Double*, ed. Guerard (Philadelphia and New York: J.B. Lippincott Company, 1967) 1-14; Hillel Schwartz, *The Culture of the Copy* (New York: Zone Books, 1996), 49-87; Marina Warner, *Fantastic Metamorphoses, Other Worlds* (Oxford: Oxford University Press, 2002), 161-203; Patrick McNamara, "Memory, Double, Shadow, and Evil" *Journal of Analytical Psychology* 39, no. 2 (1994): 233-251; Milica Živković "The Double as the 'Unseen' of Culture: Toward a Definition of Doppelgänger", *Facta Universitatis - Linguistics and Literature* 7, no. 2 (2000): 121-128; Robert Rogers, *The Double in Literature. A Psychoanalytic Study* (Detroit: Wayne State University Press, 1970).

PART IV:

MIRRORS OF ART

CHAPTER TEN

MIRRORS IN ART: IMAGES AS MIRRORS

BETH WILLIAMSON

In an essay on the subject of "Mirrors in Art" you would be disappointed if I did not discuss Velázquez's *Las Meninas* (Figure 12.3), or Van Eyck's portrait of Giovanni Arnolfini and his wife (Figure 12.2), or indeed Manet's *Bar at the Folies-Bergère* (Figure 12.4). And indeed, these images will be discussed. But I will say straight away that my interest in images that show mirrors is part of a wider interest in how pictures discuss visually the act of looking, and the effects of looking and seeing.

In my research on the religious culture of the middle ages I am interested in the phenomena of visibility and invisibility; the ways in which things were seen, or envisaged; and the ways, in painting, of representing visibility, invisibility, and revelation. I am concerned with how people thought about seeing, and how meaning was constructed in visual representation. Images which represent mirrors are therefore obviously of interest to me, as they represent and discuss explicitly the act of looking. Viewers of these images know what mirrors are, what they do, and in what ways they do it. Mirrors both reflect and construct what is seen, and mirrors within images can construct a viewer who has a particular physical and spatial relationship with the spectacle within the image. This viewer can be a particular individual or group, or a variety of less specific viewers. Spectators looking at images that contain mirrors thus pick up cues to think consciously about seeing, and about what they see and how they see it, and about the significance of what they see.

Many instances exist that demonstrate a concern with ways of seeing, and with controlling the way a spectator views a given image. Such a concern has long been recognised in the painted cycle of the Life of St Francis in the Upper Church of San Francesco in Assisi.[1] Here the scenes appear in groups of three, separated by fictive stone columns painted on the flat walls, and with illusionistic dental stonework framing the scenes.[2] The way in which the decorative stonework recedes requires that a viewer stand squarely in front of the central image of each set of three, in order to make sense of the perspectival construction. This pictorial means of controlling the viewer, by dictating the physical position that he or she will adopt on looking at the picture, constructs the scene observed by the viewer as it were through a window, on which the observer gazes, but with which he or she is not in any kind of physical contact. Images with mirrors, on the other hand, make a particular kind of address to the viewer that links the viewer with the image, in a continuum of real and depicted space. Such an involvement or implication of the viewer in the image is explicit when mirrors are depicted. However, a concern with this sort of relationship between spectator and spectacle can also be discerned in images that do not represent mirrors. Even without the explicit cue of a depicted mirror to provide a cue towards thinking about looking, some such images can nevertheless be understood as engaged with the concepts of looking and seeing, with the effects and significance of viewing, and with the embodied viewer's physical relationship with the picture, and with the scene depicted within it. These images construct an observer in a particular way without showing mirrors within the image. It is the image itself that reflects and constructs the observer. I will discuss some of this latter sort of image in the second part of this essay. But first, to some of those well-known images that depict mirrors.

The painting by Velázquez known as *Las Meninas*, "the ladies-in-waiting", (Figure 12.3), is now in the Museo del Prado in Madrid, but was designed for display in the *pieza del despacho*, a private apartment of Philip IV of Spain.[3]   It was apparently finished in 1656 when Philip's daughter, the Infanta Margarita (who stands more or less in the centre of the foreground) was five years old. The ladies in waiting were mentioned in the first written record of this work, an inventory of 1666, in which the painter Juan Bautista Martínez del Mazo, recorded the royal collection of paintings. Mazo, Velázquez's son-in-law, described a large painting "portraying" the Infanta Margarita with "her ladies-in-waiting and a female dwarf, by the hand of Velázquez."[4] However, later documents describe the painting as representing *La familia de Felipe IV* and it was only in the nineteenth century that the painting was referred to in print as *Las Meninas*.

But this painting clearly represents much more than the ladies-in-waiting, the princess, the dwarf, or the family and close courtiers of Philip IV. Most obviously, in pictorial terms, it represents Velázquez painting. This fact was noted by the Portuguese Felix da Costa, in a treatise on painting, who declared that the painting seemed "much more like a portrait of Velázquez than of the Empress."[5] In addition to representing the painter in the act of painting, the picture also represents the King and Queen, not as part of the group in the foreground of the painting, but in the mirror on the back wall of the depicted space. Although it hangs among framed paintings, this is definitely a mirror, not a painting, and is confirmed as being such by its luminous surface. This much is well-known, but there is considerable disagreement about how this painting should be interpreted, and the mirror and what it depicts has often been at the centre of the disagreement.

Michel Foucault produced an influential reading of this painting, in which he suggested that the mirror reflects that at which all the figures in the painting are looking, that which "the spectator would be able to see if the painting extended further forward, if its bottom edge were brought lower until it included the figures the painter is using as models."[6] The models are, self-evidently, the King and Queen, who must be imagined as standing in a space outwith the depicted space within the picture, and it must be they whom the painter is depicting. Foucault declares that the spectator can recognise this, and imagine the King and Queen within that non-depicted space because it is the space within which he, the observer (and the observer in this reading is definitively "he") is himself standing. This produces the effect in which Foucault is most interested, a three-way dialogue of gazes: "the exact superimposition of the model's gaze as it is being painted, of the spectator's as he contemplates the painting, and of the painter's as he is composing his picture (not the one represented, but the one in front of us which we are discussing)".[7] This apparent ambiguity has fascinated many commentators on the picture, who have discussed the shifting and paradoxical nature of what it is that we see here. Foucault goes on to say that the spectator recognises this the tripartite nature of this dialogue or overlay of gazes, and recognises at the same time that he, the spectator, has, in the act of viewing the picture, taken the place of the royal couple, the real subjects of the painting, as though by usurpation. This usurpation excites Foucault, and leading on from this observation he discusses the way in which man thus emerges (and again, it is man) as a knowing subject, a person whose presence validates the royal couple on account of the fact that their majesty would not exist, would not be effective, were it not for the observer's viewing of that majesty.[8]

This is a perfectly reasonable reading of a possible reception of the painting, in viewing conditions in which an observer of the sort Foucault is imagining—someone he calls "the passer-by"—might stand in front of this picture and consider its implications. But it probably does not describe the type of viewing which was envisaged by its creator. The development of reception theory, and its application to the consideration of meaning in art, has encouraged a welcome consideration of the construction of meaning by later observers. However, applications of reception theory sometimes neglect to consider the first generation of reception, that is the construction of meaning by a given object's first owners or observers. And while the insights of reception theory have made it clear that there is not a single or unified meaning in any artefact, and that it is not always possible to enquire into the intentions of its maker, it must not be forgotten that in an image like this, the origins and provenance of which are well known, it can be fruitful to investigate the ways in which the artist might have considered the painting's early reception. (This does not mean that the wider and longer history of the reception of *Las Meninas* after that of its first owners is not an important *part* of the whole significance of the painting, just that this later reception is not *all* that can be discerned about the painting's meaning).

The painting, created within the Royal Palace at Madrid, and presumably designed to hang in the private royal apartment in which it was noted in the 1666 inventory, would have had few casual passers-by. The usual viewers would in fact have been the royal couple themselves, who would see themselves reflected in the mirror. This presumably would have made them aware that *they* are the subjects of Velázquez's picture. In viewing this picture (which is of course the picture which Velázquez depicts himself painting) they must realise the power of Velázquez's skills of representation.[9] For they see that they are made manifest by Velázquez's painting, not in the normal way, within a portrait, upon which they look, as though at a mirror, but as real beings standing in front of this painting. The cleverness of Velázquez's composition brings the Royal couple into being, as it were, in front of this painting, the mirror being the clue and the hook which makes this obvious. In other words, they do not appear as real beings within the painted space, only as reflections in a mirror, but they are nevertheless the painting's real subject, not the Infanta, and not the ladies-in-waiting. The reflections in the mirror make it clear that Velázquez's art does not rival nature by providing a portrait that is a painted substitute for the Royal couple: it actually brings nature itself into being, by constructing their appearance for real, in front of the picture. The picture, and the specific viewers for whom it was intended (and only those viewers), become part of an installation, as it were, conceived by Velázquez. One might say that the depiction really comes to life only when animated by the presence of the King and Queen.

All this should be obvious, but it is not always acknowledged. This is partly because some analyses of the painting's reception disregard this early stage of the painting's existence, in which it was designed to create a privileged, intimate encounter for specific individuals.[10] Perhaps a few select individuals might have seen the painting in the royal apartments, but in such an environment it is unlikely that very many of them would have rationalised their encounter with the painting in the way Foucault attributes to his usurping spectator. Viewing the painting in more public surroundings, in, for example a gallery in the Prado, can allow for the reading Foucault proposes, but such a reading was presumably not intended when the painting was created.

That this is not often enough realised is partly to do with the fact that the academic or critical encounter with this painting is conditioned by our understanding of the reception of other representations, such as Manet's *Bar at the Folies-Bergère* (Figure 12.4). In this painting a mirror occupies virtually the whole background of the picture space. In contradistinction to Velázquez's painting, the viewing subject's position in front of Manet's *Bar* was intended to be taken up by unknown, multiple and anonymous spectators at the Paris salon in the 1880s. And so here, the possible relationships between the viewer and the reflection that are suggested, but not conclusively resolved, by the painting, depend to a large extent upon the shifting identity of the spectator. Much has been said about this painting,[11] and there is much to say, but for our purposes what needs to be recognised is the completely different character of the paradoxes presented by Manet and those apparently presented by Velázquez. Manet's viewer needs to ask—among other things—"who is that reflected in the mirror? Is it my own encounter with this woman that is reflected here, despite the fact that the reflection of the woman is not the reflection of the woman as I am seeing her?" But the paradoxes often attributed to Velázquez's painting ("How can I, the spectator, be viewing this painting when it is clear that the position I occupy should be being occupied by the king and queen?") largely disappear when it is understood that the spectator in Velázquez's painting *is*—or was meant to be—the royal couple. The current gallery setting of what people will, one supposes, continue to call *Las Meninas*, makes that understanding less immediate.

The double portrait of Giovanni Arnolfini and his wife, painted by Jan van Eyck in 1434 (Figure 12.1) is now in the National Gallery in London, but it was in the Spanish royal collection in the palace at Madrid at precisely the time when Velázquez was painting his depiction, or evocation, of Philip IV and Mariana.[12] It has been suggested that Velázquez may have had this painting in mind when he created his own picture.[13] However, what these two paintings do, and the role that the mirrors play within them is rather different. To begin with, the owners of this painting, its principal projected viewers, are depicted within the picture space. In the space between the two figures, on the back wall, can be seen a round mirror, in a wooden frame that incorporates 10 roundels with religious scenes. Two figures can be seen reflected in the mirror, standing at what seems to be the threshold of the room. It is normally assumed that the figure to the fore in the mirror, and therefore the one entering the room first is the artist, Jan van Eyck. This suggestion seems to be supported by the inscription on the wall beneath the mirror, "Jan van Eyck fuit hic", meaning (probably) Jan van Eyck has been here.[14]

But who are the figures depicted in the foreground, within the picture space proper? They used to be thought to be Giovanni di Arrigo Arnolfini and his wife Jeanne Cenami.[15] This Giovanni Arnolfini was the most prominent of the five members of an important Lucchese family resident in Bruges in the fifteenth century. For a long time this painting was thought to represent this couple's marriage ceremony, and that by depicting himself present in the room, as well as adding his signature, van Eyck had endowed this picture with the status of a marriage certificate. The theory that this image represents a marriage was propagated through an article by Panofsky in the 1930s which, although erudite and influential, was based upon several errors and misunderstandings. It is not any longer thought that the picture represents a wedding, but it is still, nevertheless, often known as *The Arnolfini Wedding*. Not only that, but it is now no longer thought that this represents Giovanni di Arrigo Arnolfini at all. He only married in 1447, thirteen years after this painting is dated and six years after Jan van Eyck's death, and therefore would almost certainly not have commissioned such a double portrait in the early 1430s. Lorne Campbell has suggested convincingly that the man is a different member of the same family, called Giovanni di Nicolao Arnolfini.[16] His wife was Costanza Trenta, and they had been betrothed in 1426, when Costanza was thirteen. She would have been 21 when the painting was executed, had she not died in 1433, a year before the date inscribed upon the painting. So what exactly is represented here?

Recently it has been suggested that this is, indeed, a painting of Giovanni di Nicolao Arnolfini and Costanza Trenta, but that Van Eyck's picture is a posthumous representation of Costanza.[17] This compelling, if unconfirmed, suggestion makes the best possible use of the evidence we have to date for the possible identities of the figures. So what is the implication of the mirror image in this painting? The person who is presumed to be the patron, Giovanni Arnolfini, is present in the picture, in the conventional manner, and so the image in the mirror is not needed to complete the picture. As I indicated earlier, it used to be suggested that the image of the artist (if we assume that the mirror image does indeed show van Eyck) served to show him as a witness to the marriage ceremony depicted. But since it is now not normally accepted that this image represents a marriage ceremony, or that the painting served as something like a visual marriage contract, this theory requires modification.

Perhaps the patron simply wanted the identity of the artist documented? But evidently the image in the mirror does not identify van Eyck by showing a recognisable image of him. The inscription would have been enough, under normal circumstances, to document authorship, and it is the presence of the signature itself that seems to suggest that the man in the mirror (or one of the men in the mirror) might be van Eyck. It seems that in this painting it was important to document the actual presence of the artist in this room here depicted, albeit a temporary presence and one that is conceived as being in the past. Whereas the presence of the Spanish king and queen in front of *Las Meninas* seemed to complete the painting, in the present, as they looked at it, the suggested presence of the artist in *The Arnolfini Portrait*'s mirror is a document that the artist was once present, but is no longer. Perhaps this was because the painting that we see does not actually represent a real scene, that was ever viewed by the artist exactly as it appears here. If the painting was produced in 1434, as a posthumous memorial to Costanza Arnolfini, as has been suggested, the couple might not have sat for this portrait in the normal way. Van Eyck might have been painting the portrait of Costanza from other representations, or from memory. Inscribed within the painting, however, both visually and textually, is a statement that the artist was once here, in other words that he really did see what he re-presents to the viewer. The mirror image and the inscription together evoke the past presence of the artist and attest that he was once actually present in the depicted room, and really saw the woman he has painted here, even if it was clear to Arnolfini, and to others viewing the painting, that its conditions of production meant that it could not be strictly regarded as painted from life.

In fact, although this image might seem to be concerned with portraying reality, and although it is often said that Netherlandish art of the fifteenth century was simply or principally concerned with realism, here, as with much of van Eyck's most skilful painting, it is the boundary, indeed the gap, between real and unreal, between representable reality and imaginable fantasy, that most interests the artist. He evokes his own presence in the room, in the place where the observer must be standing. If he were imagined as standing behind the observer, then the mirror would reveal this. If he were imagined standing in front of an imagined observer, the mirror would show this too. So he must be suggesting that he (once) occupied a viewing position at the threshold of this room, of this painting, in a similar way as does the later viewer. This problem cannot be resolved in the same way as in Velázquez's painting, by suggesting that the expected and "proper" viewer is identical with the person represented in the mirror, for it is obvious that the artist is not the intended regular viewer. The expected spectator must be, at least initially, Giovanni Arnolfini himself.

The artist is not to be imagined as perpetually in the presence of the patron. If the patron *did* want to represent himself in the company of the artist he could have requested this be done but he presumably wished to gaze mainly upon the joint image of himself and his wife. The artist uses the mirror here to represent not his real, continuing, or even his repeated presence in front of the object, but to represent his un-presence. He suggests that once he was there, but is no longer. The picture is his own one-off view of the scene. It states visually that what the artist saw *was* real, but is now only available through his art. This is speculative, of course, but such an interpretation would be appropriate if this were, indeed, a posthumous memorial to Costanza Arnolfini.[18] As well as representing an image of Costanza to Giovanni Arnolfini's continuing gaze, *The Arnolfini Portrait* also represents Arnolfini to himself. The painting is, in itself, a mirror. When considering the ways in which images construct meaning, we are now trained to think of what E.H. Gombrich called "the beholder's share", in other words, the collection of perceptual and psychic acts by through which the spectator brings an image into existence by perceiving and understanding it.[19] Because the act of viewing an image is not neutral, and always differs according to each spectator's knowledge of the world and of other images, we are now no longer inclined to talk of "the" observer, and the way in which "the observer" might interpret an image, but to ask "which observer?" And yet, although we do this habitually, we all-too-often forget that for a certain category of images there was an observer, or a small group of observers, whose viewing of the image was privileged in a very particular way, by their own appearance within the image.

So, for example, interpretations of a well-known image such as van Eyck's *Madonna with Chancellor Rolin*, in the Louvre, often pay surprisingly little attention to the obvious fact that the viewer for whom this painting was created was seeing not just an image of the Virgin, or a man kneeling in front of the Virgin, but an image of himself in front of the Virgin. Many questions are asked about the physical location of the painting and where it was viewed: Was it placed on an altar? Was it hung on a wall near an altar? Did it have any physical relationship with an altar at all? Was it viewed in a chapel space or a domestic space? And so on. But less often is it asked what was the nature of the connection between the real, embodied viewer outside the painting, and the depicted viewer within the painting. How did Rolin look on the image? Did he focus on the Virgin, or on himself, or on either figure, or on both at different stages of his devotions? What did he see when he looked at this representation of himself? One presumes that this image was designed to mirror Rolin back to himself not just in a reflective manner but in a constructive manner also, in the same way that textual mirrors, such as the *Mirror of Human Salvation*,[20] were supposed to offer a constructive image of what the reading subject should be or should become. This aspect of images as mirrors is the one I wish to discuss next by looking at one particular pair of images which reflect the privileged observer, the owner of the images, in a way that plays interestingly with the spectator's physical relationship with the image as representation and as object.

The Hours of Mary of Burgundy is a personal manuscript, a Book of Hours made for Mary of Burgundy, the daughter of Charles the Bold, probably in the late 1470s. It contains the normal texts for the recitation of the Hours of the Virgin together with several full-page and small miniatures. In the full-page miniature on folio 14 verso (Figure 10.1), we see a woman sitting at a casement window which seems to look into the choir of a Gothic church in which can be seen the Virgin and Child attended by four angels, by an acolyte swinging a censer, and by a group of women in contemporary fifteenth-century attire. We

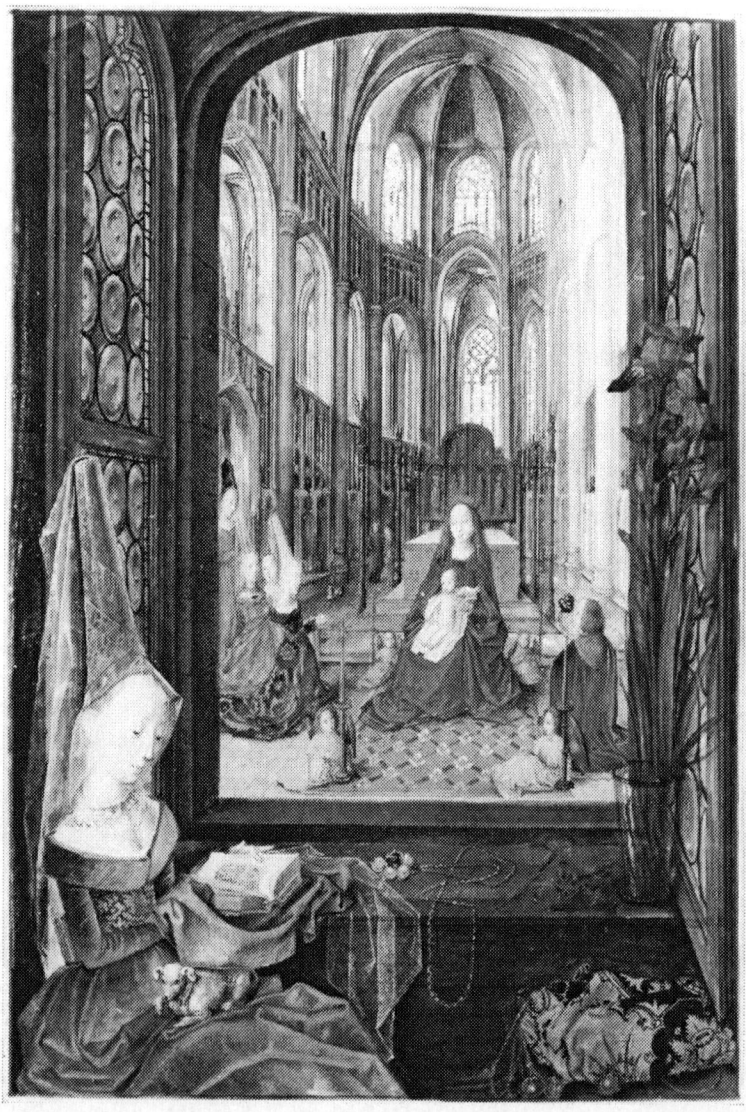

Figure 10.1. *Mary of Burgundy at Prayer*, Hours of Mary of Burgundy, late 1470s. Vienna, Österreichische Nationalbibliothek, Cod. 1857, f. 14v. Photo: Austrian National Library, picture archives.

assume that the seated woman is Mary, the owner of the book.[21] She holds a prayerbook in her hands, and is absorbed in the activity of reading. The text on the page she reads cannot be deciphered, but the large initial "O" could suggest that it is meant to be the "Obsecro te" ["I beseech thee"], a common prayer found in many books of hours. In opening this book of hours to this page the owner of the book will see in the book, herself reading a book, perhaps this very book. The prayerful concentration of the woman in the image presents a model, a mirror if you will, for Mary's own prayer and devotion. The scene through the window is not observed by the reading woman, but we are perhaps to think of this as what she sees in her mind's eye as she reads. As the real Mary proceeds to read the text opposite the depicted Mary she can keep in her mind the image of the Virgin that has just been presented to her as a suitable subject for her prayer and meditation.[22]

Later in the book, on folio 43 verso (Figure. 10.2), another window appears. It is certainly not the same window, nor the same room, and different objects appear on the sill and beside the window's frames. But the book, presumably the same book, is there, held open by a fold of its green chemise binding. But the reading woman is no longer visible. It is sometimes said, in discussions of this image, that the owner of the book, who was present in the miniature on folio 14 verso, is now absent.[23] It is true that she is not depicted in the miniature,[24] but although she is absent visually from the area in front of the window, she is *conceptually* present. The change in the orientation of the book tells us that the reader must be now facing straight on to the scene observed through the window, instead of sitting at 90 degrees to the window, as the depicted reader did in the earlier image. This development has often been commented upon as a device for increasing the spectator's identification with, or participation in, the picture. However, it is often forgotten that—as with *Las Meninas*, and *The Arnolfini Portrait*—this book of hours was designed with one particular viewer in mind. So while the compositional relationship between folio 43 verso and folio 14 verso tells *us* that the reader *we* see in Figure 10.1 has become conflated in Figure 10.2 with the real reader outside the book, this play between the two images is not, of course, designed to tell *us*, as later critical readers and observers, anything at all. The projected viewer is Mary of Burgundy, and that is the only way in which the relationship between these two images can work properly: the depicted woman within the book at folio 14 verso, and the real woman outside the book, at folio 43 verso, have become one and the same. In other words, during the course of Mary's prayer, as she has read through the book, she has moved to a higher stage of devotion. She no longer requires a pictorial model for the way she should conduct herself, but has moved closer to the object of her devotions, in this case Christ, nailed to the Cross.

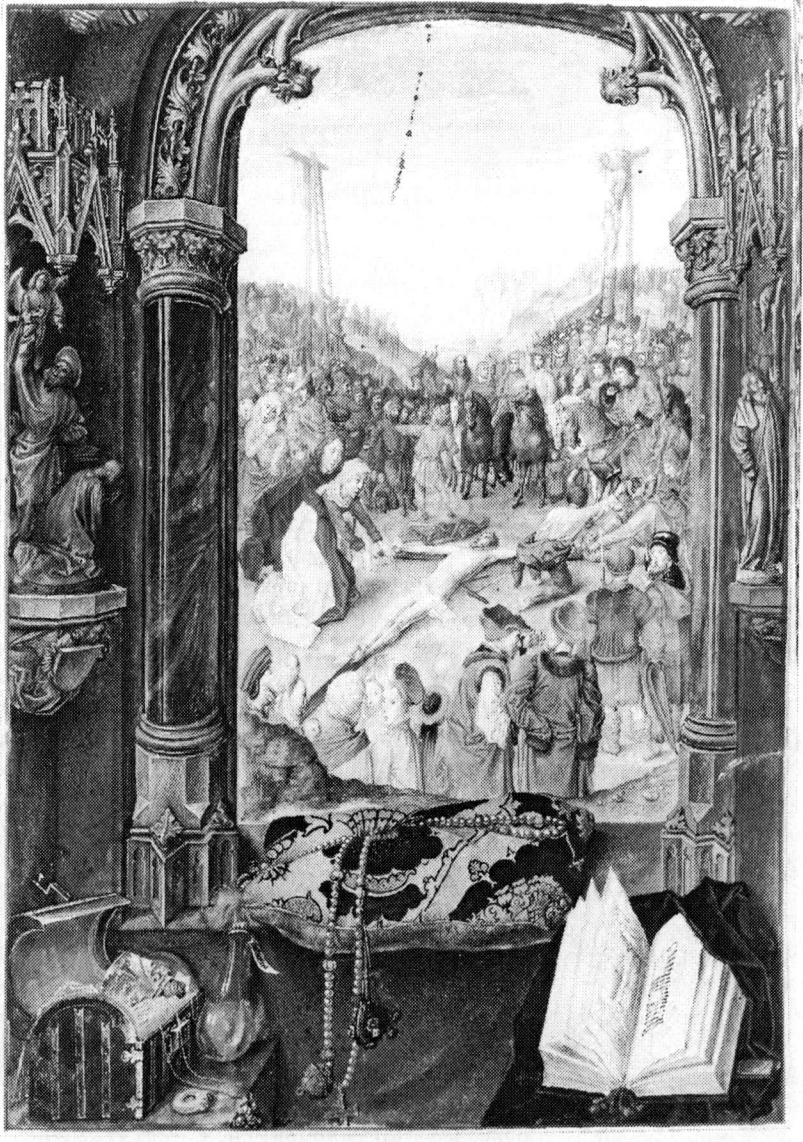

Figure 10.2. *Christ Nailed to the Cross*, Hours of Mary of Burgundy, late 1470s. Vienna, Österreichische Nationalbibliothek, Cod. 1857, f. 43v.   Photo: Austrian National Library, picture archives.

The use of images in prayer was sanctioned and encouraged where it would help a devotee to focus his or her mind, but was regarded as a lower form of devotion than image-less devotion. In this higher state, to be aspired to, a devotee could attain the right frame of mind, and create images in his or her mind, without the intervention of visual aids. The idea would be that after this stage of devotion, where the image in her book has constructed her as closer to the object of her devotions, Mary should move to the highest form of devotion, where she will no longer need any painted images at all. This stage of devotion will not be depicted in the book of hours, of course, for she will have shut the book, and will thus be able to access a higher plane of devotion than that available in the realm of painted images. This Crucifixion image constructs its meaning in relation to the earlier image of Mary reading. It depends upon an understanding of that earlier image, and works with the conventions used by that earlier image in order to create its own particular meaning. In that sense it reflects the earlier image, and depends upon it, but also develops from it.

The Crucifixion image indicates that the viewer is close to the book, and its power to enhance the viewer's involvement with the scene depicted depends upon a direct physical relationship between the viewer and the image. The viewer's visual "training", effected by having seen the earlier image, enables her to understand how she is meant to relate to the later image. Such a sequential relationship is easily manageable within a book. In other forms of depiction other strategies have to be used in order to achieve this kind of identification with the image. This can be achieved by a change of orientation of a key figure within a well-known composition, so that the artist relies upon the viewer knowing how a given scene "should" operate. For example, in viewing pictorial representations of the Annunciation spectators are used to seeing the angel approaching the Virgin, usually from the left, within an interior, or a loggia.[25] Different moments of the encounter between the Virgin and the angel are focussed upon in different images.[26] Antonello da Messina uses the viewer's extreme familiarity with the way in which the Annunciation is usually depicted, and literally turns it around. His painting of the Annunciate Virgin of about 1475 (Figure 10.3) shows the Virgin close up to the picture plane, facing out to the viewer. She has just lifted her eyes from her book, and her hand appears to be lifted in a prelude to speech. As the viewer of this panel analyses those elements of the image that make it familiar—the appearance and demeanour of the Virgin, her blue dress, her book—it becomes clear that the angel is missing, and that the viewer must be in the space usually occupied by the angel in relation to the Virgin. The viewer thus is enabled to identify with the Angel, and become part of the dialogue that effected the Incarnation of Christ.

The visual strategy employed here might be likened to the cinematic concept described in film theory as "suture". This is a means by which the viewing

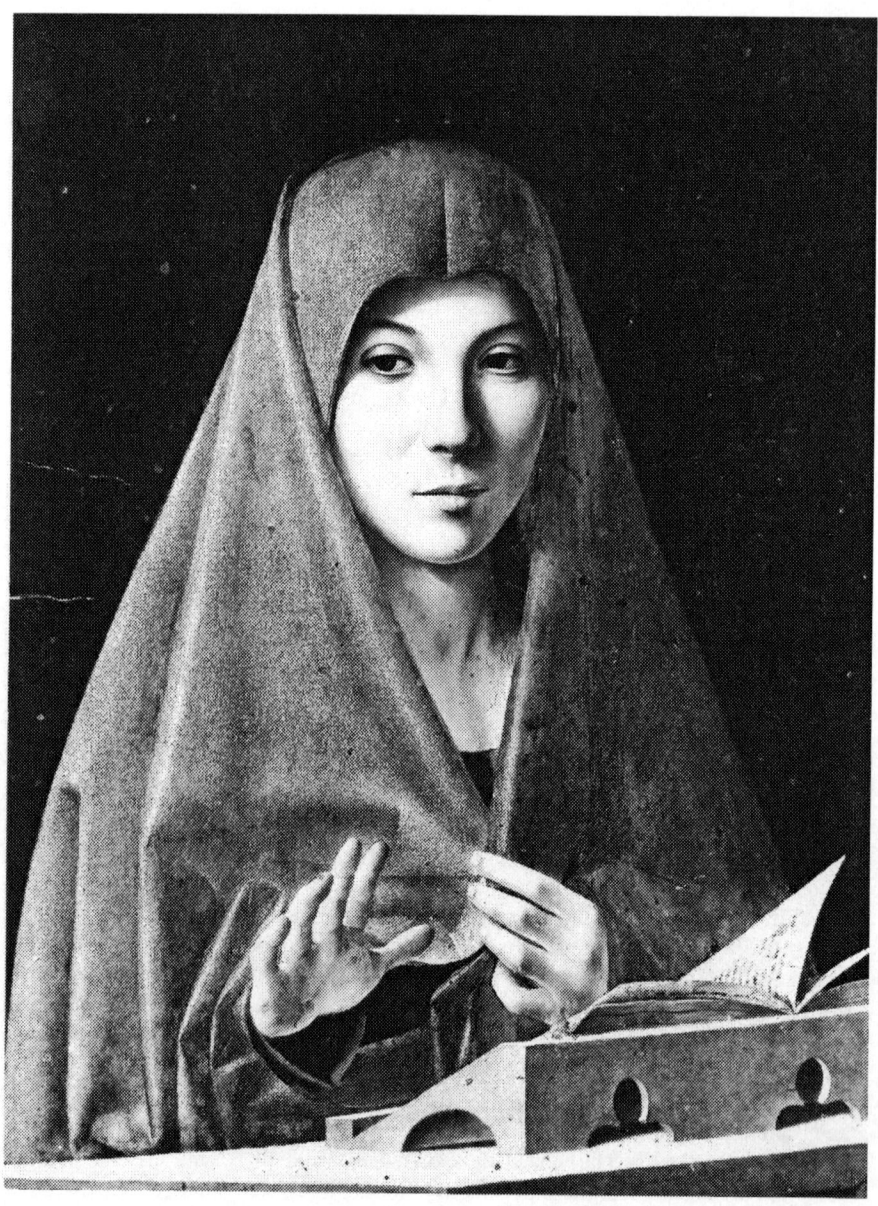

Figure 10.3. *Virgin Annunciate*, Antonello da Messina, c. 1475. Palermo, Galleria Regionale della Sicilia, Palazzo Abatellis

subject is positioned by the film: the viewer takes up a position as the subject addressed by the film, usually in dialogue with one of the characters. This is often set up for the viewer by prior sideways shots of characters in dialogue, after which the point of view shifts and the dialogue appears to take place between one of the characters and the viewer of the film. (Thus the viewer identifies with the character whose position he or she adopts). Continuity editing renders the construction of the film invisible, so that our experience of it is one of "seamlessness", thereby "stitching" the viewer into the narrative, hence the term "suture". The shift from the image of two characters in dialogue (a "two-shot") to a direct close-up shot of a single character is exactly what Antonello da Messina is doing: providing a privileged view of the Annunciate Virgin at precisely the moment that she agrees to become the mother of God, in other words at the precise moment of the beginning of human salvation.

Another example of this type of construction was produced by Leonardo da Vinci, in a now-lost painting of the Angel of the Annunciation.[27] In this composition the viewer adopts the viewpoint of the Virgin, rather than the Angel. In these two images, the viewer implied by the image is specific. The nature of the specificity is different from that of the projected viewer for the Hours of Mary of Burgundy, however. The viewer of the Mary's Hours had to be Mary, because she owned the book, and therefore the viewer implied by the images within the book was identical with the viewer of the book itself. The specificity of the implied viewers of Leonardo's *Angel* and Antonello's *Virgin* is dictated by the narrative within which these images are embedded. Therefore, in order to enjoy a participatory relationship with these paintings, the viewer must identify completely with the Angel or with the Virgin Mary.[28] There is little logical option for the viewer to do anything else in relation to Leonardo's *Angel*.[29] However, the viewer is not compelled to identify in this way with Antonello's Virgin. As John Shearman points out, "the viewer may not recognise his implied role or may choose to read his situation as external to that of the action and to think of himself as no part of the narrative, as its witness rather than as participant."[30] The unique and particular identities of the incorporeal Angel of the Annunciation and the Virgin Mother of God might possibly have made a total participatory identification with these images difficult for some viewers. My final example involves a similar reliance on a viewer's visual literacy, and, by his or her understanding of the narrative being presented, requires the viewer to witness to a fundamentally important religious event. However, rather than requiring him or her to identify with such a holy figure as the Angel Gabriel or the Virgin Mary, it allows the viewer to perform this role of witness in his or her own right.

The scenes depicting the life of St Francis in the Upper Church at Assisi represent the Franciscan Order's "official" version of the saint's life. This

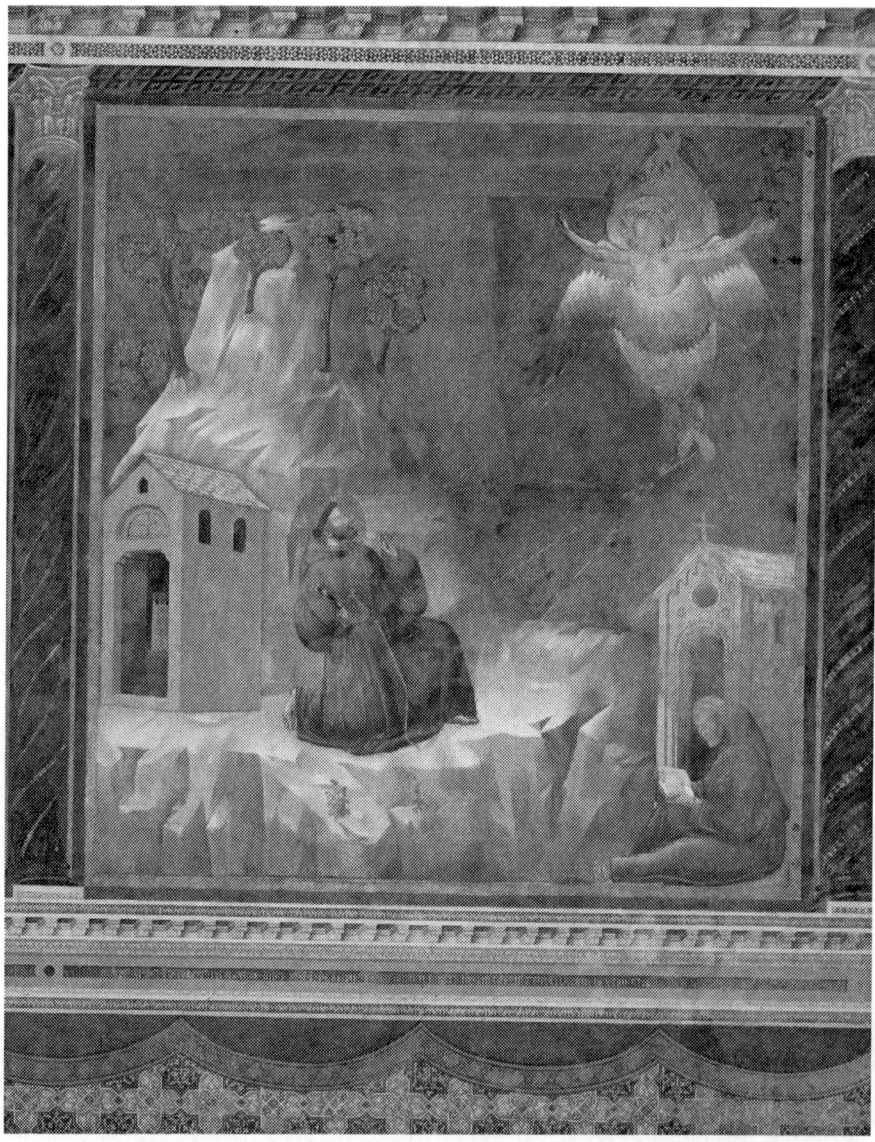

Figure 10.4. *Stigmatisation of St Francis*, Master of the St Francis Legend, 1290s. Assisi, S. Francesco, Lower Church. Photo © Alinari Archives-Florence

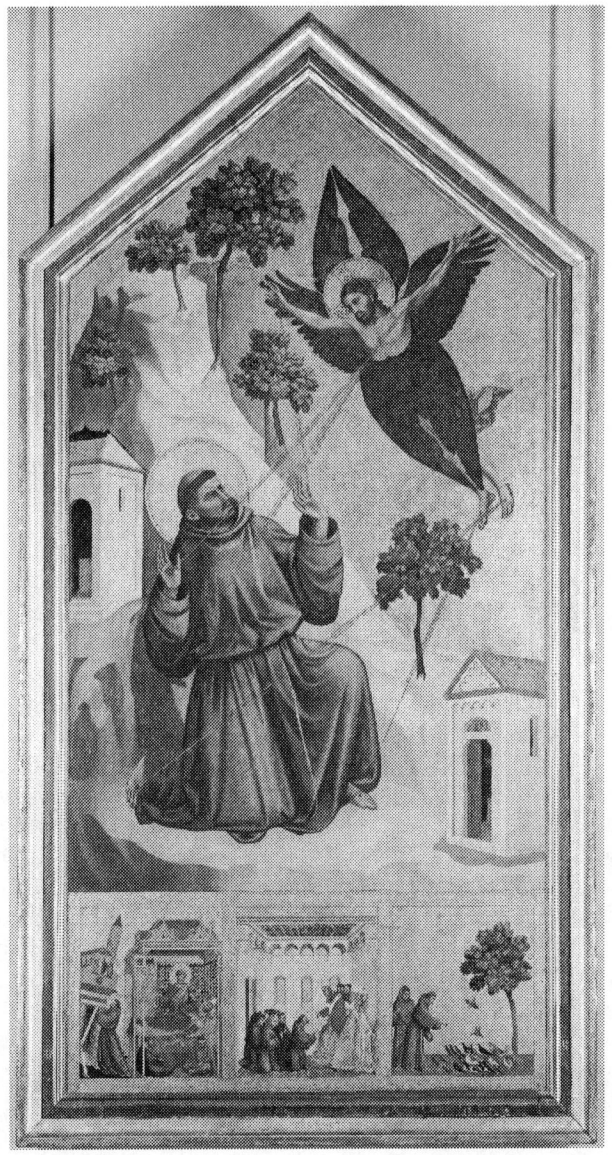

Figure 10.5. *St Francis Stigmatised*, Giotto, c. 1300-1310. Paris, Louvre
(formerly Pisa, S. Francesco)   © Photo RMN/© Jean-Gilles Berizzi.

painted cycle follows closely the "Legenda Maior", the "Life of St Francis" written in 1260 by St Bonaventure, the Minister General of the Order.[31] The nineteenth image in the cycle, that of the Stigmatisation (Figure 10.4) represents the moment of the miraculous imprinting of Christ's wounds on the body of St Francis. This image follows Bonaventure's text fairly closely. Christ appears in the form of a seraph, and each wound imprints itself upon the body of St Francis by means of golden rays from the appropriate area of the body of Christ.[32] His companion, not named in Bonaventure's text, but commonly understood to be one of Francis's closest companions, Brother Leo, is shown in the act of opening the Gospel book. In the text, just before the miracle of the Stigmatisation is recounted, Francis instructs his companion to open the book three times, and each time the book opens at Christ's passion. Soon after this, the Christ-seraph appears to him, and the Stigmatisation occurs.[33] Leo's witnessing of the event of the Stigmatisation became important in proving the veracity of the event for, as the texts make clear, St Francis was unwilling to show his wounds to anyone or to explain what had happened during his experience on La Verna. After Francis's death Leo's account was the only one which could explain the significance of the wounds found on St Francis's body.

A version of the theme on panel, now in the Louvre in Paris, but once in the Franciscan church at Pisa, is signed by Giotto and is usually dated to the first decade of the fourteenth century (Figure 10.5). It clearly depends on the Assisi cycle in many respects, both in the main scene of *St Francis Stigmatised*, and in the subsidiary scenes of *The Dream of Innocent III*, *The Confirmation of the Rule*, and *The Preaching to the Birds*. But in the Louvre Stigmatisation Leo is not present. The question raised about the absence of the witness is soon resolved in an informed viewer's mind, that is by one who is familiar with the status of Brother Leo. The viewer must reach the awareness that the truth of this miracle is no longer to be mediated through the figure of Leo, but that the spectator himself or herself must now bear witness to the truth. The viewer is drawn into a physical relationship with the image and with its significance. This relationship works by the reader becoming aware of an absent element within the image, which would be expected, and which in other versions of the image serves to make sense of the episode.

This painting has no mirror to reflect the spectator and to show where the spectator must stand or kneel; it does not even show an image of the projected spectator within the image, which would provide a mirror and a model for his or her required position and demeanour. Nevertheless, within itself, by working with reference to other images, and with the expected visual literacy of the spectator, it constructs the spectator's relationship with the painting and controls not just what the spectator should see, but how it must be seen, and what significance must be discerned through that act of looking.

Notes and References

[1] This cycle is sometimes attributed to Giotto, sometimes to "school of Giotto", and sometimes, more neutrally, to "The Master of the Legend of St Francis". It is usually dated in the 1290s, although opinions on the dating differ also.

[2] Elvio Lunghi, *The Basilica of St Francis at Assisi* (London: Thames and Hudson, 1996), illustration on 63.

[3] The literature on Velázquez, and on this painting, is vast. Some recent contributions include: Jonathan Brown and Carmen Garrido, *Velázquez: the technique of genius* (New Haven: Yale University Press, 1998); *Cambridge Companion to Velázquez*, ed. Suzanne L. Stratton-Pruitt (Cambridge: Cambridge University Press, 2002); Suzanne L. Stratton-Pruitt, *Velázquez's "Las Meninas" (Masterpieces of Western Painting)* (Cambridge: Cambridge University Press, 2003).

[4] Stratton-Pruitt, *"Las Meninas"*, 1.

[5] Ibid.

[6] Michel Foucault, *The Order of Things, An Archaeology of the Human Sciences* (London: Tavistock Publications, 1970), 8. Originally published in French: *Les mots et les choses* (Paris: Gallimard, 1966).

[7] Foucault, 14.

[8] Foucault, 15, 312.

[9] "*Las Meninas* is related to the artist's longstanding ambition to achieve noble status for himself and his art", Brown and Garrido, 184.

[10] Jonathan Brown, *Velázquez.Painter and Courtier* (New Haven: Yale University Press, 1986), 259.

[11] Again, the literature on this painting is vast. Recent contributions include: *12 Views of Manet's Bar*, ed. Bradford L. Collins (Princeton: Princeton University Press, 1996); *Manet face to face*, ed. James Cuno and Joachim Kaak (London: Courtauld Institute of Art, 2004).

[12] Lorne Campbell, *The Fifteenth-Century Netherlandish Schools* (New Haven and London: Yale University Press, 1998), 174–211.

[13] M. Millner-Kahr, "Velázquez and Las Meninas" *Art Bulletin*, LVII (1975): 225–46, 243.

[14] Campbell observes that van Eyck must have chosen this ambiguous form deliberately: ". . . if van Eyck had wished to convey his meaning more directly he would have chosen other words. He used the perfect tense, *fuit*, rather than the imperfect, *erat*; he must have done so advisedly." Campbell, 201.

[15] The definitive account of the critical history of this painting is Campbell's catalogue entry in *The Fifteenth-Century Netherlandish Schools*.

[16] Campbell, 193–198.

[17] Margaret L. Koster, "The Arnolfini Double Portrait: a simple solution" *Apollo*, 158, no. 499 (Sept. 2003): 3-14.

---

[18] The scenes around the mirror run from the Agony in the Garden to the Resurrection. As Koster has pointed out, the scenes after Christ's death are on Costanza's side of the mirror, suggesting some reference to triumph over death. Koster, 12.

[19] E.H. Gombrich, *Art and Illusion: A Study in the Psychology of Pictorial Representation* (Princeton: Princeton University Press, 1956), Part Three: "The Beholder's Share".

[20] Adrian Wilson and Joyce Lancaster Wilson, *A Medieval Mirror* (Berkeley: University of California Press, 1984).

[21] Most scholars agree that the reading woman is Mary of Burgundy, although it is sometimes suggested that this figure is Mary's step-mother, Margaret of York. The book may have been commissioned by Margaret for her step-daughter. See Anne Hagopian Van Buren, review of Otto Pächt and Dagmar Thoss, *Die Illuminierten Handschriften und Inkunabeln der Flämische Schule II'*, *Speculum* 68 (October 1993): 1187–90.

[22] It has been suggested that the kneeling woman, closest to the Virgin, is also an image of Mary, and thereby provides a mental vision for Mary of herself attaining devotional access to the Virgin and Child. Others maintain that this kneeling woman is Margaret of York.

[23] ". . . while once again *we* see the book, its owner now is absent." Erik Inglis, *The Hours of Mary of Burgundy: Codex Vindobonensis 1857*, Vienna Österreichische Nationalbibliothek (London: Harvey Miller Publishers, 1995), 28.

[24] It is sometimes suggested that the woman wearing pale blue, with a blue and gold hat, in the foreground of the scene visible through the window, is Mary of Burgundy, an equivalent figure to the kneeling figure close to the Virgin and Child on f. 14. This is unlikely.

[25] David M. Robb, "The Iconography of the Annunciation in the Fourteenth and Fifteenth Centuries" *Art Bulletin* 18 (1936): 523–26.

[26] Michael Baxandall, *Painting and Experience in Fifteenth-Century Italy* (Oxford: Oxford University Press, 2nd edition 1988): 48–36.

[27] Known from sketches and from a copy in Basel (Öffentliche Kunstsammlung).

[28] ". . . in Leonardo's [painting] we share the angelic salutation with a unique person, to the extent that we share, in the manner of the spiritual exercises, the Virgin's joys and sorrows, and here we share particularly a whole range of possible reactions, from surprise, and wonderment, to fear." John Shearman, *Only Connect: Art and the Spectator in the Italian Renaissance* (Princeton: Princeton University Press, 1992), 35.

[29] There might be different devotional and meditative possibilities for male and female viewers here.

[30] Shearman, 36. Perhaps the implications of identifying with the Angel might be more problematic.

[31] "Major Life of St Francis" ("Legenda Maior") in *St. Francis of Assisi, writings and early biographies: English omnibus of the sources for the life of St. Francis*, ed. Marion A. Habig, (3rd revised edition, London: S.P.C.K., 1979).

[32] "Life of St Francis", Chapter 13.3, Habig, 730.

[33] Ibid., 729–30.

CHAPTER ELEVEN

IN THE LOOKING GLASS: THE PAINTER FADES

JUDIT G. VARGA

The curious Self-Portrait by the seventeenth century Austrian painter, Johannes Gumpp, has mainly been considered in discussions of representation, reflection and authorship, but its meaning as a self-portrait has not been essentially problematised. Through focusing on the use of a mirror in the painting and analysing the gaze in the painter's portraits, this essay reconstructs the ways in which the painting itself crucially modifies its assigned meaning as a "self-portrait".

Victor Stoichita, in his discussion of the fictionalisation of the authorial self in self-portraits, mentions Johannes Gumpp's name with reference to his oil painting entitled *Self-Portrait* (Figure 11.1). This picture, which dates from 1646, is now to be found in the Museo degli Uffizi in Florence. Soichita indirectly alludes to the problems in defining the painter's identity as he hesitates between naming him "Gumpp" or "Wümpp".[1] This self-portrait is currently the only creation which is definitely attributed to Johannes Gumpp, although his authorship is possible in the case of the frescoes in the Lustheim Palace in Schleisheim, Bavaria. This latter ceiling painting is attributed to Johann Anton Gumpp, who might therefore be the same person as that who appears in the self-portrait under the name of Johannes Gumpp.[2] In the *Self-Portrait* the only sign of Gumpp's identity is a "*trompe l'oeil*" *cartellino*, a piece of note pinned on the upper part of the canvas that bears the painter's portrait: "*Johannes Gumpp (Wümpp?)/ 20 Jare/ 1646 (1659?)*". Such inscriptions usually serve as evidence that the portrait is a representation of the painter; they are commonly expected to be an indication that the work is a self-portrait. The painter whom we identify as the author is usually marked out by a collection of verbal and visual signs that through the interpretations of a given community come to denote him/herself. In the case of Johannes Gumpp critics have not reconstructed the biographical author and only unclear references exist to either Johann Anton Gumpp or a certain Franz Gumpp, suggesting that the painting possibly represents one of them.

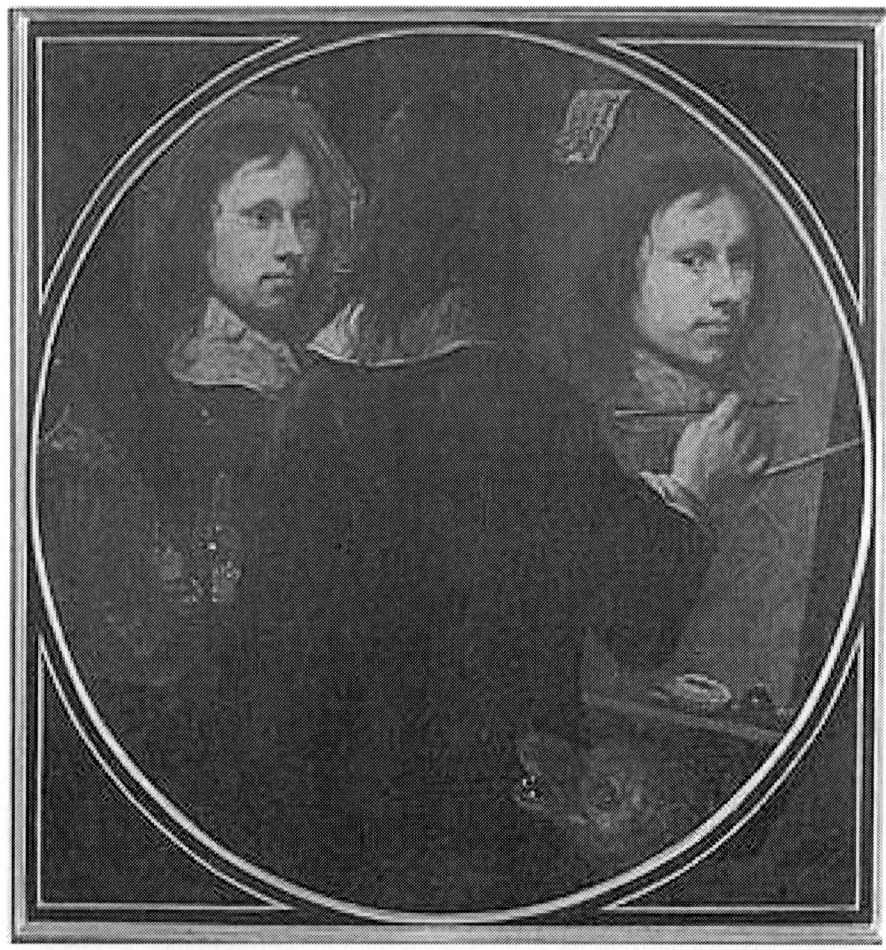

Figure 11.1. Johannes Gumpp. *Self-Portrait*, 1646. Galleria degli Uffizi, Florence.

There is a strong probability that Johannes Gumpp was a member of a famous architect family of Innsbruck in Austria. The tradition of naming in this family causes a difficulty in distinguishing its male figures, as everyone's name is a combination of the first names of their fathers, grandfathers and uncles. There is a variation of Christian, Johann, Georg, Anton and Franz; each male in the family carrying a part of his predecessor through his name. Each one of them was directly or indirectly contiguous with all other male members; rendering the possibility of the straightforward isolation and definition of Johannes Gumpp's identity ontologically questionable. There were two painters among the talented architects of the family, who went by the names of Franz Gumpp and Johann Anton Gumpp. Franz Gumpp died aged twenty-four in 1663, one year before the date shown on the *cartellino*; his authorship of the *Self-Portrait* is therefore generally rejected.[3] The creation of frescoes and maps is attributed to Johann Anton (1654-1719), but his authorship is debatable on the basis of his age: he was not 20 years old in 1646 or in 1659, the dates given by the *cartellino*. The only piece of identification we have of this Johannes Gumpp is his *Self-Portrait* (Figure 11.1). He is literally known from this canvas, yet his name only appears in the inscription pinned to the painted portrait on the easel. Gumpp's identity is forged in a self-portrait that foregrounds questions of identity, resemblance and reflection rather than the portrayal of its author.

The *Self-Portrait* shows the mirror image on the left and the painted portrait of a young man on the right. In the middle, occupying most of the foreground of the painting stands the figure of the painter at work. He turns his back to the viewer and appears on the axis between the specular image and the painting, dividing and at the same time connecting the two images. The two representations of his portrait in progress occupy the upper third, while a cat and a dog that are trying to tear each other apart are shown in the lower section. The painter is standing with his head turned towards the mirror and holds a brush in his right hand, which shows that he is in the process of transferring the image in the mirror to the canvas. The two images do initially look very similar, almost identical, apart from their difference in size; the one on the canvas is slightly bigger than its mirror counterpart, and the position of the eyes introduces a significant fracture between them: the gaze of the mirror image is directed towards the painter, whereas the image on the canvas is looking out at the spectator.

The number of frames and surfaces is strikingly apparent in the picture, as Stoichita points out, a polygonal mirror, a rectangular canvas and a round painting are included in a richly ornamented, gilded rectangular frame.[4] The different borderlines of the surfaces in which they appear, further disrupt the identity between the two faces. The diagonal lines of the canvas, disappearing in the dark depth of the background and the triangular composition of the three heads make the structure of the painting appear perspectival: its lines tend towards a single vanishing point, the geometric centre of the painting. The viewer stands facing this point, and occupies a position from which the whole painting and all elements of it can be seen. The duplication of the painter's face undermines the painting's interpretation as *a* self-portrait, and the complications involved in seeing the two images as reproductions of the same face underline this. The painting's nature of existence questions its own *raison d'être*: it is not only a self-portrait whose aim is to represent the painter, but it also generates a questioning of the status of its own meaning, through becoming a platform for discourses on representation, self-representation and meta-pictures.

The understanding of the painting as a self-portrait has been founded on the knowledge of iconographical conventions, which have been formulated during the long representational tradition of Western culture. A portrait, claims Shearer West in her *Portraiture*, represents a unique individual and is concerned with the likeness of the sitter's physical features, inner life, and social position, and it involves a series of negotiations between the sitter or the commissioner and the painter.[5] Victor Stoichita puts it more simply that if a painted figure is looking in the spectator's direction and his physiognomy is individualised, it is a self-portrait. Painters have been appearing in their paintings as "characters" or "visitors" from the early Renaissance; a famous example of the former is Caravaggio's *David and Goliath*: the severed head in David's hand bears the painter's face. Dürer's *The Martyrdom of Ten Thousand Christians* has the painter inserted in the image as a "visitor": he is an alien body in the painting, announcing his own authorship.

When a painter appears as neither a "character" nor a "visitor" in his painting, the independent self-portrait is born.[6] Self-thematisation can be made explicit with the addition of the painter's name – the insertion of written text as an explanation of the painterly context. Yet the *cartellino* in Gumpp's painting, with the unclear date (1646 or 1659?) and the ambiguous name it contains, counteracts the attempts to define its author. Gumpp's work offers the self-portrait as what it is, namely, a painting. It does not play with the idea of passing for a mirror, like the famous painting by Parmigianino, whose frames coincide with the frames of the convex mirror bearing the painter's reflection. Gumpp's *Self-Portrait* robs the self-portrait of its *trompe l'oeil* nature by implanting not only the painter but his mirror image as well, and presents his self-portrait as another representation, foregrounding the artificiality and subjectivity of artistic creation instead of the identity of its creator.

The seemingly identical duplications of the painter's face arrest the viewer's gaze as the bright complexion stands out against the painting's lustreless background. If we accept that the image on the left is a mirror reflection the logic of similarity leads us to conclude that the person standing in front of the looking glass has the same features as those in the mirror, so the face in the mirror is that of the painter in the act of painting. The identity of the figure turning his back to us, and the meaning of the portrait in the canvas both originate in the octagonal mirror. The reason for us to identify the surface as a mirror is based solely on convention, as the portrait that is supposed to be its copy differs from it in small but significant details. We perceive it as a mirror on the basis of its shape and lustre, which we recognise because we have seen mirrors depicted before. Therefore, our perception is formed by an identification based on iconographical conventions rather than the justifiable similarity between the image reflected in the mirror and the painted portrait. Due to the hiding of the painter's face, the painted portrait remains the only source of interpretation. The words in the *cartellino* attach the name Johannes Gumpp to the face emerging in the canvas, whose features have been assigned to the figure of the painter despite the ambiguousness of its similarity to the mirror image. An imaginary painter is created from the name in the *cartellino* and the features appearing in the looking glass. All this indicates that in addition to the fact that Johannes Gumpp's name is problematic and his physiognomy elusive, his identity is based on the questionable resemblance of two images. His identity, therefore, becomes increasingly difficult to grasp. By the challenging representation of the painter's self, the painting raises questions in connection with the authenticity of interpretive methods that are based on the *a priori* truth of the existence of a positive reality, the truthfulness of representation, the transparency of painting and language, and the Western need to achieve a complete, reassuring meaning.

By showing the process of its creation, the painting invites its spectators into the privacy of the painter's studio and reveals the secrets of self-portrait creation. In order to paint his self-portrait, a reflecting surface is necessary for the painter, since he needs to see himself as others see him to be able to transfer his likeness to a canvas. Not the painter's soul, psyche or mind, but the virtual image he sees will become the origin of his painting. In Gumpp's *Self-Portrait*, the diversion between the two images confuses the process of representation. During the transportation from mirror to canvas, the connection between the mirror image and the painted portrait has been lost; questioning the status of the reflection in the octagonal mirror as the origin of the self-portrait. The unlikely position of eyes supports this proposition: sightlines drawn from the portrait and the mirror image suggest that the portrait in the canvas is the copy of a reflection *other* than the octagonal mirror image. If the original of the mirror image were identical with the original of the portrait, they should necessarily occupy the same place, and the two portraits should be looking towards that one point outside the canvas. Gumpp's mirror image, however, faces the painter, while the portrait looks towards the point to be occupied by the beholder. Showing the painter immersed in self-observation conjures up the illusion of the original scene of the painting's production. In order to create this reality effect, however, Johannes Gumpp had to alter the position of the eyes in his mirror image. If he was to faithfully represent himself while looking into a mirror, Gumpp would have had the mirror image look towards where he was standing, the space that is now occupied by the spectator: the space where the portrait's gaze is directed. As Nicole Lawrence observes in the catalogue entry of Gumpp's painting in *Self-Portrait: Renaissance to Contemporary*:

> . . . the artist would not be seeing an angled view of himself in the mirror: he would, rather, be viewing his face straight on. He is therefore transposing onto the canvas not what he observes in the mirror, but what the external viewer sees. This mirror is not, therefore, a symbol of truth, but a sign of deceit.[7]

By contradicting the basic principles of mirroring, Gumpp's mirror image has become an unfaithful representation, and his attempt to create a reality effect has resulted in disrupting it.[8]

The shift from an external to an internal point of view, induced by the gaze of the mirror image and the self-portrait, underlines the inscrutability of the painter's figure by introducing a split between the painter's and the author's perspective. Clad in a black mantle and turned away from the viewer, the painter is looking at his reflection in the octagonal mirror. In this act of viewing he repeats what the viewer of a self-portrait does, with the only difference being that the viewer, instead of seeing himself, sees another. The black figure can be understood as the viewer's double, offering an internal, intimate viewpoint for the beholder. There is however, another point of view established in the space facing the canvas, at the end of the portrait's gaze. This position, now occupied by the spectator, belonged to the *author*, the creator of Johannes Gumpp's *Self-Portrait*. By implying a distinction between the *author* and the *painter* Gumpp's painting destabilizes the viewer's position. It stages the self-portrait as a mirror image that was transposed onto the canvas by the painter. The mirror first loses its claim to truthfulness and verisimilitude when it does not reflect back the person looking at it, and secondly when it is misleading about the painter's identity.[9] Due to the artificiality of the painted mirror image, the painter that the self-portrait ultimately aims to picture will remain elusive; just as reflections disappear when the observer steps away from the mirror. Therefore, the attempt to maintain the unity between the self and its mirror image proves to be a delusive act, as the mirror image in the painting proves to be just as interpreted an image as its counterpart appearing in the canvas.

Stoichita calls paintings where the painter paints himself as if looking over his own shoulder "scenarios of production in the third person".[10] In these situations the viewer sees the painter's back, as he is turned towards the canvas that exhibits his work to the beholders' eyes. The painting's structure implies a fundamental split between the author and the painter, by the painter's creating an image of himself as *other*. In his description of Gumpp's *Self-Portrait* Stoichita states that while the *cartellino* identifies the portrait in the canvas, the actual author of the painting has been quietly ignored.[11] By extending Johannes Gumpp's name to the figure of the author, we blur the structural distinction between the author and the painter, and replace the author with the highly fictional figure of the painter. The author of the painting is characterised by his occupying an external position to the *Self-Portrait*. As implied in Stoichita's analysis, he could be a second painter who observed Gumpp in the process of painting his self-portrait and depicted the whole scene as he saw it. He copied Gumpp's back, his mirror image and his portrait, and complemented it with the image of the cat and the dog. Apart from the ambiguous message in the *cartellino* naming not even himself but the portrait in the canvas, this hypothetical painter disappeared almost completely, leaving his ambiguous meta-painting behind. In addition to the unsettling mirror image another controversial mark of his presence is the lack of any claim of authorship over the painting, which is in pronounced opposition to the emphasized presence of the inscription on Gumpp's portrait.

For the painter to assume overall authorship of the painting the creation process had to involve at least two mirrors. In order to paint his own shoulders turned towards spectators Gumpp had to be able to see his own reflection from the back. The standing figure in black mantle has, therefore, to be a copy of a mirror reflection, a virtual figure devoid of material, time, and origin, similar in characteristics to the reflection of the painter's face in the octagonal mirror. The author, whether we attribute this role to Johannes Gumpp or another, unknown painter, is literally ungraspable in both cases. If it is Gumpp, his origin is a virtual image. If it is an unknown painter, he exists as an absence in the non-presence of his signature. It is through the metaphoric logic of the viewer that Johannes Gumpp, the author of the self-portrait, is constructed when he assumes that the painter shares the author's identity under the name defined in the *cartellino*. The author of the *Self-Portrait*, therefore, is always a mirror image, similarly to the painted self-portrait in the canvas and the reflection in the octagonal mirror – the longer we look at them the less real they seem to be. By the de-stabilising of the author's identity the status of the painting as a self-portrait falters considerably: how could it become a portrait of a self whose identity is impossible to ascertain? Despite the repeated efforts with which this painting strives to represent a person, its attempts fail; instead of showing him, the painting hides the author from the viewer, binds him in the mirror and presents him in the guise of the painter. It shows a failure to preserve the author as a visual representation and stages a disbelief in the verisimilitude of painting instead. By telling the narrative of the impossibility of representing the author's self the painting challenges the belief in knowledge through vision and in the existence of a world outside representation that can be grasped and copied onto a canvas. The author it produces is always already a representation, no matter if it is visual (mirror image) or graphic (the name in the *cartellino*).

The viewer is denied access to the painter's identity by the black-mantled figure's posture, who turns away and hides his face. He is contemplating his mirror image evoking an imaginary unity based on a dyadic relationship between the image and the painter. This ideal relationship, based on mutual correspondence, is undermined when the painted image appears in the canvas. Emerging there, it becomes a sign already accommodated in the system of representation that defines the tradition of self-portrait painting. During the mirror image's transformation into a painted portrait, which implies its become a subject through the discourse of representation, a part of the author's self has already been necessarily lost. The quality of blurring the portrait's referent leads to the spectators' questioning of their own role in the viewing situation, as the painting challenges viewers' reception technique *via* its denial of the *a priori* criteria: the existence of an authorial self as the origin of the self-portrait.

In her book on Dutch painting, *The Art of Describing*, Svetlana Alpers opens a problematising discussion of the strategies of Renaissance pictorialisation. She claims that the interpretative methods of art history were developed with reference to the tradition of the Italian Renaissance; she mentions influential art historians like Heinrich Wölfflin and Ervin Panofsky and evokes the Horatian doctrine *ut pictura poesis* [as is painting so is poetry].[12] This formula created an analogy between visual and verbal arts and defined painting and poetry as ideal imitations of nature and human action. Art was believed to provide a way to get to the real through faithful representation, the understanding of painting as "the mirror of life" flourished as the founding principle in Western culture.

The works of Leon Battista Alberti and Giorgio Vasari support this theory by emphasizing the narrative, allegorical and expressive material in painting. They thus steer the viewer away from the potentially problematic details that could threaten the formation of a narrative. According to Alberti, the task of the viewer was to recognise himself in the *istoria* of the painted scene: "The *istoria* will move the soul of the beholder when each man painted there clearly shows the movement of his own soul."[13] The emphatic connection between viewer and painting is complemented by the spatial correspondence performed by Alberti's perspective construction, when "both the beholder and the things he sees will appear to be on the same plane."[14] This remark proposes that painting is a continuation of the viewer's reality with *imitation* being its founding structural element. In her paper on Vasari, Alpers remarks that he often described an unseen face in a painting and assigned meaning to it based on his previous knowledge of the scene from literary sources. [15] She shows how Vasari recurrently focuses a painting's meaning outside of its picture frame. Gumpp's *Self-Portrait*, however, does not refer to narratives outside itself, it confines meaning to the space barred by the rectangle of its richly ornamented frames. It addresses the viewer by means of the portrait's gaze and by the repetition of his/her own spatial and postural features in the figure of the painter: "the beholder, when looking at the painting, will occupy the same position as the painter in the middle of the canvas." [16] Although the Albertian connection between viewer and painting is made possible by the element of self-recognition due to the *Self-Portrait*'s multiple viewpoints as opposed to Alberti's fixed viewing structure, this painting cannot be conceived of as the continuation of the beholder's reality.

If paintings are imitations of nature, the self-portrait, being an image copied from the truthful, reflecting surface of a mirror, is potentially the ultimate imitation. "Mirror to life" par excellence, the self-portrait is expected to look like its subject, the painter/author. Often, the aim is likeness, and even if the painter's physiognomy is not recognisable, the connection is established on the basis of literal or metaphorical correspondence with the mirror image, a reflection only accessible to the painter. When his/her likeness is transposed onto the canvas, the reflected image disappears, only the title implies the existence of a reflected image of the self which is a prerequisite to the self-portrait. Joanna Woodall claims that "This lifelike reflection will disappear when the living subject is no longer physically there to look." [17] Self-portraits that represent "scenarios of production" retain the painter's image in a painted mirror, so his reflected image is present to confirm the lifelikeness of the portrait. In Gumpp's painting the painter's portrait in the octagonal mirror disrupts the identity between reflection and representation; its presence leads to a split between the painter's and the author's self, it dislocates the viewer and questions the foundations of the self-portrait.

The frames of Parmigianino's famous *Self-Portrait* in a convex mirror coincide with those of the mirror image. Stoichita claims that in this case the "mirror is in the place of an absent reality", [18] implying that having turned metaphorically into a mirror, the painting is a reliable source of the real. Parmigianino's *trompe l'oeil* painting assumes the characteristics of the convex mirror image, disguising itself as an exact copy, a *simulacrum* of the virtual image. Ontological reasons question the representability of the mirror image. The materiality of the painted image makes this process impossible: a mirror image cannot be cannot be reflected by another mirror, since it reflects the object itself, [19] and it cannot be depicted either. It is non-graspable because virtual; once given substance it ceases to be a mirror image, and the principle of its verisimilitude becomes invalidated. The Parmigianino *Self-Portrait* therefore deceives viewers by pretending to be "in the place of an absent reality", while it can only attempt to create the *effect* of the real.

Norman Rockwell's *Triple Self-Portrait* (Figure 11.2) can be understood as being a playful replication of Johannes Gumpp's work, as both paintings exhibit the unreliability of the self-portrait as a source for the identification of the painter by showing discrepancies between the mirror image and the actual self-portrait in the canvas. While the eyes in Gumpp's *Self-Portrait* act as sites of difference, both of Rockwell's portraits look in the direction of the spectator, who is compelled by the portrait's direct gaze. Although the mirror image's gaze is covered by semi-transparent, opaque spectacles, the sightlines drawn from these partly concealed eyes and from the painted portrait's engaging look undoubtedly converge in a point in front of the canvas where the spectator stands. The implied viewer's position coincides with the artist observing himself in the mirror, which causes the merging of the two selves. When brush and paint scattered on the floor lead the spectator's gaze back into the painting along the painter's tilted body, it meets the painter's problematic mirror reflection. The angle between the mirror and the canvas prevents the mirror image from matching the sitting painter. It disguises itself as the painter's point of view, while the laws of reflection attest that the mirror image was designed from someone else's position, who is neither the painter nor the viewer, in a way that interrupts the structural hierarchy of the self-portrait. Although its general organisation evokes Gumpp's *Self-Portrait*, the easel on the right stretches into the mirror's surface, and like the painter's body that connects the two spheres, suggests the suspension of boundaries between the space of representation and reflection, further questioning the candidness of mirroring. Rockwell's painting implies the presence of an unknown point of view, which like the divergent sightlines in Gumpp's *Self-Portrait*, lead towards a spatially separated painter and author, implying that both paintings problematize the figure of the painter as author.

As the painter's objectification is inscribed in the structure of a self-portrait, the split in the painter's character remains inherently sustained. In maintaining this breach, a self-portrait enacts two grammatically exclusive meanings of the word "subject": the painter is the grammatical subject of the "scenario of production" and the phrase; "he paints". He is also the reflexive object of the utterance "he paints himself", at the same time as he is the semantic "subject" of the painting that the phrase describes. In this case the denotative "subject" meets its grammatical opposite: the "object". As the painter paints his self-portrait and turns to look in a mirror to see himself from the outside, he enacts the transition from *grammatical* subject to *semantic* subject, and becomes the *object* of his own work. This linguistic puzzle at the heart of the self-portrait is forgotten when the self-portrait, the painter and the author are identified under one person's

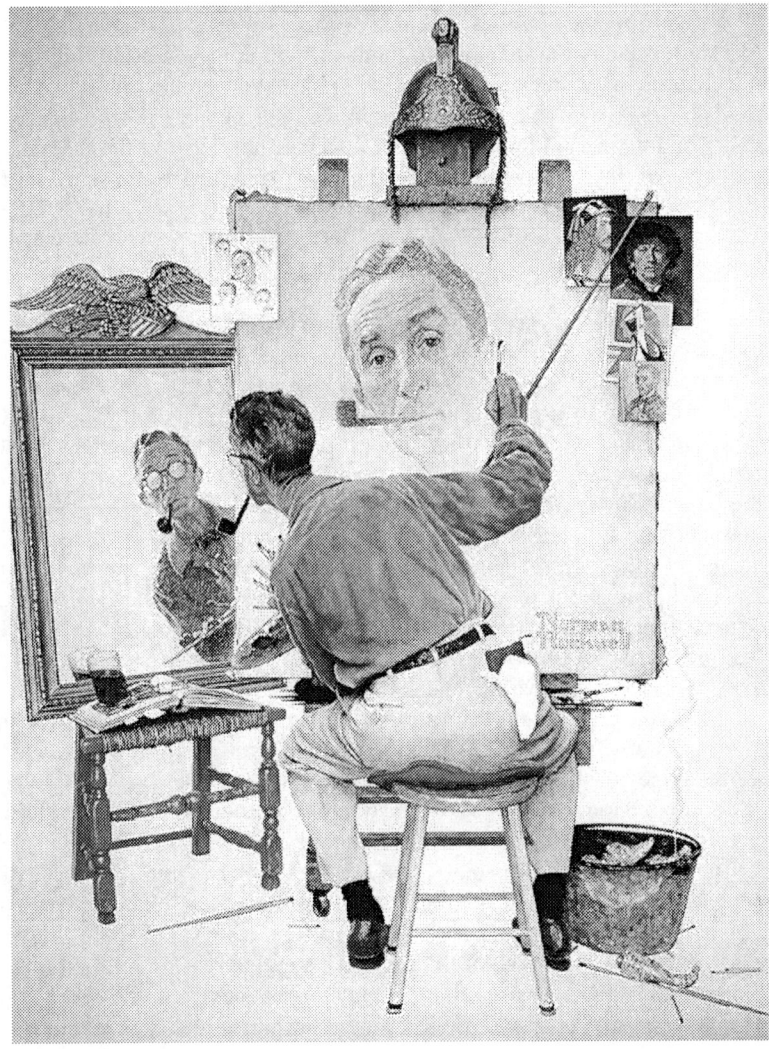

Figure 11.2. Norman Rockwell. *Triple Self-Portrait* 1960.   The Norman Rockwell Museum at Stockbridge, Massachusetts.

name, the creator of the painting. The mirror image, therefore, functions not as an iconic sign of the painting's creator, but as a symptom of the interruption of semantic identification between painter as subject and author as object, that alludes to the *impossibility* of defining "him". The painted mirror image in Rockwell's or Johannes Gumpp's self-portrait does not perform the role of the idealised, trustworthy guarantee of meaning, as described by Alberti in *De Pictura*:

> I do not know why painted things have so much grace in the mirror. It is marvellous how every weakness in a painting is so manifestly deformed in the mirror. Therefore things taken from nature are corrected with a mirror.[20]

Alberti establishes the tradition of the mirror as the judge of artists' creation, and as an example to follow to reach the highest level of imitation. Questioning this stance the painted mirrors in Gumpp's and Rockwell's self-portraits, function as sites of discrepancies in the paintings' structure. Alberti explains that "the painter is concerned solely with representing what can be seen", his relation to the world therefore is essentially optical, and his task is to create the perfect copy of things seen.[21] Norman Bryson claims, however, that this means the painter achieves his goal when the image minimises its material existence and becomes transparent in front of the viewer's eyes. Bryson concludes that the Albertian picture is not a part of *vision*, as since it follows strict mathematical rules to construct perspective, it remains the artist's careful design.[22] Alberti's picture theory conceives of reality as a non-changing, transcendent entity, and envisages a painter who witnesses all but does not interpret. He, however, leaves unnoticed that the construction of the perspectival system inscribes the painter's interpretation via the monocular viewing structure it produces.[23] What Alberti's treatise forgets to mention acts as the point of reference in Gumpp's *Self-Portrait*: interpretation distorts not only the viewers' reception but also the painter's founding perception. Svetlana Alpers summarises Johannes Kepler's theory of vision with the famous saying: "ut pictura, ita visio" ["sight is like a picture"],[24] explaining that Kepler, like Alberti, imagined vision on the basis of the *camera obscura* [dark chamber], the popular visual device of the age. Kepler claimed that when we actually see, the image is formed at the back of our eyes, the retina, just as it would appear on the wall opposite the small hole in a dark room. He called this image a picture, which implies that our vision is a representation, *separate* from the object seen: a *picture* on the retinal screen of our eyes. Visual perception itself became an act of representation (picture),[25] challenging the primacy of the Albertian painter-viewer continuum as the aim of viewing. Due to the appearance of reality as a *representation* an ontological breach between the perception and reception process of a painting opened up. Without the transcendental guarantee of the synchronic identity of nature or reality it was impossible to repeat the founding perception, impossible to see the painting as the artist conceived it. As Jonathan Cray observes; the age of *camera obscura* is aware of the dependency of the organisation of space on the perspective employed and it sees human vision as potentially distorting.[26]

Since both Kepler and Alberti based their theories on the working principles of the *camera obscura*, the physical characteristics of the mirror image in Alberti's treatise, and the Keplerian *camera obscura* image coincide at crucial points. Both are reflections of objects outside themselves, exist externally to the viewing subject and are defined as atemporal and spatially bound.[27] This analogy, applied to Gumpp's *Self-Portrait*, results once again in the wavering of the mirror image's status as the source of truth. Claiming that the image is necessarily a distortion underlines the painting's critical attitude towards the mirror as the judge of painting. It challenges the belief that since painting represents the world in a truthful, mirror-like way and looking at a painting is like looking through a window, painting is the continuation of the artist's and viewer's world. The *Self-Portrait* confronts Alberti's famous metaphor of painting as a "transparent window" and draws attention to its own materiality.[28] Mirror and painting, identified as the ultimate agents of reflection, turn metaphorically around, and work against the verisimilitude of the painting, once the mirror image appears *painted*.

Therefore, the *Self-Portrait* of Johannes Gumpp is about the hidden delusiveness of vision: the eyes in the artist's portraits betray the discrepancy between the reflected and the painted portrait, and the viewers' eyes hesitate between an external or internal viewing position, rendering Gumpp's *Self-Portrait* impossible to be seen as a whole. Viewing becomes a partial, fragmented activity creating a painting that exists momentarily; reproducing itself for each glance instantaneously as a series of provisional views. It introduces diachrony in the process of vision as opposed to Alberti's idealised atemporal vision theorised as the union of the painter's founding perception and the viewer's reception. Bryson calls this viewing experience the "flickering, ungovernable mobility" of the glance, which, as opposed to centring on the founding gaze of the painter, addresses vision in the "durational temporality" of the viewing subject.[29] In the case of the *Self-Portrait* it implies the questioning of the primacy of vision as the *rue royale* towards knowing and representing the world. Its visual strategy underlines the inscrutability of the painter's self-image through the abandoning of resemblance and, consequently, disables the viewer to perceive and interpret identity on the basis of the analogy between self and its picture. It presents mimesis as a construction, implying that to resemble is to approximate, to attempt to overcome the distance between copy and original. Complete resemblance (mirroring) would mean the reproduction of the original at the expense of resemblance, therefore, in order to retain its resemblance, a portrait has to differ, and it is this distance, this difference from the original that constitutes the core of its meaning.

Notes and References

I would like to thank David Punter for his encouragement, Beth Williamson for her availability to discuss my questions and the invaluable suggestions she made, and Nicole Hegener for her kind support and helpful feedback on this essay.

[1] Victor Stoichita, *The Self-Aware Image: An Insight into Early Modern Meta-Painting* (Cambridge University Press, 1997), 192.

[2] In one of the latest articles on the painting, Nicole Hegener mentions the painting's author as "probably" the son of Christof Gumpp (1600-1672), whose last appearance is dated from Florence in 1646. "Johannes Gumpp (1626 - nach 1646): Selbstbildnis mit Spiegel und Staffelei" in Ulrich Pfisterer und Valeska von Rosen, *Der Künstler als Kunstwerk. Selbstbildnisse vom Mittelalter bis zur Gegenwart*, (Stuttgart: 2005), 84-85, 201.

[3] Anthony Bond and Joanna Woodall, *Self-Portrait: Renaissance to Contemporary* (London: National Portrait Gallery, 2005), 213.

[4] Stoichita, *The Self-Aware Image*, 206.

[5] Shearer West, *Portraiture* (Oxford University Press, 2004), 165.

[6] Stoichita, *The Self-Aware Image*, 205.

[7] Nicole Lawrence, "Johannes Gumpp: *Self-Portrait*" in *Self-Portrait: Renaissance to Contemporary* (London: National Portrait Gallery, 2005), 123.

[8] Jean-Luc Nancy sees the snarling cat that is shown near the mirror as indication of the mirror's unfaithful quality: "le chien, situé sous le portrait et au premier plan, symbolise la fidélité, tandis que le chat, sous le miroir et plus en arrière, indique, sinon l'infidélité, du moins une fidélité moins nette ou moins vive." Jean Luc Nancy, *Le Regard du Portrait* (Paris: Galilée, 2000), 42-43.

[9] Shearer West calls self-portraits compelling and elusive both because they involve the creation of an objectified double of the artist and because their viewer, on looking at the metaphorical mirror, sees not his own but the painter's reflection. West, *Portraiture*, 165.

[10] Stoichita, *The Self-Aware Image*, 227.

[11] Stoichita, *The Self-Aware Image*, 247.

[12] Svetlana Alpers, *The Art of Describing: Dutch Art in the 17th century* (The University of Chicago Press, 1993).

[13] Leon Battista Aberti, *On Painting* (New Haven and London: Yale University Press, 1966), 77.

[14] Alberti, *On Painting*, 56.

[15] S. L. Alpers, "Ekphrasis and Aesthetic Attitudes in Vasari's *Lives*," *Journal of the Warburg and Courtauld Institute* 23 (1960): 190-215.

[16] Anthony Bond, "Performing the Self?" in *Self-Portrait: Renaissance to Contemporary*, 33 (London: National Portrait Gallery, 2005).

[17] Joanna Woodall, "Every Painter Paints Himself: Self-Portraiture and Creativity", in *Self-Portrait: Renaissance to Contemporary*, 23 (London: National Portrait Gallery, 2005).

[18] Victor Stoichita, *The Self-Aware Image*, 192.

[19] Richard Gregory explains that when two mirrors are facing each other, the second mirror does not reflect the non-existent image of the first mirror. It receives light from the object via the first mirror and reflects the object itself. Richard L. Gregory, *Mirrors in Mind* (New York: Freeman Spektrum, 1997), 81. Richard L. Gregory also discusses this in chapter 7 of this book.

[20] Alberti, *On Painting*, 86.

[21] Alberti, *On Painting*, 43, 89, 95.

[22] Norman Bryson, *Vision and Painting: The Logic of the Gaze* (London: Macmillan, 1983), 106.

[23] Telling of the importance of the artist's interference with the construction of perspective are phrases such as "I inscribe a quadrangle of right angles, as large as I wish…" or "Here I determine as it pleases me…" that can be found throughout Alberti's text.

[24] Alpers, *The Art of Describing*, 28-59.

[25] Kepler's theory of vision, reflection and refraction elaborated in his *Supplement to Witelo* in 1604 means a significant discontinuity with the traditional view of Greek philosophers like Plato and Euclid carried on through the Middle Ages, according to which it was our eyes that emitted visual rays which then encountered daylight and the colours and shapes of the objects they met were reflected back towards the eye where the image was formed. This view shows the conception of the world as part of human vision and includes the certainty that true knowledge could be acquired through sight.

[26] This model, however, still offers a *monoscopic* paradigm of vision, and therefore is not, according to Jonathan Cray, a real break in the discourse on vision, as that will come in the nineteenth century with the changes in the role and status of the "observer". Further discussion on the paradigm of vision can be found in Jonathan Crary, *Techniques of the Observer: On Vision and Modernity in the Nineteenth Century* (London: MIT Press, 1991).

[27] The mirror will reflect the person in front of it even without him/her actually looking into it. The mirror image therefore exists externally to human vision; it is there even if its subject looks away from it.

[28] Alberti, *On Painting*, 56.

[29] "The glance is a furtive or sideways look, whose attention is always elsewhere. It shifts to conceal its own existence, capable of carrying unofficial messages of hostility, collusion, rebellion. The painting of the glance addresses vision in the durational temporality of the viewing subject." Bryson, *Vision and Painting*, 94.

CHAPTER TWELVE

REFLECTING ON THE TEXT: APOLLINAIRE'S MIRROR

KATHERINE SHINGLER

Published in the summer of 1914, "Cœur couronne et miroir" (Figure 12.1) was one of the first of Guillaume Apollinaire's visual poems combining word and image—a genre that he referred to first as "idéogrammes lyriques", and later baptized *calligrammes*. As the title of the poem indicates, words are arranged to figure a heart, a crown, and a mirror, and it is the multi-layered significance of this last section of the poem that will be my focus here. Following the word-fragments clockwise, the mirror reads, "Dans ce miroir je suis enclos vivant et vrai comme on imagine les anges et non comme sont les reflets" ["In this mirror I am enclosed alive and real as one imagines angels and not as a reflection"].[1] And Guillaume Apollinaire—or rather his name—is indeed enclosed within the oval-shaped frame of the mirror.

Apollinaire tells us that he is not merely reflected in the mirror, but contained within it, "alive and real as one imagines angels". This is no ordinary mirror: rather than simply reflecting reality, it appears to allow transcendence, giving access to an ideal realm situated through the looking-glass, in which the poet becomes associated with the divine. The mirror as a window onto the ideal is an unmistakably Symbolist motif, associated particularly with the poetry of Stéphane Mallarmé, in whose celebrated "Sonnet en –x" sense could only emerge in a transcendent realm glimpsed via the mirror. As Peter Read has pointed out, in another of his poems, "Les Fenêtres", Mallarmé proclaims, "Je me mire et me vois ange!" ["I look at my reflection and see myself as an angel!"] , making it a likely source for Apollinaire's mirror-poem.[2] This reading of the mirror also ties in well with the interpretation of the mirror also ties in well with the interpretation put forward by Alain-Marie Bassy and Willard Bohn, both of whom see the poem's progression from heart to crown to mirror as symbolic of the poet's apotheosis, or his movement from man to king to saint, with the mirror doubling as a halo or mandorla surrounding the poet's

Cœur couronne et miroir

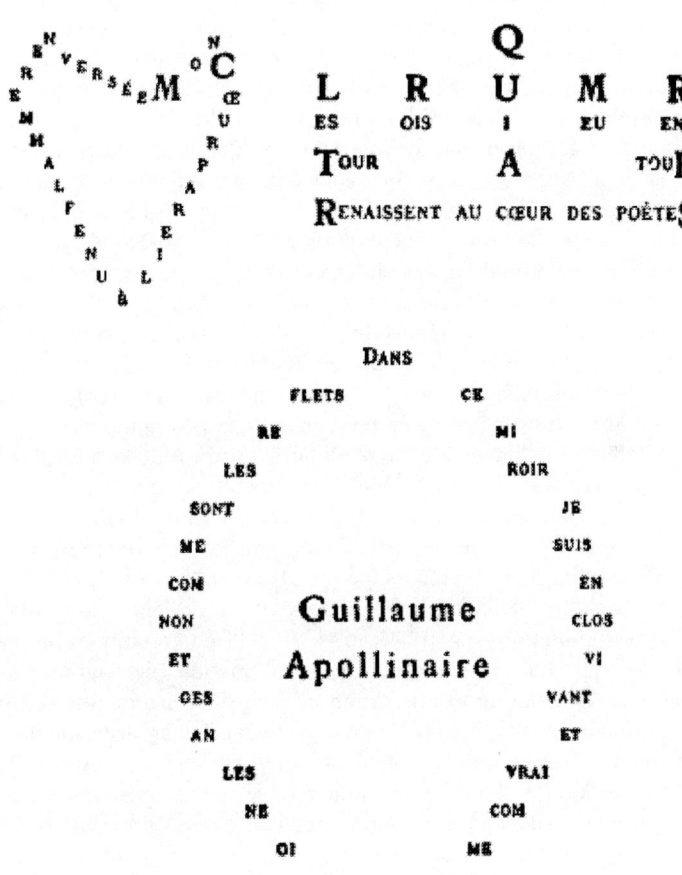

Figure 12.1. "Cœur couronne et miroir", Guillaume Apollinaire, 1914. *Œuvres poétiques*, edited by Marcel Adéma and Michel Décaudin (Paris: Gallimard, Bibliothèque de la Pléiade, 1965), 197. Reproduced by kind permission.

body.[3] "Cœur couronne et miroir" may therefore be seen as an enactment of the kind of artistic practice described in Apollinaire's monograph on the Cubists written the previous year, for it is an example of a work in which the creator "se donn[e] le spectacle de sa propre divinité" ["gives himself the spectacle of his own divinity"].[4] This concept of artistic divinity not only implies mastery over the chosen medium, but also, since "chaque divinité crée à son image" ["each divinity creates in his own image"],[5] imagines art as a process of self-affirmation and immortalisation—essentially, a pouring of one's self into the work that is aptly figured by the reflected self-portrait offered in this poem.

Apollinaire's mirror may well represent a window to an ideal realm in which the poet is canonised, and the interpretation that is to follow will draw on this idea, while insisting that it by no means exhausts the mirror's significance. Apollinaire, a poet at the forefront of pre-war modernism, had rejected the poetic Symbolism of the previous generation as far too closed-off from modern reality, declaring his attitude in his statement that "On ne peut pas transporter partout avec soi le cadavre de son père" ["One cannot carry one's father's dead body around everywhere"].[6] He is thus a rather unlikely candidate to be borrowing a conventional Symbolist trope without modifying it or endowing it with any new meaning. Sure enough, there is at least one crucial respect in which Apollinaire's mirror-poem can be seen to depart from the putative model offered by Mallarmé: whereas we see the latter's mirror only as a mental image conjured up by words— that is, we see it only in the mind's eye—Apollinaire gives his mirror shape on the page, representing it both verbally and visually. The innovation is by no means trivial, and places Apollinaire's poem in dialogue not just with literary precursors, but also with the visual arts. Although I will come back to Mallarmé as a key point of reference and formative influence for Apollinaire's poetry, I think that "Cœur couronne et miroir" should also be read (and viewed) with an eye on possible pictorial models, and more specifically in relation to a tradition of pictorial mirrors. Viewed in this context, Apollinaire's mirror gains a new significance as an instrument of *mise en abyme*—which, after all, is often understood as an internal mirror, reflecting back onto the work of art—and as an emblem of self-conscious artistic creation.

That Apollinaire intended this kind of reading is confirmed by the title of the collection in which "Cœur couronne et miroir" was originally to feature: *Et moi aussi je suis peintre* ["I too am a painter"]. The art-historical reference of this title (Correggio is said to have uttered the phrase, overcome with admiration and ambition, when he first saw, when he first saw a work by Raphaël) makes it clear not only that we are expected to view the poems as well as to read them, but moreover that we are expected to view them in relation to painterly traditions.[7] *Et moi aussi je suis peintre* did not make it to the presses due to the outbreak of war, but as Daniel Grojnowski has shown, the same concern with pictorial models permeates the "Ondes" section of *Calligrammes*, in which "Cœur couronne et miroir" and other poems written prior to the war were eventually published in 1918.[8]

Apollinaire's poetry has frequently been compared to Cubist painting, and indeed there is something of the Cubist still life in the two-dimensional figures and dislocated space of "Cœur couronne et miroir". However, I wish to argue that the relevant pictorial models for Apollinaire's mirror are to be found in a set of paintings that depict mirrors, notably Jan van Eyck's *The Arnolfini Portrait* (1434), Diego Velázquez's *Las Meninas* (1656), and Édouard Manet's *Un Bar aux Folies-Bergère* (1882) (Figures 12.2–12.4). I have settled on these three paintings as likely models for Apollinaire's poem for two reasons. Firstly, the mirrors in these paintings do not contain—or rather do not only contain—reflections of people and objects that are also represented in the picture space in front of the mirror. They do not simply duplicate figures in the painting, giving us an alternative view of them; like Apollinaire's mirror, they all reflect people or objects that are located outside the represented picture space, on the spectator's side of the picture plane. These pictorial mirrors allow things to be seen that could not otherwise be seen. Secondly, these are (and were in Apollinaire's time) well-known, even canonical paintings. Apollinaire, an art critic as well as a poet, would almost certainly have been familiar with all three, and it is likely that he had some or all of them in mind as models for his visual poem. Although there is no mention of *The Arnolfini Portrait* or its creator in any of his writings, we do know that Apollinaire saw and greatly admired *Un Bar aux Folies-Bergère*, and there is also evidence that he saw a copy of *Las Meninas*.[9] It would therefore be difficult to reject his poem's visual reference to these pictorial mirrors as purely accidental or unintentional.

I do not aim, within the limited scope of this essay, to fully unpack the varied implications of the mirror in each of the three paintings. Nevertheless, some very basic and limited remarks about their shared meanings and functions are appropriate. Mirror-images are representations of reality, and the mirror-image in each of these works is a representation within a representation. Mirror-images might be seen, if not as a special sub-category of representations, then at least as carrying certain connotations as standard: their reflections are faithful to reality, delivering precise (albeit inverted) copies of whatever is presented to them. We are justified in saying, then, that in all of these paintings, and "Cœur couronne et miroir" alongside them, the mirror almost automatically connotes the mimetic ideal in art: the perfect copy of reality. As an emblem of mimesis, the mirror functions within these works of art to provide a putative standard of representation—a standard against which the work of art itself must be judged. Of course, this is not to say that these artists are necessarily *recommending* the mirror as a model of the relationship in which art does or should stand to the

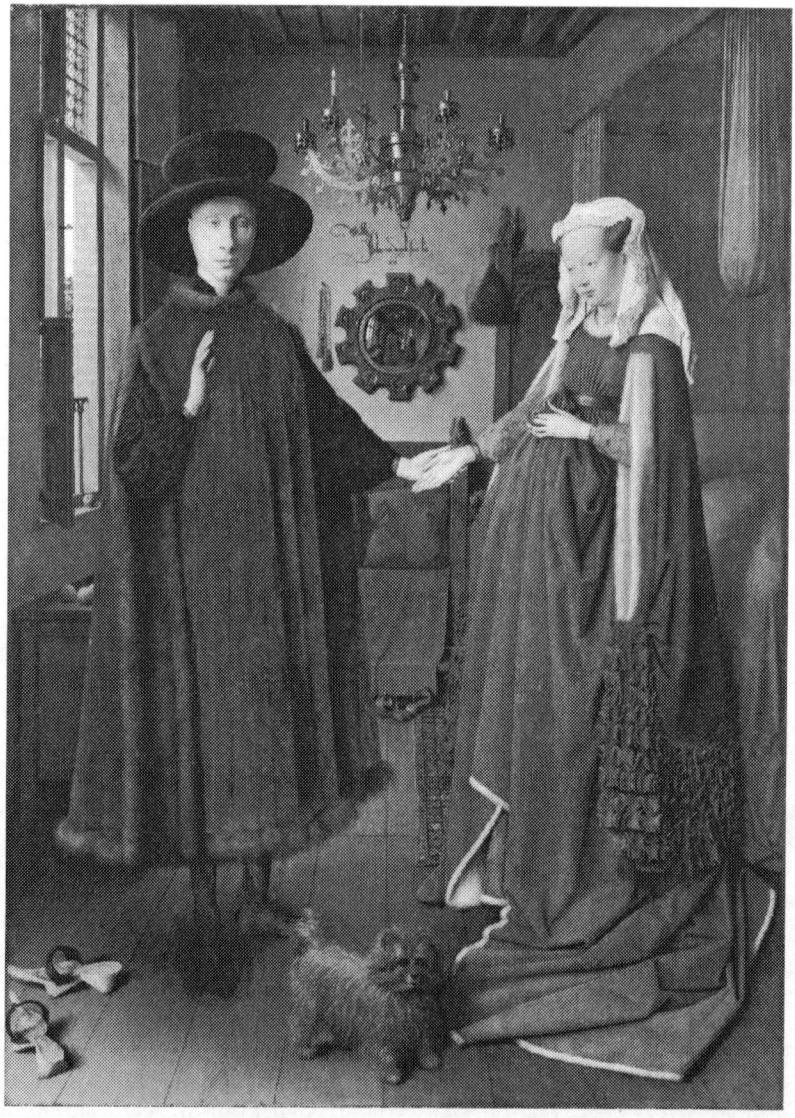

Figure 12.2. *The Arnolfini Portrait*, Jan van Eyck, 1434. London: National Gallery

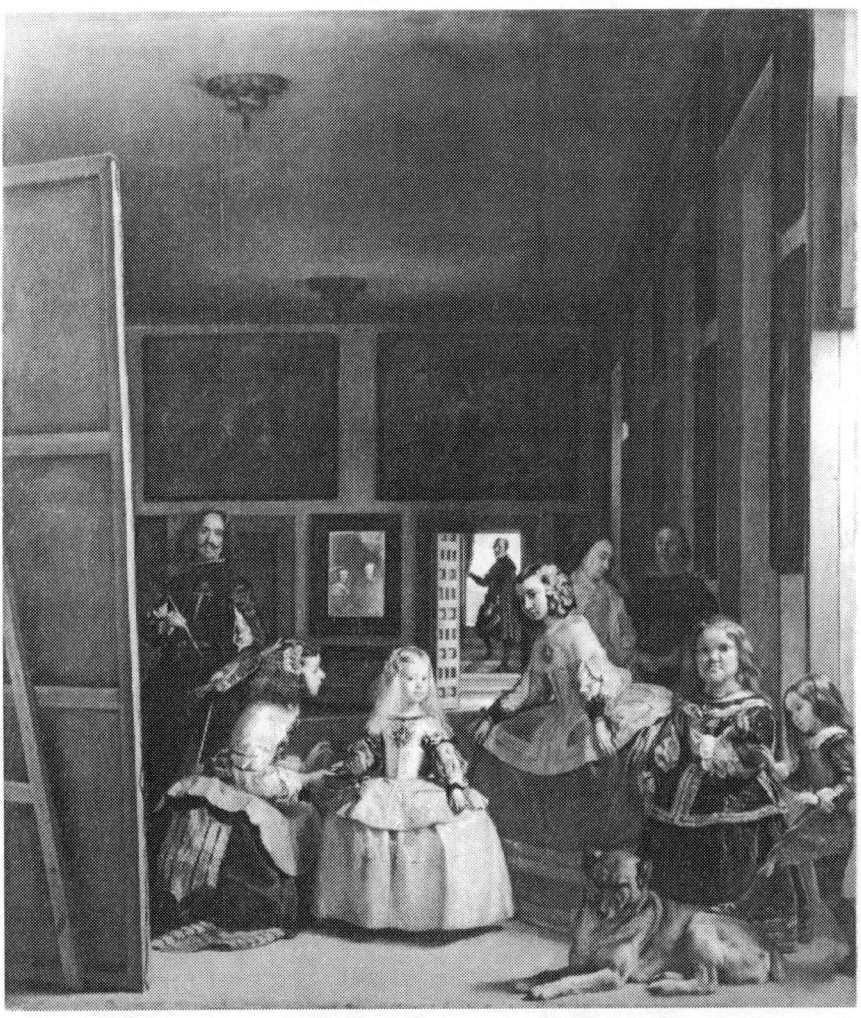

Figure 12.3. *Las Meninas*, Diego Velázquez, 1656. Museo del Prado, Paris

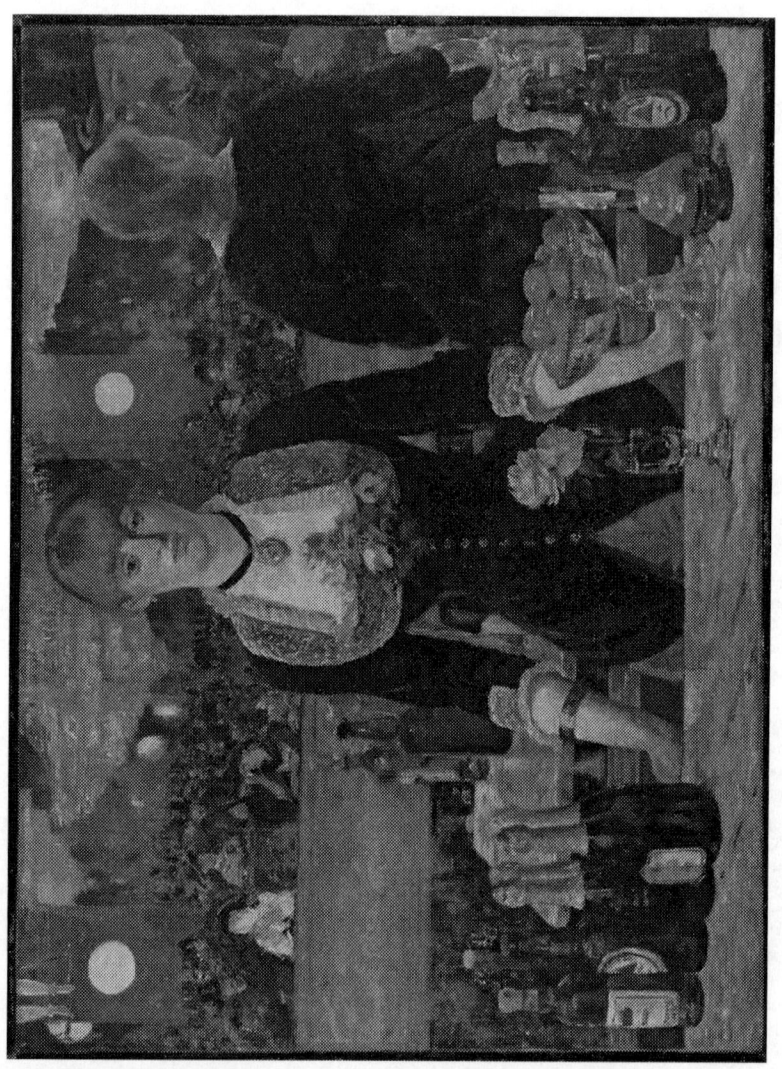

Fig.ure 12. 4. *Un Bar aux Folies-Bergère*, Édouard Manet, 1882
The Samuel Courtauld Trust. Courtauld Institute of Art Gallery. London

world. Rather, the inclusion of the mirror acts as a cue to us (the spectator) to think about the way in which art reflects the world, and the very legitimacy of the mimetic ideal. Manet's mirror in particular appears to deliberately subvert this ideal, for what we might expect to provide a faithful copy of the scene turns out to offer a somewhat distorted image which fails to make sense in relation to its model. For example, given the frontal perspective of the implied spectator, and the fact that the mirror is positioned parallel to the picture plane, we would expect the reflection of the barmaid's back to be more or less hidden behind her, but find it positioned way off to the right.[10] The spatial relationships between the bottles on the left of the painting do not seem to have translated into a faithful mirror-image, and the whole group is represented in the mirror on the wrong edge of the counter. Such spatial discrepancies between the mirror-image and its model might be taken to imply that no representation, not even a reflection, can claim to provide a copy of reality, and that the mimetic ideal in art is a false and misleading one.

Apollinaire's own pronouncements on aesthetics reveal him to be profoundly anti-mimetic in outlook—as one might expect from a champion of the Cubists and of early abstract art. In an interview given in 1918, he stated,

Je suis tout à fait hostile à l'art mercenaire de l'imitation . . . Je suis, oui, partisan d'imiter la nature, mais seulement par l'imagination, pas du tout par la photographie. La création est par essence et par force le contraire de l'imitation; la première correspond aux talents supérieurs, la seconde aux êtres subalternes.[11]

[I am quite hostile towards the mercenary art of imitation . . . Yes, I agree with imitating nature, but only through the imagination, and never photographically. The essence and strength of artistic creation is its opposition to imitation; the first corresponds to superior talents, the second to lowly beings.]

Similarly, in *Les Peintres Cubistes*, to which I referred earlier on, Apollinaire argued that "les photographes seuls fabriquent la reproduction de la nature" ["only photographers manufacture imitations of nature"], and that "la vraisemblance n'a plus aucune importance" ["real resemblance no longer has any importance"].[12] In both of these statements, photography, conceived as a mechanical process of copying involving no creative input from the photographer, doubles for the mirror as an emblem of mimetic representation, against which Apollinaire defines true art—the kind of art which does not merely imitate reality, but modifies it through the creator's imagination.

In the light of these statements, one might expect to be able to align Apollinaire with Manet, and to read his mirror as a highly ironic emblem of mimesis. Indeed, the words making up the mirror constitute, as Peter Read puts it, "[un] refus des reflets, c'est-à-dire du trompe-l'œil et des aspirations mimétiques en art" ["a refusal of reflections, that is to say of *trompe-l'œil* and mimetic aspirations in art"].[13] And yet like many of Apollinaire's *calligrammes*, "Cœur couronne et miroir" gains part of its meaning from the basic relationship of resemblance between each of its visual forms, and objects in the world. Its effectiveness is partly dependent on the ease with which we identify its shapes with those of certain objects, although admittedly at times we need guidance from the text, and some forms can be identified with more than one object—our mirror-mandorla is a case in point. Of course, we are not dealing here with a *trompe-l'œil* pictorial representation, or a convincing illusion of visual reality; yet at the same time, each part of the poem schematically mimics the form of an object.

This aspect of Apollinaire's visual poetry is even more striking when set against other typographical experiments of the period. The poetic experimentation of Italian Futurism (a movement with which Apollinaire sympathized on many counts, publishing the manifesto *L'Antitradition futuriste* in 1913) for the most part refrained from figuration. There is some debate over whether or not Apollinaire came into contact with Stéphane Mallarmé's 1897 visual poem, *Un Coup de dés jamais n'abolira le hasard*, prior to the composition of the first *calligrammes*; in any case, both employ very different visual strategies.[14] Mallarmé's arrangement of text-fragments in seemingly random positions over the double-page works something like a Rorschach test: the poet intended his readers to see in the layout a faint suggestion of the poem's motifs—a constellation, a keeling vessel[15]—but seeing those motifs is more a matter of imaginative projection than of easy recognition. The *calligrammes*, given the simple and easily identifiable forms of everyday objects, distance Apollinaire from contemporary practices in both experimental poetry and the visual arts—which in avant-garde circles were tending increasingly towards abstraction—and instead visually recall Classical and Renaissance examples of shaped verse, such as Rabelais's "dive bouteille".

The *mise en abyme* set off by the inclusion of the mirror cannot be seen as purely and straightforwardly ironic, since the poem itself does not stand in absolute opposition to the mimetic ideal in representation. Nor does Apollinaire's mirror subvert the mimetic ideal by distorting reality as Manet's does. In fact, when set against the three paintings mentioned earlier, Apollinaire's mirror turns out to be the only one capturing the artist himself— the very figure one might reasonably expect to locate beyond the picture plane, as an onlooker of the represented scene. (What I mean by this can be elucidated by reference to photography: a photograph of a room containing a mirror will— unless the mirror is positioned at an angle—reflect the photographer himself; one might by analogy expect these pictorial mirrors to reflect the painter in the act of painting. Of course, this expectation arises as a result of precisely the sort of assumption about the nature of pictorial representation that is brought into question by the mirror.) And yet what we see in Apollinaire's mirror is also rather unexpected, for here we have a picture of a mirror whose reflection is *verbal*, not pictorial, in nature. A talented draughtsman, Apollinaire could quite easily have sketched his own likeness in the centre of the mirror, and in fact he employed both line drawing and arrangements of words in some subsequent *calligrammes*.[16] The poet nevertheless chose, in this instance, to substitute his name for his portrait in the mirror. Like Cubist collage, which often used pasted text as a shortcut to representation, Apollinaire's punning substitution of word for image here is playful, pointing up the hybridity of his new genre. But it also indicates a certain stance in relation to the poem's dual means of representation—visual and verbal—and their relative values. A self-portrait inserted into the frame of the mirror would refer to or represent the poet by virtue of its resemblance to him, and hence, at least by the standards implied by the mirror, would be superior to the poet's name as a purely arbitrary means of designation. Apollinaire's choice of word over image in this instance indicates a rejection of the kind of mimetic pictorial representation that would have him contained in the mirror "comme sont les reflets", as a pale imitation of himself; words, on the other hand, have the power to place the poet in the mirror not as a mere reflection (or imitation of reality) but "vivant et vrai". This also suggests that while the poet's likeness is ephemeral, his name serves as a more stable and enduring marker of identity.

What further problematizes the poet's substitution of name for portrait, however, is the fact that "Guillaume Apollinaire" is itself a pseudonym—a substitute for the poet's real name, "Wilhelm de Kostrowitzky", abandoned partly because it marked him out as a foreigner, and partly because, as I wish to show now, taking on a specifically literary persona allowed him to create and affirm his own identity through his writing. Personal identity is almost omnipresent as a concern throughout Apollinaire's writings, and his placing of himself inside the mirror in "Cœur couronne et miroir" might be seen as a response to this—an instance of self-affirmation, if not of poetic narcissism. Coming back to the three paintings into whose tradition Apollinaire's mirror is implicitly inscribed, it is interesting to note that all of the painted mirrors reflect onlookers, or internal spectators, whose spatial location in relation to the depicted scene corresponds to our own position as spectators of the painting. In *Un Bar aux Folies-Bergère*, the mirror reflects an anonymous gentleman talking to the barmaid, and whose position we appear to share, given the way the barmaid's gaze addresses us. The mirror of van Eyck's *Arnolfini Portrait* reflects—along with the backs of the couple standing in the room in front of the mirror—two figures standing in a doorway; again, what these reflected *internal* spectators see corresponds to what we see from our position as *external* spectators of the painting. The reflected spectators in *Las Meninas* have been identified as specific individuals, Philip IV and Queen Mariana, and thus present a slightly different case[17]; but once again, what these internal spectators see corresponds to what we, as spectators of the painting, see. Thus, while obviously we do not occupy the *same* space as these internal spectators (we are in a gallery, while they are involved in the represented scene), our positions are similar, or analogous, and because of this we are drawn into a complex process whereby we not only view the painting, but view it "through the eyes of" the reflected spectators. We are made to identify with the internal spectator, whose presence is indicated by the mirror, and become imaginatively involved in the scene.[18]

Apollinaire's mirror-poem stands in contrast to these painterly representations of the mirror, which function to imaginatively involve the spectator of the painting in the painting's narratives. By so unambiguously placing *himself* as creator in the mirror, Apollinaire displaces us from the sort of participation demanded by the paintings. We are not allowed to look into the mirror ourselves, even though it is positioned frontally so as to capture our reflection. Rather, like Echo watching Narcissus, we look at Apollinaire look at himself in the mirror, as we so often do, in a sense, when we read poems such as "Cortège", which relates the poet's quest to discover "enfin celui-là que je suis / Moi qui connais les autres" ["finally who it is I am / I, knowing others"].[19]

The poet's presence in the mirror should not, however, be brushed aside as mere vanity. The mirror with the literary pseudonym as its reflection bespeaks a conception of poetry as a mechanism for the author to work out and ultimately affirm his personal identity.[20] This identity is a literary one, intimately bound up with words: it is both constructed through and designated by them. It is also worth noting that Apollinaire's indication of his own creative presence in the poem is a quality that is actually shared by the three paintings. Although none of the three painters actually represent themselves reflected in their pictorial mirrors, they are nevertheless present in their works in some way. Velázquez includes his self-portrait within the picture space in front of the mirror, where he depicts himself in the process of painting another work. Van Eyck, meanwhile, gives us a cheeky "I was here", inscribed by the mirror on the wall at the back of the room. It has also been suggested that there is a resemblance between Manet himself, and both the gentleman talking to the barmaid and the male figure located in the left of the reflected background of the *Folies-Bergère*, who seems to stare at the barmaid from the distant balcony.[21] Without wishing to dismiss this altogether, I would suggest that if Manet's presence *as artist* can be discerned within this work, then it is through his rough, non-illusionistic brushwork, which serves as an indexical sign of his creative activity. In all of these cases—and Apollinaire's poem is included in this—the artist's presence within the work brings into question the ideal of mimetic representation, which implies direct, unmediated "mirroring" of the world. The artist's presence reminds us that works of art are not mirrors of reality, but products of human agency, and are created by individuals who have it in their power to manipulate reality through their representations. Apollinaire, along with the three painters, indicates his presence, giving us "the spectacle of his own divinity", not as a narcissistic gesture but as a manifestation of self-conscious artistic production, with the mirror as its emblem.

Apollinaire's mirror is a polysemous emblem, symbolizing mimetic standards of representation yet also, in drawing attention to the relationship between these standards and the poem itself, embodying the poem's reflexivity—the way in which the work reflects back upon itself. One should exercise caution, however, when placing Apollinaire's visual poetry in relation to poetic Modernism, understood as a tendency towards reflexivity or self-referentiality. This tendency is perhaps best exemplified by the poetry of Stéphane Mallarmé, who described his "Sonnet en –x" as a purely self-referential work: "un sonnet nul et se réfléchissant de toutes les façons" ["an empty sonnet that reflects back on itself in many ways"]. For Mallarmé, meaning is not dependent on linguistic reference. He imagines the poetic work as a closed-off interior, detached from the harsh realities of modern life, with its meanings generated entirely internally, "par un mirage interne des mots mêmes" ["through an internal mirage/mirroring of words themselves"]. [22] Now, Apollinaire's *calligrammes* may be seen as an inherently self-conscious genre, their use of space and typography drawing attention to the qualities of the printed medium; in "Cœur couronne et miroir", this reflexivity becomes even more acute as the mirror implicitly discusses its own dual means of representation. The poem does not for all that shun reference to reality, or retreat into an allegory of itself as Mallarmé's poetry has so often been characterized as doing. Indeed, the mirror may also refer to Apollinaire's conviction that poetry—as indeed the visual arts—should strive to fully take account of the modern world in which it is produced, "reflecting" all aspects of everyday life. For Apollinaire, anti-mimetism does not necessarily equate to art's withdrawal from modern reality. Incorporating the language of the street and of publicity bulletins, as well as often taking on the forms of banal everyday objects—a pipe, a pair of glasses, a pocketwatch—Apollinaire's poetry is in this sense a mirror of modern life. *Calligrammes* such as "Cœur couronne et miroir" reflect not only back upon themselves, but also beyond the page to include the world that they linguistically and pictorially evoke.

In sum, Apollinaire's mirror cannot be reduced to a critique of the mimetic ideal in art. While the verbal content of the poem might imply resistance to that ideal, its pictorial qualities place it in a slightly more ambiguous position. We are involved in a subtle and complex play of reflections on the poem's visual and verbal means of representation, with the mirror-emblem both highlighting those means and bringing them into question without wholly undermining them. The upshot of the preceding discussion, however, is that even at this very early stage in the development of the *calligrammes* as a poetic genre, Apollinaire seems to be asserting the superiority of the arbitrary word over the mimetic image as a means of representation. This stance is suggested by his rejection of the pictorial self-portrait in favour of a verbal designation that distils the essence of the poet's identity—an immutable ideal ego both established and maintained for posterity by his writerly production. The poet is immortalized in the mirror of his work, "as one imagines angels and not as a reflection". Despite its prominent visual aspect, and Apollinaire's desire to bring the reader's experience of his poetry into closer contact with picture perception, "Cœur couronne et miroir" effectively reminds the reader that words are the poet's primary medium, and the means by which he ultimately affirms his identity.

Notes and References

[1] All translations are my own.

[2] Peter Read, "Un Ange dans le miroir: reflets et vérité dans l'esthétique d'Apollinaire", *Que Vlo-ve ?* 23 (1996): 72. The quotation from "Les Fenêtres" is from Stéphane Mallarmé, *Œuvres complètes*, vol. 1, ed. Bertrand Marchal (Paris: Gallimard, Bibliothèque de la Pléiade, 1998), 10.

[3] Alain-Marie Bassy, "Forme littéraire et forme graphique: les schématogrammes d'Apollinaire", *Scolies*, nos. 3-4 (1973-4): 187-88; Willard Bohn, *The Aesthetics of Visual Poetry, 1914-1928* (Cambridge: Cambridge University Press, 1986), 56.

[4] Guillaume Apollinaire, *Méditations esthétiques. Les Peintres Cubistes*, in *Œuvres en prose complètes*, vol. 2, ed. Pierre Caizergues and Michel Décaudin (Paris: Gallimard, Bibliothèque de la Pléiade, 1991), 7. The latter volume will hereafter be cited as *Pr2*.

[5] Apollinaire, *Méditations esthétiques. Les Peintres Cubistes*, *Pr2*, 8.

[6] Apollinaire, *Méditations esthétiques. Les Peintres Cubistes*, *Pr2*, 6.

[7] *Les Soirées de Paris*, 26-7 (July–August 1914) contains an advance order form for the collection, giving the title as *Et moi aussi je suis peintre*, and describing it as an "Album d'idéogrammes lyriques coloriés", indicating that the poems were to be coloured.

[8] Daniel Grojnowski, "'Et moi aussi je suis peintre': 'Ondes' dans *Calligrammes*", in *Apollinaire : Les Actes de la Journée Apollinaire, Université de Berne 1981*, ed. Pierre-Olivier Walzer, 43-55 (Fribourg : Éditions Universitaires Fribourg Suisse, 1983).

[9] Apollinaire mentions *Un Bar aux Folies-Bergère* in a review of June 1910 ("La Vie artistique. Exposition Manet", *Pr2*, 213-14). In two articles of 1909-10, Apollinaire talks about seeing copies of the Velázquez paintings that were in the Prado Museum in Madrid ("La Vie artistique. Peintures de Graznow", *Pr2*, 240-41; "Vladislav Granzow", *Pr2*,

124). It is likely that these included *Las Meninas*, which had been in the Prado since 1819.

[10] The initial sketch for *Un Bar aux Folies-Bergère*, as well as X-rays of the finished work, reveal that Manet in fact moved the reflection of the barmaid further to the right during the process of composition. See Juliet Wilson-Bareau, "The Hidden Face of Manet: An Investigation of the Artist's Working Processes", *The Burlington Magazine* 128, no. 997 (April 1986): 79 and 86.

[11] Apollinaire, "*La Publicidad* [Interview par Pérez-Jorba]", *Pr2*, 992.

[12] Apollinaire, *Méditations esthétiques. Les Peintres Cubistes*, *Pr2,* 8–9. Similar comparisons between photography and realist representation are drawn in Guillaume Apollinaire, *Les Mamelles de Tirésias* in *Œuvres poétiques*, ed. Marcel Adéma and Michel Décaudin (Paris: Gallimard, Bibliothèque de la Pléiade, 1965), 865 and 882. This volume will hereafter be cited as *Po*.

[13] Read, 71.

[14] Apollinaire claimed, in a letter of late July 1914, to have laid eyes on *Un Coup de dés* only a couple of days beforehand, meaning that it cannot have influenced his first calligrammes. Letter cited in Michel Décaudin, *Apollinaire* (Paris: Librairie Générale Française, 2002), 129–30. However, Pierre Reverdy later indicated that Apollinaire knew Mallarmé's poem at least by the time that *Alcools* was being prepared for publication, in 1913. Pierre Reverdy, *Le Voleur de Talan* (Paris: Flammarion, 1967), 166–67.

[15] On the motifs figured by the spatial arrangement of *Un Coup de dés*, see Mallarmé to André Gide, 14 May 1897, in Stéphane Mallarmé, *Correspondance complète 1862–1871. Lettres sur la poésie*, ed. Bertrand Marchal (Paris : Gallimard, 1995), 632.

[16] See, for example, "Madeleine", *Po*, 239.

[17] On the identity of the figures in *Las Meninas*, see José López-Rey, *Velázquez: A Catalogue Raisonné of his Oeuvre* (London: Faber & Faber, 1963), 204. Jonathan Brown and Carmen Garrido, *Velázquez: The Technique of Genius* (New Haven and London: Yale University Press, 1998), 181. Our knowledge of the identity of these internal spectators will obviously enter into the way in which we imaginatively identify with them in our viewing.

[18] My analysis here is heavily indebted to Richard Wollheim's account of our imaginative identification with the "spectator in the picture". It should be noted that Wollheim's account does not apply solely to pictures which indicate the presence of an internal spectator through a mirror. See Richard Wollheim, "The Spectator in the picture: Friedrich, Manet, Hals", in *Painting as an art* (London: Thames and Hudson, 1987), 101–85.

[19] *Po*, 74.

[20] Although I have not framed my own analysis in psychoanalytic terms, "Cœur couronne et miroir" is clearly open to readings relating it to Lacan's "mirror-stage" in the formation of the self. A Lacanian perspective might also be brought to bear on another figured mirror by Apollinaire, which forms part of "Poème du 9 février 1915" (*Po*, 409), and in which the lover is conceived as a mirror enabling the formation of the poet's ideal ego.

---

[21] Jack Flam, "Looking into the Abyss: The Poetics of Manet's *A Bar at the Folies-Bergère*", in *12 Views of Manet's Bar*, ed. Bradford R. Collins, 179 and 182 (Princeton, NJ: Princeton University Press, 1996).

[22] Mallarmé to Henri Cazalis, 18 July 1868, in Mallarmé, *Correspondance complète 1862–1871. Lettres sur la poésie*, 392–93 for both quotations. "Mirage" in the second quotation is related to the verb "(se) mirer" (to reflect), and thus refers to mirroring and reflections as well as to a "mirage" in the sense of an illusion.

LIST OF CONTRIBUTORS

MARK PENDERGRAST is the author of *Mirror Mirror: A History of the Human Love Affair with Reflection*, as well as other books, including *For God, Country and Coca-Cola; Victims of Memory;* and *Uncommon Grounds*. He is currently working on a history of the Epidemic Intelligence Service. He lives in Vermont in the United States and can be reached at markp@nasw.org.

MELANIE GILES is a lecturer in archaeology at the School of Arts, Histories & Cultures, University of Manchester, where she teaches on a variety of courses, including MAs in 'Complex Societies' and 'Archaeological Field Practice'. Her main research interests are the Iron Age of Britain and Ireland, with publications on themes such as identity, landscape and material culture.

JODY JOY is undertaking a PhD at the University of Southampton that is being funded by the AHRC and he has recently been appointed to the Iron Age Curatorship at the British Museum. His research is focused on British Iron Age mirrors and asks the question of what mirrors can tell us about later Iron Age society. He utilises innovative theoretical approaches, such as the biographical approach, to examine prehistoric material culture.

CRYSTAL ADDEY is completing a PhD at the University of Bristol. Her research focuses on the role of oracles and other forms of divination in late antiquity, particularly in the development of late Platonist philosophy. She has presented her work at several national and international conferences, including meetings of the International Society for Neoplatonic Studies and the Classical Association. Forthcoming publications include an article in the Conference Anthology, International Society for Neoplatonic Studies 2005.

ROSS HULKES received his PhD from the University of Bristol, where he has taught courses on Latin Language and Roman imperial discourse. He has presented papers on various aspects of antique culture at both national and international conferences. His research interests are mainly concerned with the theory of ideology and its place within ancient Roman society and the history of intellectual thought.

MARK KAUNTZE is a doctoral student in the Department of Historical Studies at the University of Bristol. His research on the twelfth-century cosmological poet, Bernardus Silvestris, is funded by the Read-Tuckwell Foundation for the Study of the Afterlife.

MIRANDA ANDERSON is currently based at Osaka University (on a JSPS Fellowship) where she is undertaking research into cognitive and neuroscience with Hiroshi Ishiguro. She undertook a PhD at Edinburgh University in English Literature on the topic of 'Early Modern Extended Minds and the Shakespearean Subject of the Mirror'. She was previously awarded a Monbugakusho research scholarship for cultural studies of the mirror in literature. Her research focuses on representations of cognition and subjectivity in literary and cultural texts.

JACOMIEN PRINS is based at the University of Utrecht's Research Institute of History and Culture. Her research focuses on the transmission and reception of ideas about cosmic harmony in Plato's *Timaeus* during the Italian Renaissance. She recently organised a symposium on the tradition of the harmony of the spheres at the Research Institute and papers from this will be published by Uitgeverij Verloren [Verloren Publishers] in a Dutch volume entitled *Harmonisch labyrinth [Harmonious labyrinth]*. She is also the author of several articles on the philosophy of Marsilio Ficino and Francesco Patrizi.

RICHARD L. GREGORY started thinking about and experimenting on perception 50 years ago at the University of Cambridge. He has studied visual illusions, and developed a general theory of vision, perceptions being regarded as predictive hypotheses, much like hypotheses in science. He has invented a number of instruments and written fifteen books and hundreds of research papers. He co-founded the Department of Artificial Intelligence at the University of Edinburgh and founded the first Hands-on Science Centre in Britain, the Exploratory. He is a Fellow of the Royal Societies of England and Scotland.

LYNN HOLDEN is a research fellow at the University of Edinburgh, where she completed her PhD in Comparative Mythology. Her publications include Forms of Deformity: A motif index of abnormalities, deformities and disabilities of the human form in traditional narrative; Encyclopedia of Taboos; Taboos: Structure and Rebellion; and journal articles on diverse topics such as biblical folklore, ghost narratives and the uses of deformity. At present she is examining the theme of the phantom lover and demon possession for a festschrift in honour of the Scottish ballad scholar and ethnologist Dr Emily Lyle.

BETH WILLIAMSON is Senior Lecturer in the History of Art, University of Bristol. She has published on Italian and Northern European painting of the fourteenth and fifteenth centuries, and she has a special interest in imagery of the Virgin Mary and in altarpieces. She is the author of *Christian Art* in the "Very Short Introductions" series for Oxford University Press.

JUDIT G. VARGA is a research student at the University of Bristol. Her work focuses on the theoretical questions raised by the representation of vision in literary texts and in paintings. She has recently presented conference papers on Iris Murdoch's *The Unicorn*, Johannes Gumpp's *Self-Portrait* and Velasquez's *Las Hilanderas*.

KATHERINE SHINGLER is a doctoral student with the Centre for the Study of Visual and Literary Cultures in France, which is based at the University of Bristol. Her research takes an interdisciplinary approach to the visual poetry of Stéphane Mallarmé, Blaise Cendrars and Guillaume Apollinaire. She examines the poets' engagement with the visual arts and uses both contemporaneous and more recent research in experimental psychology to assess the notion of visual-verbal simultaneity that underpinned their experiments in *mise en page*.